Roots of Elvis

CALUMET
EDITIONS

Minneapolis
FIRST EDITION March 2022

Roots of Elvis: The True Origin Story Revealed by DNA & New Research

This book is not affiliated with Graceland, Elvis Presley Enterprises, Elvis Presley or any of the historical persons about whom this book is written.

Printed in the United States of America.
10 9 8 7 6 5 4 3 2 1

ISBN: 978-1-950743-77-3

Cover and interior design: Gary Lindberg

Roots of Elvis

THE TRUE ORIGIN STORY REVEALED
BY DNA & NEW RESEARCH

Gary Lindberg

CALUMET
EDITIONS
Minneapolis, Minnesota

Also by Gary Lindberg

Nonfiction

Letters from Elvis
Brando on Elvis
The Power of Positive Handwriting

Fiction

The Shekinah Legacy
Sons of Zadok
Deeper and Deeper
Ollie's Cloud

For my son, Scott, and my sister, Bonnie

Table of Contents

Introduction

The Briar Patch

Almost all Elvis Presley fans know the myriad mysteries surrounding his celebrity. Did he fake his death? Were any of the "Elvis sightings" genuine? If he is still alive, where is he? Multiple conspiracy theories have evolved in the years since Elvis "left the building." According to some, his stillborn twin brother actually survived and regularly performed as the superstar on stage. Some fans profess that Elvis had other hidden siblings. Many say that Elvis left behind a string of illegitimate and unknown offspring.

These mysteries and fanciful theories have helped sustain popular interest in an entertainer who left us back in 1977. Nothing fascinates the public like controversy about a popular figure's death. Consider the assassination of JFK and the death (or murder, or suicide) of Marilyn Monroe.

For Elvis, these and many other provocative theories have nearly obliterated the more important issue of how the standard biography of Elvis is largely a movie set, a false front that fools you into thinking it's the real thing. Within the canon of the Elvis story is a vast quantity of wrong assumptions, errors of logic, distortions, critical omissions, lies, and erroneous family stories blessed as gospel and passed down for generations, in some cases by those who had never met Elvis. This mudslide of misinformation, made worse by a rain of errors published by careless or misinformed authors, has swallowed up the true story of Elvis Presley and his family, which is unfortunate since a much more fascinating narrative, populated by a cast of deliciously eccentric characters, is just now emerging from the dustbin of history.

In the briar patch of Elvis Presley's family, thorny bloodlines twist around each other, identities shift like phantoms and prickly questions of morality and legality are choked by the weeds of practicality. But uncovering some of the truth by finding Elvis's ancestors and relatives can be difficult. Poor people and new migrants often leave little trace of their passage. Inadequate public records cannot chart the convoluted branches of this family tree; they can only provide tantalizing clues to the intricate relationships and abundant dysfunctions of the players in this overgrown garden.

Stripped of embellishment, however, Elvis's origin story surfaces as a stirring melodrama. Out of the intersecting plotlines, an unlikely star of epic proportions arises to change the face of popular culture in America.

Untangling the Mess of Myth

An investigator from outside the tight-lipped community of Tupelo, Mississippi—Elvis's birthplace—has little chance of unlocking the long-held secrets of his friends and family or discovering what those closest to the vein of truth may not know. So much has been forgotten, or perhaps was never fully known or understood at all. For many years there was no need for anyone to understand Elvis's family because he was nobody. But then, suddenly, he was somebody and no one remembered his history correctly, or they inflated their own roles, or they died without telling necessary facts, or they didn't want inconvenient truths revealed. After he became famous, it seemed too late to debunk the legend of Elvis with the facts.

To get at the truth of a person or their history, biographers often use the subject's letters as a source of insights. With Elvis, this is a challenge. Elvis's fundamentalism, based on unchallenged assertions, suggests that Elvis seldom wrote anything down. Perhaps a song lyric or two, maybe a note to an associate, sometimes a greeting or a signature on a card—but letters? No way.

And then, one day in 1988, I was shown a box containing sixty-five letters handwritten by Elvis Presley to his secret confidante, Carmen Montez. After thirty years of corroborating the letters' contents and subsequent authentication by a world-renowned handwriting analyst, I published a book, *Letters from Elvis,* about the Elvis letters and another two hundred letters to the same recipient by three other celebrities. Clearly, the established "truth" about Elvis had been wrong. He did write letters—lots of them. Long ones too.

The information in Elvis's letters to Carmen Montez also contradicted some hardened beliefs accepted by nearly everyone. In one of his earliest letters, Elvis claimed that Vernon Presley was not his biological father. When I read this letter written in Elvis's matter-of-fact style, I was dumbfounded. But Elvis had written it as fact.

Letters from Elvis came out in November of 2018. In early December, after receiving death threats caused by the "heresy" of my book, I received a call from a man named Julian Riley who lived in the small town of Verona, Mississippi, about four miles south of Tupelo. The Verona town hall is where Vernon and Gladys Presley were married on June 17, 1933.

I was half-expecting this caller to rage at my foolish decision to challenge the fundamental truth of Elvis's parentage and other things. In a deeply articulated Mississippi accent, he got right to the point. "I just read your book. You wrote that Vernon was not Elvis's father."

I had no defense for that charge, so I admitted, "Yes, I did. That was a claim Elvis made in one of his letters."

"Well, I just want you to know..."

He paused and my hand tightened into a fist. I was ready to defend myself.

At last, he continued. "...I believe that's true. Vernon is not Elvis's daddy. In fact, coming from one of Elvis's letters, that helped me accept that the letters were genuine. Who else would know that—or dare say it?"

My fist relaxed. Here was an older gentleman who lived in the Tupelo area and believed that Vernon was not Elvis's biological father. "You sound pretty confident about this. In fact, it sounds like you knew this before you read my book."

"I did. But unfortunately, I can't prove it yet scientifically."

"Do you have any theories about who Elvis's father really is?"

"I do, but I can't reveal that yet either."

"Is this just a hunch of yours?"

"More than that. I've been researching Elvis's family for close to fourteen years. Built an online family tree with about thirty-eight thousand entries. Adding to it all the time."

"Did you say thirty-eight thousand names?"

"More than that, actually. But that's not all."

He seemed to be waiting for an invitation to continue.

"What else were you doing?" I asked.

"For the last few years, I've been collecting DNA samples from all the branches of the family tree. No one has ever done this for Elvis. Amazing what you can learn when you do something like that."

"I can't even imagine."

"Seems like we're heading in the same direction with this Elvis thing," he said. "I've lived in Tupelo all my life."

It suddenly dawned on me that this man, Julian Riley, could be my bridge into the social network of Tupelo and provide a body of information that would take me a lifetime to accumulate.

"Why such an intense interest in Elvis?" I asked.

"Got my reasons, same as you. We can get into that later. Maybe we should work together."

"I think so."

"Okay, then I will send you my book," Julian said.

The good news hadn't stopped. "You wrote a book?" I asked.

"Hardest thing I ever did in my life. I was a CPA in a previous life, so I'm pretty good with numbers, but putting words together... that nearly killed me. The book's almost a decade old now and real out of date. I've learned so many new things. I wasn't even doing the DNA when I wrote it. Now I have nearly a hundred samples."

I hesitated to speak for fear that I would break this dream if that's what it was. Finally, though, I feebly said, "Sure, send the book."

Eventually, Julian and I became trusting friends, and I have spent hundreds of hours with him on the phone and in Tupelo. The results of our combined efforts and skills are in the book you are holding. It is our fearless attempt to tell the true, authentic origin story of Elvis Presley and correct the historical record in countless important and entertaining ways.

This book is filled with new facts. In some cases, though, we speculate about motives and thought processes. When we do this, we always take full credit for our theories so you can distinguish fact from, well... from informed opinion.

I hope you enjoy the fruits of our labors.

GPS Locations

Throughout the book, we have placed the GPS locations of sites of interest, many of them hard to find without guidance. These coordinates can be used in conjunction with Google or other mapping sites to help you quickly find locations on a map. Look for references such as: (GPS location 34.51671, -89.50227).

If you are reading on a Kindle, these numerical coordinates will be live hyperlinks. Click the coordinates and your mapping tool will open, showing you the precise location of that site.

If you are reading a printed version of this book, open Google Maps (or your mapping tool of choice) and enter the numerical coordinates into the search box exactly as you would enter an address.

Writing Conventions Used in This Book

Words matter, and some terms have different meanings for different groups. Two terms in particular are used throughout this book with specific meanings, and because the intent of these terms may be misconstrued, I will list them here.

American Indian

"Indian" and "American Indian" are the standard terms I have decided to use when referring to the indigenous peoples of America. Some groups may prefer terms such as "Native American" or others, but trying to use all the alternatives makes the book less readable. I have many Indian friends, and they all prefer the simplicity of "Indian" or "American Indian." It is how they refer to themselves and their culture. There is no other reason than this for my choice.

American Civil War

The "American Civil War" is a nearly universally recognized reference to the war that began in the United States in 1861 after decades of simmering tensions between northern and southern states over slavery, states' rights and westward expansion. Emotions still run high about the cause and meaning of this war, particularly among many residents of the southern states who prefer calling it the "War for Southern Independence."

With no political intent, I have generally standardized on calling this conflict the "American Civil War" because that is the term by which most Elvis fans and readers around the world know this event. Standardizing usage, I believe, can help eliminate confusion about what is meant by the term.

Black and White

There are many references to African Americans in this book. I have standardized on referring to them and their cultural aspects as "Black people," "Black music," "Black influence," etc. This is in conformance to the preference of the *Chicago Manual of Style* for capitalizing "Black" when the term refers to racial and ethnic identity. Also when the term "white refers to such identity, I capitalize White to distingish it from other uses.

The Appendices

I have placed several useful appendices at the end of this book.

Appendices A through G organize the major blood lines that lead directly to Elvis Presley. Each family line begins with the first immigrant to America. Where known, the locations and dates of birth, death and marriage are shown along with exposition to help clarify relationships and the timeline of the family's genetic momentum toward the birth of Elvis Presley.

Appendix H is a list of all the GPS locations available in the book.

Chapter 1
The Riley Factor

The Guide

Since publishing *Letters from Elvis,* I have been drawn into a murky world of contradictory information and conspiracy theories about every aspect of Elvis's life from the moment of birth to the end. I have been approached by a legion of claimants to the Kingdom of Elvis... potential offspring, siblings and cousins. Each had a fascinating story about how they were related to the King. Another throng came armed with evidence of uneven credibility to validate their beliefs in the survival of Elvis's stillborn twin, Jesse; the existence of other Elvis look-alike siblings; various crimes and deceptions of Elvis's manager, Tom Parker—the list goes on and on.

I suppose the nature of my book, which detailed numerous unknown Elvis relationships and atrocities inflicted upon him, unintentionally made me seem less of a traditionalist and more sympathetic to the fringes. Few of my new sources, however, appreciated that I had invested thirty years in proving my own various Elvis claims, a rigorous process that strengthened my desire for evidence to support the tales I was being told.

Oddly, the story of Elvis's family and early years had remained largely unscathed by revisionists. The generally accepted biographies of Elvis and his ancestors had become the bedrock of his legend, seemingly beyond reproach. And yet my own research had suggested there were many mysteries and discrepancies in the recorded history. Penetrating that world of the early 1900s in Mississippi might turn up astonishing insights, but how could I hope to turn over some of that fertile soil from my desk in Minnesota a century later?

I would need a guide to lead me into this new terrain, of course. Ideally, that guide would possess deep knowledge about Elvis and Tupelo, have countless personal connections in the area, share my strong desire to solve mysteries and be highly analytical.

My first conversation with Julian Riley piqued my interest. The more I learned about him, the more I realized there was perhaps no other person alive who could do a better job.

The Angel

If this section were a Facebook page, the profile picture would be an angel. Not just any angel, but the angel that surprised Julian and me at the Priceville Memorial Gardens, a cemetery in Tupelo. This angel offers the ideal icon to represent Julian's invaluable qualities.

On a warm Mississippi afternoon in late September 2019, Julian introduced me to the numerous plots where Presley kin were buried. As we meandered from one square cemetery plot to another, he explained that many fans believe Elvis's twin, who reportedly died in childbirth, was buried in an unmarked grave in this cemetery. He pointed out a couple of the more popular locations.

We ended the tour at the family plot next to Sales Presley and his wife Annie Cloyd Presley, the site favored by Julian for the stillborn infant. Sales Presley was Vernon Presley's first cousin who married after Elvis and Jessie were born. As Julian was explaining his rationale for baby Jessie lying in an unmarked grave, he stopped suddenly and said, "Well, will you look at that?"

Confused, I asked, "At what?"

"This big angel here just landed," he said. "I was out here two weeks ago, and that angel was not here. I swear to God."

An angel appeared in the family plot next to Sales Presley and his wife Annie Cloyd in the Priceville cemetery.

At over four feet tall, it's unlikely Julian would have missed this angel on his previous trip. "It's huge," I said. "Would've taken a truck with a hydraulic arm to move that concrete statue onto this plot."

Julian nodded. "I wonder if some fan, thinking that little Jessie was buried here, brought this angel out here as a tribute," he said, stepping closer to study the angel's face. "Looks familiar to me... like a young picture of Elvis I have."

I laughed, then realized he wasn't joking.

Later, Julian showed me a picture of three-year-old Elvis. I admit, the angel looked a lot like the boy in the photo. Another unsolved mystery? I think that's when it occurred to me that I had a priceless asset in Julian. If the historical record about Elvis was going to be corrected and updated, Julian and I would be the ones to do it.

Tupelo Connections

Frank and Leona Richards' home at 509 South Maple Street as it looked in 2021. Gladys and Elvis lived here for a time. Photo: Gary Lindberg.

Julian's roots in the Tupelo area were as deep as Elvis's, perhaps deeper. Though he never knowingly met Elvis, his roots were entangled with the King's in surprising ways, some of which I would discover much later. In fact, my search for Elvis's true roots would become mysteriously interwoven with the unearthing of Julian's own story. Julian was born in Tupelo in 1942, and his family lived on South Spring Street in the same part of South Tupelo where Gladys, Vernon and Elvis lived from 1938 until the summer of 1943.

In 1938, Gladys and Elvis had lost their home on Old Saltillo Road after Vernon had been sentenced to the infamous Parchman Prison for forging a check. They lived temporarily in several different places until finally moving in with Gladys's second cousin, Frank Richards, and his wife Leona on Maple Street (GPS location 34.25218, -88.70591) near the Tupelo Garment Factory.

When Julian was just two years old, his family moved for three years to Grandpa Noonan "Noon" Riley's big farmhouse on Chesterville Road just west of the Tupelo airport. Julian and his brother Larry enjoyed having close family around all the time.

The farmhouse of Jullian Riley's grandfather Noonan "Noon" Riley. Photo: courtesy Julian Riley.

"I was one spoiled little boy," Julian confessed. "This was probably the same kind of family life Elvis experienced as a child. Gladys had relatives in South Tupelo, and there was little Elvis getting all the attention from his mother and other family members. Maybe that's why he wanted to be the focus of attention all his life."

Julian's father, Wade Julian Riley, in front of Tupelo Hardware.

Julian's father, Wade Riley, worked for the local newspaper, the *Tupelo Daily Journal*. His beloved grandfather, Noon Riley, was a bit of an entrepreneur. He straddled the changing times, owning a mule barn and one of the first used car lots in Tupelo at which his second son, Julian's Uncle Lawrence Riley, sold automobiles. Interestingly, the car lot was on the street that Gladys Presley walked every day on her way to work at the garment factory—and again on the way home. It is likely that Lawrence Riley, a handsome young man with an eye for pretty women, and Gladys Presley, herself a pretty young woman just a year younger than Lawrence, struck up a friendship as she frequently passed by the car lot.

Julian's Uncle Leon, just fourteen years older than Julian, was still living in the farmhouse and to Julian felt more like a big brother than an uncle. Leon worked at Tupelo Hardware, which traced its roots back to the Raymond and Trice Company founded in Richmond. "Uncle Leon knew where every item in the store was located," Julian told me. "If Tupelo Hardware didn't have it, he could tell you where to find it."

Leon, who worked at the hardware store for fifty years, was the man who told many Elvis fans the story about Gladys buying Elvis a guitar for his birthday. Elvis received this guitar for his eleventh birthday in January 1946. Several months earlier, Elvis had performed at the Mississippi Alabama Fair and Dairy Show, placing fifth. The second-place winner sang and played a guitar, but Elvis did not own an instrument, which he believed was a disadvantage. For his next birthday, Elvis got his guitar. A clerk named Forrest Bobo sold it to Gladys at the hardware store. In a small town like Tupelo, it is perhaps no great coincidence that Forrest's sister, Audrey, was married to the son of Duskey Presley, a cousin of Vernon Presley.

"As a child," Julian said, "any trip we made to Tupelo meant a visit to Tupelo Hardware. I remember standing at the large display case full of pocketknives and dreaming of having one."

During the summer of 1948, Julian and his family moved from Grandpa Noon's farmhouse to their own house in Verona. Several months later, in November, Gladys and Vernon moved their thirteen-year-old son Elvis to Memphis in the middle of the night. The reasons for this move have been a mystery for decades but is finally solved in "Chapter 11: Memphis Bound."

Aunt Evie Hodges (Leon's older sister) owned a small country grocery store in Verona with her husband. It was basically a large house in which the family lived in the back and groceries were sold in the front, a common practice before the 1960s. Local

The Hodges grocery store in about 1950. Proprietor Tyson Hodges stands beside his son Joe, who would become a Vietnam War hero, and his daughter Linda Susan. Joe and Jullian Riley were close friends growing up.

folks called in their orders, paid on store credit, and Evie or her husband, Tyson, delivered the groceries at no charge. Many of the local kids hung out at Hodges Grocery Store in the 1950s.

Julian explained: "Our little gang included my first cousin, Joe Hodges, who was just eleven days older than me, and also my brother Larry, a kid named Mike West, and Jimmy Williams, a friend from Plantersville about four miles down the road." Jimmy Williams's great-grandfather coincidentally was the Justice of the Peace who married Vernon and Gladys in Verona.

The old Verona Town Hall as it appeared in 2022. Photo: courtesy Julian Riley.

Julian eventually would own the Verona Town Hall where that marriage took place (GPS location 34.19399, -88.71619).

Fortunately, the boys had plenty to do. Chartered in 1860, Verona is the oldest town in Lee County and had plenty of old buildings to explore and fabulous places to ride horses. Noonan made sure that Julian, Larry and Joe Hodges had good horses.

Shake Rag was the name locals had given to a section of town north of Main Street and east of the Gulf, Mobile & Ohio railroad where the poorest Black families lived. It had dirt roads, and the derelict shacks had no indoor plumbing. Noon Riley owned a livestock trade barn in Shake Rag approximately where the Bancorp South Arena is located today.

Shake Rag got its name, according to Mississippi Blues Trail historical markers, from a colloquialism about people "shakin' their rags" while fleeing a fight. But the term may also be related to Shake Rag's location next to the railroad tracks. Prior to trains making regular station stops in Tupelo, people would signal for the engineer to stop a train by shaking a rag. Shake Rag had a few churches and businesses but was also notorious for gambling and bootlegging.

The Shake Rag district in Tupelo.

Some historians claim that Elvis acquired a taste for Black music in Shake Rag, but locals say this is unlikely because there was very little music going on in that poor section, and Gladys never would have let Elvis roam around Shake Rag at night. Some writers have mistakenly considered all the Black areas of Tupelo to be "Shake Rag," but this is not so.

Before pulling up stakes and suddenly moving to Memphis, Vernon's family lived temporarily on the corner of Commerce and East Main Street in a house facing Main. This was on the edge of Shake Rag but not in it as some writers have claimed.

By the time Julian was a few years old in 1947, Vernon was working for L. P. McCarty, a wholesale grocery business, and the Presleys lived across the street. After a short time, the Presley family moved to a nearby house on Mulberry Alley behind the McCarty building and the Cockrell Banana Company. Both homes were within two blocks of downtown Tupelo and within easy walking distance of Gladys's and Vernon's jobs.

The local bus was a source of excitement for Julian and his friends. Several times per day, it would make the short trip from Verona to Tupelo and back. The bus picked up at the Hodges Grocery Store and cost a dime each way.

"When we were old enough to ride the bus without our parents, we felt grown-up," Julian told me. "Every Saturday we went into Tupelo to see a movie at the Lyric and the Tupelo theaters. These were the theaters where Elvis watched their favorite stars on the big screen. We could see a double feature for a quarter and then go to see Uncle Leon at Tupelo Hardware."

On Sundays, Grandpa Riley would take his grandchildren to feed and water the animals at his livestock barn. When he had a good horse available, he'd saddle it up and let the kids ride it around Shake Rag.

Gladys Love Smith, Elvis's mother, had been friends with one of Julian's aunts for a long time. Gladys and Zora Mears had lived near each other east of Saltillo when they were younger and went to the same school. The families of both girls had struggled to survive. A few days after she turned seventeen, Zora married Jewel Daves, but the marriage didn't last very long.

In 1937, Zora married Lawrence Riley, Noon Riley's son, who had been working at the used car lot, thus becoming Julian's aunt by marriage. After Vernon Presley was sent to prison a few months later, Zora often rode in Noah Presley's school bus with Gladys and Elvis to visit Vernon at the Parchman Penitentiary about four hours away.

In a 1997 interview in the *Northeast Mississippi Daily Journal*, writer Michaela Morris reported Zora as saying, "My mother, Daisy Mears, was called on to help when Gladys Presley went into labor with Elvis and his twin brother. My mother pinned the first diaper on Elvis. Elvis's music talent began showing up when he was just a small child. He would drag out buckets and lids, turning them into a drum set. He was always singing and jumping around. He always wanted to be in school plays. During the bus rides to visit his father … young Elvis would raid the box lunches packed by the girls for the trip. Half the time he would eat the dinner before we got there. After the Presley family moved to Memphis, they would come back to East Tupelo and visit with us. We would have hamburger suppers. They were good times. I remember Elvis would go rabbit hunting with my sons. Elvis was a good child, and he told me that he would always be an East Tupelo boy."

Julian Riley's lifelong interest in history began, he believes, when he was a five-year-old on his Grandpa Westmoreland's farm near Richmond, Mississippi, less than fifteen miles from Tupelo. "I remember that my aunt had come in from the cotton field carrying an Indian arrowhead she had just found," he told me. "Something about holding that ancient arrowhead in my small hand ignited an interest in history that, at times, has been all-consuming."

Over the next fifty years, Julian accumulated one of the largest collections of Indian artifacts in Mississippi. In 1980, he co-authored with friends Buddy Palmer and Steve Cook a research paper on the locations of previously unknown and unnamed Chickasaw Indian villages, a valuable resource for Chickasaw Nation researchers. Buddy Palmer personally knew many members of Elvis's family, a fact Julian didn't know at the time but which would become useful later.

Another vivid memory of Julian's frequent visits to the Westmoreland farm was attending Sunday School and church services at Andrews Chapel, the small church just north of

Richmond that many family members of Elvis had attended. Julian's mother, Jewell, would bring along peanut butter sandwiches and jugs of water for the children to help calm their inevitable restlessness. "There would be all-day singings and dinner on the ground," Julian remembered, "and many walks through the old church cemetery, which to us was just a bunch of dead people we didn't know."

While attending Mississippi State University, Julian authored a term paper about the history of Richmond, the nearest town to the Westmoreland farm. Founded in 1840, Richmond is one of the oldest towns in present-day Lee County. He discovered that many founding families of Verona and Tupelo had previously settled in Richmond, but he would not understand until much later the numerous connections between Richmond and the Elvis Presley story.

In 1991, Julian's interest in local history led him to buy two of the three oldest buildings in Verona and, in fact, in all of Lee County. The first building had served as the Verona Post Office until 1951, and the second building was the first bank in Lee County. When it came up for sale in 2004, Julian bought the third historic building, which had been used as the Verona Town Hall from 1860 until 1976. Most recently, the building had been used as a church downstairs with a Masonic Lodge upstairs. After purchasing this third building, Julian embarked on an ambitious restoration project.

Then, in 1983, he entered politics. After a bitter electoral dispute that went all the way to the Mississippi Supreme Court, Julian ran for office a second time and was elected Chancery Clerk and Registrar of Lee County. "I got to know practically everyone," he told me. "So, I know where the bodies are buried, so to speak—even the Presley bodies—and where to find all the records. That was my job as chancery clerk… the records." For a researcher, there is no better way to learn the facts about a county and its residents than from the public records.

Julian's research had uncovered the true story of how Vernon and Gladys had run off to Verona on June 17, 1933, to get married in the building Julian now owns. As Julian explained it to me, Vernon's father, Jessie Dee, didn't like his son, Vernon, very much and would not give permission for Vernon to marry. Vernon was only seventeen years old, which could have caused a problem in either Lee County or adjoining Itawamba County. So, the couple went to Pontotoc County where they were not known, lied about their ages and purchased a marriage license. They were driven back to Verona by Marshall Spencer Brown, a distant cousin of Gladys, and his wife, Vona Mae Presley Brown, Vernon's first cousin. Justice of the Peace Robert Emmitt Kelly had previously married the Browns, so Marshall and Vona Mae knew the procedure. The Presleys were finally married in the Verona Town Hall by Kelly, who records show had signed the marriage license and could only perform marriages in Verona.

After proving the details of this story, Julian was incensed at how certain untruths had contaminated the historical record. In the 1985 book *Elvis and Gladys* by Elaine Dundy, based on unverified family stories, the author claimed that Gladys and Vernon were not married in Verona but rather in Pontotoc, Mississippi.

"Why don't people check things out before publishing these things?" Julian complained to me as we were recording an interview at the Tupelo Public Library. "Yes, I know, back then they didn't have all the research tools that we have today, like the Internet. But why are we still arguing about things like this? The truth is so elementary."

I wondered how Julian could be so sure the wedding of Gladys and Vernon had taken place in Verona.

"Because that's where Vernon himself said they were married. I'd call him an eyewitness."

"Vernon said that?"

"Yes, and the evidence is in a letter. I found it over there in that file cabinet." He pointed to a row of cabinets against the library wall. "In the letter, researcher Roy Turner and biographer Elaine Dundy make it clear they knew Vernon and Gladys were married in Verona. Why Dundy wrote otherwise is a mystery, but I suspect politics was behind the decision. Tupelo likely wouldn't want its small neighbor, Verona, to become known as the marriage place of Gladys and Vernon. I think we should set the record straight when we find out the truth."

Fortunately, a local TV station story about the Elvis Presley connection to Verona attracted a special visitor to the Town Hall—Rachel Ann Harden, a local resident with an abundance of historical knowledge about Elvis and a thirst for more. Eventually, she and Julian teamed up on a more structured process of gathering historical information that included local meetings in which individuals could share their personal stories. This work led to the publication of *The Roots of Elvis Presley* in 2010.

Several years later, Julian embarked on his most ambitious project—collecting DNA samples from all branches of the Elvis family tree to finally determine who is related to whom and how. The number of DNA samples voluntarily submitted is now close to a hundred, and the results are astounding. The family tree is being revised. The true parents of DNA donors are being found. New family members are being identified. And the authentic roots of Elvis Presley are finally being discovered with scientific certainty.

Julian Riley is the real hero of this journey of discovery. I could have no better guide.

Chapter 2
The DNA Factor

What is DNA?

Much of this book is about the use of DNA to untangle the genetic roots of Elvis Presley. Doing this is not a simple matter. To understand our use of DNA to clarify family branches and match one person genetically to another, it's essential to understand what DNA is and how it works. For the geeks among you, here is a quick summary.

DNA, or *deoxyribonucleic acid,* is the hereditary material in humans. Nearly every cell in a person's body contains the same DNA, and yet, astonishingly, every person's DNA is different. This is why we are able to compare the DNA of two genetic samples and determine if they are from the same person, from a relative or from a nonrelative.

The information in DNA is stored as a chemical code made up of about thirty-three billion different chemical bases. The distinctive order in which these bases are assembled provides the genetic code for each person. Imagine that each of those chemical bases were like a letter of the alphabet. Assembling them in a different order could produce an unlimited number of words and sentences. Of course, DNA has billions of additional "letters" to work with. The only way a person could have significant duplicate DNA from another person is to inherit it.

In the body, DNA attaches to two long strands that form a spiral famously called a double helix. Then it forms twenty-two different autosomal chromosomes. Conveniently, these are numbered from 1 to 22, and each chromosome contains specific DNA from the individual.

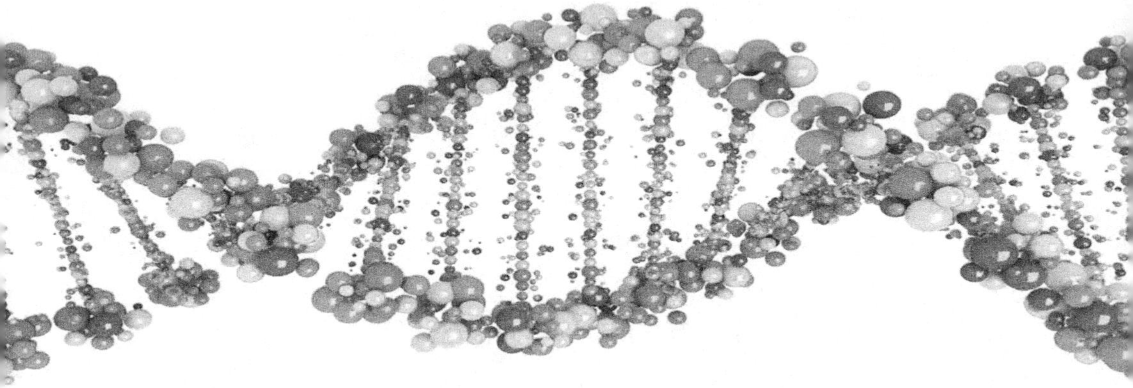

DNA attaches to two long strands to form a spiral called a double helix.

Matching DNA Samples

Finding matches between DNA samples requires a researcher to look for exact matches on DNA "segments." A DNA "segment" is a chunk or string of DNA found on a chromosome. When a DNA segment of one sample matches a segment from another sample, those shared segments are comprised of DNA inherited by a common source (unless they are so small as to be coincidental matches).

The location of a segment on a chromosome is identified by a starting location and an ending location measured in units called centiMorgans (cM). Numerous segment matches can occur between DNA samples as shown in this chart of matched segments between a parent and a child.

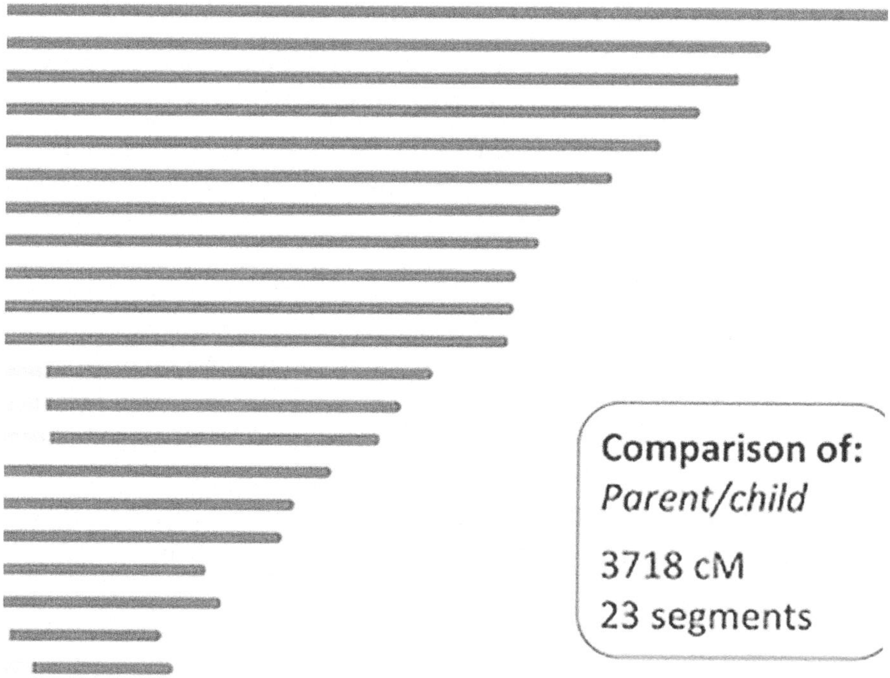

In the previous chart, the lengths of all shared DNA segments add up to 3718 cM showing that the two samples are a parent and a child. Add in the unmatched segments and all twenty-two pairs of chromosomes add up to a total length of about 7000 cMs. For offspring, then, approximately half of a child's DNA is inherited from the father and the other half from the mother in a manner represented by the following chart showing four generations:

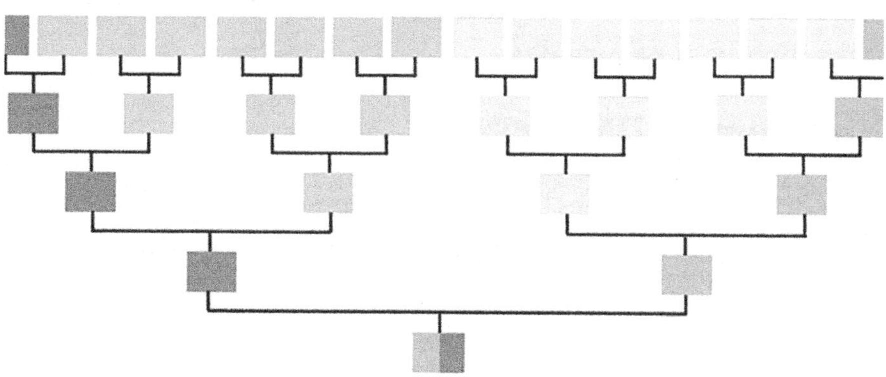

The total length of all the *shared* DNA segments discovered in two DNA samples reveals the closeness of the family relationship between the two DNA donors. The following range of average values can be used as a reference for the length of shared segments between an individual and a relative:

- Identical twin: 7000 cM
- Parents: 3350 - 3600 cM
- Full siblings: 2300 – 2900 cM
- Grandparents and aunts/uncles: 1300 – 2200 cM
- First cousins: 600 – 1200 cM

Keep in mind that the above values represent average ranges. In some cases, matches can have slightly higher or lower centiMorgan values. But DNA cannot distinguish between the grandparents or aunts/uncles of an individual DNA donor or between identical twins. There is some additional fuzziness that occurs between other family relationships such as second and third cousins. For these instances, it is necessary to have additional family tree data that can help clarify the true relationships. Family information can help clarify DNA results, and DNA data can help verify the information recorded in family trees.

Julian Riley's enormous family tree of Elvis Presley's roots combined with the authentic DNA results of nearly a hundred individuals, most of whom are family members who collectively represent every branch of the tree, has produced the most complete and accurate picture ever created of Elvis's family, and it is getting better every day.

Using Popular DNA Services

If you do not have access to a law enforcement DNA lab, the most convenient way to have DNA analyzed for possible relatives and ethnicity is to send a DNA sample to one of the popular companies like Ancestry.com, 23andMe, Family Tree DNA or

MyHeritage. These companies process DNA samples and do much of the matching work. Unfortunately, the only way to find DNA matches in one of these databases is to be in its database.

Ancestry and 23andMe do not allow transfers of outside DNA kits into their systems. Considering that these two companies have only 75 percent of all the DNA tests that have been processed, being in the database of just one of these DNA giants means you could be missing out on dozens or even hundreds of potential matches. For our Elvis DNA project, most of the authentic family DNA samples that were obtained by Julian Riley use coded names for anonymity so no one else can find them.

Decentralizing DNA Research

An online service called GEDmatch provides a partial solution to the decentralization of DNA kits by allowing uploads from nearly all of the companies that process DNA plus law enforcement and penal systems in most states. However, it is still up to each DNA donor to choose whether he or she wants to upload DNA information to GEDmatch. Today, GEDmatch has only about 10 percent of ALL the processed DNA test kits.

GEDmatch is used by millions of individuals. Users must "opt in" to allow their DNA kits to be accessed by law enforcement. We have chosen to restrict governmental access.

Once a DNA kit has been processed, we upload it to GEDmatch to match it against:

1. All our previous kits, most of which are from authentic family members for whom we know specific relationships.
2. All other kits uploaded to GEDmatch by other users, which means hundreds of thousands of samples not available in the databases of the direct-to-consumer DNA companies.

3. All kits uploaded by everyone to the original DNA processing company.

This allows us to find ancestral matches from among the largest possible number of DNA samples. It also allows us to scout new DNA submissions every day, scouting for fresh samples that match someone in our Elvis database. This is the second way we expand the Elvis DNA project. The first way, which is how Julian began the project, is through personal contact—reaching out to known family members or people contacting us with evidence or a belief that they are a member of the growing Elvis family tree.

We regularly supply a free DNA kit to individuals who have a compelling story that leads us to believe they may belong in the Elvis family tree. When asked, we also provide a non-disclosure agreement (NDA) that restricts us from sharing the results of their DNA test with anyone without their permission. In some cases, especially when a potential family member has already had their DNA processed, we help them download the raw DNA file we need for GEDmatch.

Elvis's DNA

It is common knowledge that Elvis's DNA is not available for comparison. It is said that Elvis Presley Enterprises bought up all the potential samples of his DNA to avoid future lawsuits from newly identified relatives claiming a share of his estate. Perhaps there is a sample of his DNA locked away in the Graceland vault, but that is no help to researchers.

The truth is, however, that we do not need Elvis Presley's DNA to accurately determine if or how someone is related to Elvis. The amount of family tree data on file combined with the unsurpassed amount of analyzed DNA in our collection from all branches of the family tree gives us the ability to use a process called DNA triangulation to pinpoint an individual's familial relationship to Elvis and all his other kin.

Remember that Elvis's DNA is an inherited hodgepodge of shared DNA segments from a variety of direct ancestors. From these forebears, he inherited his traits, talents, inclinations, physical characteristics and even some health issues.

Who are these kin? Most fans are unfamiliar with many of them and how they are related to each other. Fortunately, we have identified them, and we have DNA from all of the main branches of the tree. We have Presley DNA, Smith DNA and Mansell DNA. We have DNA from the Tacketts, the Loyds, the Gilmores, the Hargetts and Husseys and Browns and Spencers and Hodges... and more. We have solved many family DNA puzzles and discovered unknown family members. We have even helped an adopted relative locate her biological father who was a member of the expanded Elvis Presley family. For several remarkable Elvis Tribute Artists (ETAs), we have scientifically answered serious questions about whether they were Elvis's offspring.

Our primary mission, however, continues to be correcting the garbled and unreliable public record of Elvis Presley and presenting to the world the real man and his fascinating family free of folklore, brand influence and conspiracy theories.

Noah's Ark

Here is an example of how DNA has helped define an Elvis storyline and sort out a theory of unknown parentage.

In 1918, when Noah Presley, Rosella Presley's son and Elvis's great-uncle, was raising a big family, he bought a farm near Tremont in Itawamba County for six hundred dollars. We know this historical fact because Julian found records of the transaction. But we then noticed that a year later Noah sold the farm for five hundred dollars—a hundred-dollar loss. Noah never even got a crop in before suddenly packing up his whole family and all their stuff, a kind of Noah's Ark moment, and moving to East Tupelo in Lee County.

Like me, Julian loves a good mystery. "Something important must have happened to Noah's family at that time," he told me. "But I was having a hard time figuring out what it was. Selling your farm for a loss is not something a rational person is going to do."

And then Julian's research turned up an interesting tidbit. "I discovered that Noah had registered for the World War I draft," he said. "Well, if he got called up, his family would be in a heap of trouble. Noah's got a wife and mother and about five kids to take care of. So, he had to find a way to not get drafted."

Julian could only think of one way in which Noah could stay out of the war and be with his family. He had to appeal to someone with the political clout to keep him out of the military. Who could that be?

"Tom Hussey," Julian explained. "Tom was one of the wealthiest men in the county. I'd heard a story about how the overseer of Hussey's farm had been drafted, so Tom Hussey rode his horse into the courthouse and demanded that they take the man's name off the list. And they did! The man had clout."

Tom Hussey (left) and his brother, Charles Hussey.

But why would Noah Presley expect wealthy landowner Tom Hussey to help him out? For a long time, Julian had been theorizing that Tom Hussey may have been Noah's father. If they were father and son, then Tom Hussey would have a strong motivation to help out his son. However, Noah's mother, Rosella, had never married, and the various fathers of her children all chose to be anonymous.

Julian continued. "So, it occurs to me... Noah probably thinks Tom Hussey is his father. And Hussey probably knows he is Noah's daddy. I can imagine Tom saying to Noah, 'I can't help you with your draft issue over in Itawamba County because I have no clout over there. But if you move here to Lee County, I can fix it for you.'"

Records tell us that Noah moved his family to East Tupelo, and he took a building owned by Tom Hussey, setting up a grocery store. "You can see why I thought Tom was Noah's father, right?" Julian asked. I nodded.

"But then, I started putting together all these DNA pieces," Julian said. "I got some Hussey DNA and matched it with Noah's DNA—and guess what?"

"You were right," I suggested.

"No, Tom Hussey was *not* Noah's father. DNA sometimes provides big surprises. But fortunately, I had also collected DNA from the Morris family. Tom Morris was another big landowner. It turns out Noah's father was Tom Morris and not Tom Hussey. Noah's story ended with a twist—and the truth. The only mystery left in this story is whether Noah ever knew who his real father was. I certainly hope so."

There were other related mysteries, of course. DNA would eventually show that Tom Hussey was the father of numerous relatives of Noah and at least one half-sibling. But that's a story for another chapter.

Ask Us for Help

If you believe you or someone you know may fit into the Elvis family tree, please contact us at elvisdna@calumeteditions.com. If you just want to know the straight story about Elvis and the colorful family who literally made him what he was, read on.

Chapter 3

The Geography of Elvis's Roots

You will find many references throughout this book to a variety of geographic places in Mississippi, Elvis's home state. When I began working with Julian and gathering historical information about Elvis's family, I was immediately confused by these names. I didn't know how they related to each other geographically. The accompanying simplified maps show the principal locations mentioned in this book and their approximate locations.

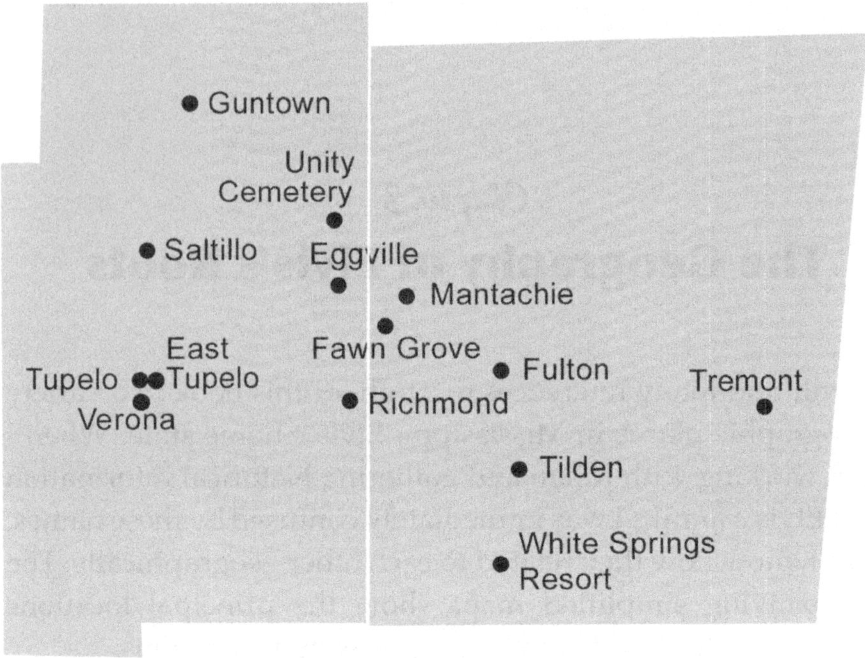

Places frequently referred to in Lee and Itawamba Counties.

Rooted in Itawamba County

One of the most startling discoveries of Julian Riley's research was that Tupelo has very little to do with Elvis's family tree, which is rooted in the county next door. All of Elvis's relatives on the Presley, Wallace and Hood branches are from Itawamba County. Most of the people in his tree who made an impact on his life story were from Itawamba County or passed through it. Elvis Presley was not even born in Tupelo; he was born in East Tupelo, a separate town with its own government in the year of his birth.

More than a different name separated these two towns, which were geographically divided by the one mile stretch across the Town Creek bottom. East Tupelo was a rough, blue-collar town literally on the wrong side of the tracks. The unfortunate, poverty-riddled residents lived there with their outhouses and dirt roads. It was not Shake Rag, where the poorest Blacks lived, but close to it with a reputation for rowdiness.

This is not how East Tupelo began life, however. During the Civil War, the hills around the townsite were chosen as a campsite for Confederate soldiers. The higher altitudes, good air and fresh water made the site more desirable than the swampy terrain on which Tupelo was located. At one time, about thirty thousand Confederate soldiers encamped there. But after the Battle of Nashville, military defeats and hunger had shrunk the ranks of the Army of Tennessee to about ten thousand men, many of them malnourished and barefoot in the winter of 1864.

Tupelo, on the other hand, though situated on swampland, had the virtue of sprouting up where the railroad crossed an old Indian trail from Pontotoc west of town all the way to Fulton in Itawamba County. All the towns in Lee County, in fact, were located where Indian trails crossed a railroad track. When Lee County was formed in 1867, Tupelo was chosen as the county seat because it was near the center of the county.

By 1900, two families, the Longs and the Martins, had gained ownership of the land where East Tupelo is located today. William Snipes and Ruben Martin built the first two homes, and Mrs. Wade Hampton Long eventually bought the Snipes house and the farm on which it was located just north of East Main Street. The fledgling settlement of East Tupelo was originally called Longtown or Longville because the Long family owned so much of it.

A dress manufacturer known as the Tillie Murphy Factory opened at 201 South Canal Street in 1911. The factory provided regular employment for local women, a major motivation for them to move there. The factory continued operations until the town of Red Bay, Alabama, built a new plant for the owner and the dress factory moved there in 1937.

A few miles east, near Richmond, Tom and Charles Hussey owned a very large farm. They eventually purchased the original Martin home and over sixty acres of land on the south side of East Main Street. In April of 1917, Tom gave the land and the house as a wedding present to his daughter, Tee Hussey. Her husband, Sam Long, was the youngest son of Wade Hampton Long and would become a prominent Tupelo attorney.

These are not just meaningless historical facts. The Hussey farm will play an essential part in the Elvis family story.

Cotton is King

Cotton was the white gold that drove the economy throughout the southern United States. Mills in the Tupelo area would bring in the cotton and then cut and compress it into bales. "If you're shipping a lot of cotton," Julian explained, "that fluffy cotton takes up a lot of space. So, they used huge steam-operated presses to squeeze the cotton down into smaller bales, kind of like a garbage compactor. After banding it to keep it tight, the bales would take up about a third of the space of uncompressed cotton."

Back in the early twentieth century, running the big cotton compressors had not required a lot of labor, and the labor was mainly men. But as the industry evolved toward the sewing of garments, workforce needs favored females—and children.

"So, you get whole families moving down to South Tupelo to work at the cotton mill, and there was a lot of child labor going on," Julian explained. "I've got pictures of twelve-, thirteen-, fourteen-year-old children working long days."

The cotton could be efficiently warehoused right here in the Tupelo area until customers were identified, and then it would be shipped out. "Well, since we had the cotton mill here, and the cotton," Julian told me, "it made sense to some smart people to turn some of it into thread—before long, a lot of thread. And then they started turning that thread into fabric."

But they couldn't sell all the fabric they made, so someone had the bright idea to turn the cloth into garments. It was a natural progression.

In 1923, the Meridian Cotton Mill incorporated the Tupelo Garment Company as a separate business, which bought about fifty sewing machines to start making dresses, men's shorts, nightwear and underwear under the Chevette brand. W. B. Fields, who preferred to be called Buchanan and had experience in managing factories, was persuaded to run the new business, which in several years expanded to about 180 sewing machines. Buchanan was given a seat on the board of directors. He and his son leveraged the business into an interest in various banks and a number of other factories, some of which they owned individually.

Company Town

To find enough women to run the sewing machines, "they sent buses into the countryside every morning to pick up farm girls and bring them to the garment factory," Julian explained. Gladys was one of the women who rode the company bus to work, and she made lasting friendships on the bus and at the factory. One of them, Faye Harris, remained her friend for life.

"Eventually, though, it made sense to have workers near the factory," Julian explained, "so the company built a bunch of little houses nearby for its employees. They did a really good job of painting them and fixing them up over time, so in those days they were pretty good places for people to live in."

Mr. Joshua Heard Ledyard, the president of the Tupelo Garment Factory, went even further. Each house had its own vegetable garden and fenced yard. There were tennis courts, a baseball field and basketball court. For social and public events, Ledyard built an outdoor stage with a grandstand. The company gave free medical treatment to all employees and their families. Ledyard also founded the Ledyard School and hired the best teachers so families would have a place to educate their children well. Elvis attended this school in the first grade and possibly part of the second grade.

The Wrong Side of the Tracks

Because the settlement was just a mile east of Tupelo, it became colloquially known as "East Tupelo" as early as 1921, but the only charter Julian found for the town is dated February 22, 1934. Before it was chartered, however, it was the location of a consolidated school system for the eastern part of Lee County. In September of 1925, a school for students from Priceville, Briar Ridge, Oak Hill and East Tupelo was constructed on land that had once belonged to Tom Hussey. Elvis would have attended this school starting in the third grade.

Tom Hussey, one of the wealthiest and most influential men in the area, built the first movie theater in Lee County on property owned by Sam and Tee Long at the corner of Main Street and Lake Street. People would come to East Tupelo from all over Lee County to watch a real moving picture show. Julian thinks Tom Hussey would have liked the silent westerns. The movie house later became a bowling alley and then a nightclub called The Tavern.

By the early 1930s, a public dance hall opened, followed by a few other nightspots. One of the first dance halls was the Owl's Roost, a popular gathering place just off Main Street on Highway 6. Another dance hall called Melrose, on the southeast corner of Old Highway 78 and Feemster's Lake Road, had an open-air dance floor that extended over Feemster Lake.

Elvis's great-uncle, Noah Presley, was elected mayor of East Tupelo and served for two years beginning January 7, 1934. During Noah's term, community water and sewer systems became operational. No longer did residents have to use outdoor toilets or draw well water.

By late 1934, just several months before Elvis was born, The Tavern shut down and became an Assembly of God church. Bootleggers from out of town, who were selling illegal alcohol in East Tupelo, were a big reason the town was earning a reputation as a rough and lawless place. Perhaps seeking less sinfulness in their community, local churchwomen began speaking out angrily about activities in a cluster of buildings on the west side of Highway 6.

In a special election on September 30, 1946, residents voted 110 to 77 to approve the annexation of East Tupelo by Tupelo, hoping the union would gain more personal acceptance for East Tupelo residents and improve the district's repute. Even today, though, acceptance has not improved much. It is now called Presley Heights, but that old East Tupelo stigma still lingers in the older residents.

As Elvis was growing up with this stigma, Julian believes he probably found it difficult, perhaps impossible, to overcome attitudes about his East Tupelo origins. Some Tupelo folks in the 1950s must have found it hard to accept the extraordinary success of a poor boy from the wrong side of the tracks whose father was an ex-convict.

"Many of them just could not believe that rock 'n roll was here to stay," Julian told me, "and that Elvis was the King."

Hold in your thoughts the people mentioned in this chapter. Many of them have unwittingly contributed to the Elvis family tree. They will return for encore performances in future chapters.

Chapter 4
Ground Zero

Effie

A few months after the start of the new millennium, perhaps inspired by the notion of a fresh start on old commitments, Julian Riley was at work on his personal family tree and wondering about some of its murky intertwining with the Elvis family.

"I remember driving out to visit the quaint cemetery next to Andrews Chapel near Richmond in 2000 to look up some family names and dates," he reminisced. "When I was growing up, Andrews Chapel was my church, and the cemetery was my quiet place… when it wasn't full of church people and potluck dinners on the grass."

As a child, Julian had played among the headstones in the adjoining cemetery and joined Sunday outdoor singings. He knew that his grandparents and a few other relatives were buried on the grounds, but not once had he wondered who the other dead people were. "Just local folk who had died," he explained. "A bunch of names I didn't recognize."

It was now 2021, and I was in the passenger seat of his car as we approached the chapel for my first visit to Andrews Chapel Cemetery (GPS location 34.22678, -88.56241). He continued telling me about his family as he walked among the grave markers to the area where his ancestors were clustered. Then he stopped and pointed out a weathered concrete tombstone inscribed with words that had suddenly reached out to him back in 2000:

EFFIE
DAUGHTER OF R.L. & DOLL SMITH
BORN JULY 21, 1904
DIED SEPT. 17, 1905
GONE BUT NOT FORGOTTEN

The headstone for Effie Smith, Gladys Smith's sister and Elvis Presley's aunt.

The names of Effie's parents (*R. L. & Doll Smith*) had resonated like a church bell in his mind. "And then it dawned on me," Julian said. "Robert Lee and Doll Smith were Gladys Love Presley's father and mother. They were Elvis's maternal grandparents! The *Effie* buried there must have been Gladys's sister."

Julian recalled a sudden shiver despite the heat and mugginess of that day two decades ago. "'My God,' I thought. 'Elvis Presley's aunt is buried right over here, close to where my relatives were laid to rest. They probably knew each other.' This was a real wake-up call. Something I didn't understand was going on here in this old cemetery."

Effie Smith had died when she was about one year old. For her to be buried in Andrews Chapel Cemetery probably meant Effie's parents, "Bob" Smith and Octavia "Doll" Mansell Smith, lived nearby at the time. Julian knew that Elvis's grandmother, Doll Mansell, was a gateway to a branch of Elvis's family tree that threaded backward directly through Julian's mother, Gladys.

Mary Jane

In 2006, about two years after buying the old Verona Town Hall building in which Vernon and Gladys were married, Julian returned to the Andrews Chapel Cemetery with an acquaintance. He had been continuing to investigate Elvis's local roots, but his attempts to find information about Rosalinda Presley, Elvis's paternal great-great-aunt, had come to an impasse. There was very little in the public record about her.

As he was leading his friend to the crumbling Effie Smith tombstone, the main purpose of the drive to Richmond, he passed a tombstone bearing the name Mary Jane Presley.

"Hey, there's a Presley buried right here," his friend remarked.

"Don't know who that one is," Julian said. "There are some others around the cemetery too. Wish they could talk to us."

"Only way is through their headstones, I guess… if somebody would listen."

"Well, they'll be waitin' a long time. Not many visitors come here anymore."

Mary Jane Presley's headstone at the St. Andrews Chapel Cemetery.

Though he had seen the Mary Jane Presley headstone

countless times growing up, this time it stirred up questions about who this mysterious woman could be.

Back home, Julian resumed attempts to uncover more information about the enigmatic Rosalinda Presley. He knew that the contemporary story of Elvis Presley actually began with two sisters in Itawamba County, Rosalinda and Rosella Presley. Rosella was generally regarded as Elvis's paternal great-great-grandmother, and while her life was full of contradictions and mysteries, much more was known about her than Rosalinda, who seemed to defy inquiry. One of the many family mysteries was the location of the graves of these two sisters.

Researchers knew Rosella's largely unknown sister by the name Rosalinda, so Julian doggedly analyzed cemetery books and census records for any reference to the name Rosalinda, or Rosa, or even Rosella. "Genealogy work can be very frustrating," Julian explained. "Records often contain mistakes that can hide what you're looking for. And sometimes records are missing."

One day, haunted by the mysterious Mary Jane Presley tombstone, Julian was carefully going through lists of cemetery plots at the library. One name caught his attention, a name misnamed "Rosie Presley" and listing a burial site at Ridge Cemetery in northeastern Itawamba County. He believed this might be a reference to Rosella Presley. "My modest dyslexia helped me out," Julian joked.

The Ridge Cemetery grave marker for Rosella Elizabeth Presley, great great grandmother of Elvis Presley.

The following Monday, Julian drove an hour

to Ridge Cemetery for a firsthand look at the headstone, and there it was with the wrong first name and misspelled middle name (GPS location 34.45013, -88.17990).

"Obviously, the headstone had been there since Rosella's death," Julian said. "I'm sure close family members in Itawamba County knew where her grave was, but no researcher had ever bothered to ask them—including me. A little gumshoe work could have saved me a lot of library time."

Later, from family members Julian tracked down, he learned that the original homemade marker had simply read "Our Mother" and was replaced by this granite marker with incorrect information. Based on census records, Julian determined that the date of birth was wrong. The year should have been 1863. Family members had told Julian that an unmarked burial space near Rosella's gravesite was the grave of a grandchild, a close cousin of Elvis, who most likely died before being named.

Julian was still haunted by the Mary Jane tombstone. This was the opposite kind of mystery from Rosella's. In this case, he had a gravesite but didn't know anything about the person in it. Back at the library, Julian began the laborious task of studying pages of county census records looking for "Rosalinda" or "Rosa" or "Presley." He found the name John A. Presley in Monroe County, a man the family called "Big John" because of his height.

One of the few things known about Rosalinda was that she had a son named John A. Presley, so Julian probed further into the census record to discover the names of others who were living in the same household. Most of them were John's siblings, but one female was much older. "That woman must have been John's mother, but her name wasn't Rosalinda—it was Mary Jane."

Apparently, Rosalinda's given name was actually Mary Jane. Rosalinda was probably a nickname. In a flash, Julian knew that he had found Rosalinda Presley's grave beneath a marker in Andrews Chapel Cemetery that was engraved with her real name—Mary Jane Presley. The headstone had no dates for her birth or death on it, so Julian went to W. E. Pegues, the Tupelo funeral home that probably had buried her. "The ladies there were nice enough to go upstairs and get the cemetery books for me. And in one of those books, I found her name—Mary Jane Presley. Pretty easy when you have the right name to look for!"

Family members at the gravesite of Rosella Presley. Standing from the right: her son Joseph W. Presley, Joe's wife Delma L. Jackson and Rosella's daughter Robbie Presley with unnamed children.

Julian also found the date on which Mary Jane had died, November 16, 1932, less than two years before Elvis was born. The cemetery book stated she was sixty-eight years, three months and four days old when she passed away. Backtracking from her date of death, Julian calculated that Mary Jane was probably born Christmas Day, December 25, 1863.

Rosalinda had not disappeared from the records—she had just been misidentified. Now that Julian knew her various names (one record even misspelled her first name as "Ross," which also implied a change of gender), he would be able to discover more of her story and how she unwittingly contributed to the roots of Elvis Presley.

The Hussey Farm

As Julian put the pieces of history together, the story of the cemetery emerged. The chapel and the cemetery were located on land adjacent to the massive "Hussey farm" owned by Tom Hussey and his younger brother Charles. Numerous workers had toiled on Hussey land, many of them reduced by hard times from homesteaders to the dreaded status of sharecropper. Sharecropping meant that these workers were not paid a wage for their labor but instead earned a small "share" or percentage of the profit from selling the crops they had raised.

As workers died, they were buried in the cemetery adjacent to the Hussey farm, Andrews Chapel Cemetery. The cemetery book served as a kind of roll call for all those souls who once lived and worked together, went to the same church, married into each other's families and finally died just as poor as they had begun. They had all moved here to work the Hussey farm even though living conditions were harsh.

After Julian and I arrived in 2020 for my first glimpse of the cemetery, Julian looked out wistfully at the expanse of tombstones and said, "They look like little houses, don't they? All lined up in neighborhoods. Westmorelands over there, Presleys here, some Mansells to the left, Tacketts and Smiths…"

I started photographing headstones as Julian wandered from grave to grave as if seeing it all for the first time.

"This is not just the story of the Presleys," Julian continued. "It's the story of how all of these families loved each other and had kids together and buried each other. My family story is interwoven with all these others, and this graveyard is where these folks all came together one last time." He paused, perhaps listening to the stories swirling around him.

"I always thought the Priceville cemetery in Tupelo was where most of the family members were buried," I said.

"Some of the more recent ones, yes," Julian explained. "But this is where we find the roots of Elvis Presley. This is Ground Zero."

As the wind picked up, I could almost hear the stories too.

Chapter 5

John Wallace and the Presley Sisters

The real story of Elvis Presley starts with the two Presley sisters, Rosella and Mary Jane "...who most people called Rosalinda just to confound me," Julian joked. But there would be no story without a man named John Wallace, a colorful and mysterious figure who genetically pollenated the Presley line and without whom there would be no Tupelo honey called Elvis.

Julian began a search for John Wallace in 2006 because of clues suggesting that this man, considered to be a mythical character by many, could have fathered Elvis's grandfather, Jessie Dee.

Discovering the identity of Jessie Dee's father had confounded researchers for decades. In 2006, the only person to seriously research Elvis's family was Roy Turner, a Tupelo resident, and most of his attention had been on Gladys's side of the family, the Smiths and Mansells. Turner's research, done without benefit of modern research methods and tools such as the internet, had been scooped up uncritically and dispensed by Elaine Dundy in her 1985 book *Elvis and Gladys*.

A Hidden Cousin

After speaking about his Elvis research at an Itawamba Historical Society meeting in 2006, Julian was approached by a woman who gave him the name and phone number of a man she said was related to the great-grandfather of Elvis Presley. "I didn't know what to make of this," Julian told me. "Could this story be true? How could information of this magnitude not have been recorded and reported already?"

It took several months, but Julian finally contacted Mackey Hargett, the man who claimed to be an unknown relative of Elvis. At Mackey's home in Fairview, a small town in Itawamba County, he told Julian an astonishing story. "After Elvis became popular, my grandma, along with her brother and sisters, told the family that they were related to Elvis Presley," Mackey told Julian. "Grandma said she had a half-brother named Jessie Dee McDowell Presley, who was Elvis's grandpa."

Mackey's grandmother, it turned out, was Elnora Wallace Yarber, the oldest daughter of a man named John Wallace and his wife Almira. Jessie Dee, Mackey claimed, was the son of John Wallace by a woman named Rosella Presley who was not his wife.

Julian knew that Rosella Presley, though never married, had birthed numerous children, all of whom had taken her Presley name because they didn't know the identities of their fathers.

Over time, Mackey gave Julian family photographs and detailed information about his family and his developing relationship with Elvis. Julian became convinced that Mackey was no crackpot and that the mythical John Wallace was in fact robustly human.

With a name and additional information to target his research, Julian discovered that the real John Wallace was born August 1, 1853, six miles south of Fulton in Itawamba County to parents Hugh and Lydia who had been married less than a year. John had two sisters, Mollie and Malinda, and a brother, Willis. His mother Lydia had died shortly after Willis was born.

"I have not located Lydia's burial site, but it should be somewhere near Tilden in Itawamba County," Julian told me.

John's father remarried a couple of years after his mother had died. John worked the family farm and lived in the Tilden community until he was about twenty-two. Julian does not believe he could read or write. "On several documents I found that John made an X for his signature," Julian explained.

John Wallace Moves to Texas

After the War for Southern Independence, as some Southerners refer to the American Civil War (1861–1865), the South was living under forced reconstruction during which the US government attempted to integrate nearly four million formerly enslaved people into society. Many young men, including John Wallace, left Mississippi and migrated to Collin County, Texas, just northeast of Dallas. In 1877, twenty-four-year-old John married eighteen-year-old Rachel Barlough from Hickory Hill, Texas, just thirty miles north of Gladewater, which would become a favorite haunt of Elvis decades later.

Rachel had two older sisters. Her father, John Hamilton Barlough, was a US Army veteran who had received a land grant in Texas. A widower, he had remarried three years before Rachel married John Wallace. John Barlough's second wife, Paralee Simmons, was nearly the same age as his oldest daughters. It was common at this time for younger women to marry much older men because the supply of young men had been diminished by the war.

In 1878, John and Rachel Wallace had a son, George Hugh Wallace, but John is listed on the June 1880 census as a widower in Collin County. "Rachel may have died from the complications of childbirth, not uncommon in those times," Julian suggested. "Also, I cannot find their son, George, on any later census report. Family members reported that George died at an early age."

John Wallace had a brother named Willis. "It seems clear that both brothers had a crush on pretty Rosella," Julian told me. "Willis went a long time before getting married and during that time he was almost always within arm's reach of Rosella." In the 1880 census report, John Wallace's immediate family (his brother Willis, his aunt and his grandmother) were living just three houses away from the Presley sisters on White Springs Road.

It appears that sometime after the 1880 census was taken, John Wallace packed up his little boy and moved back to Tilden, Mississippi, probably with the encouragement of his relatives back home. If he had not moved back to Mississippi, we would not have had an Elvis Presley.

A Young Man with No Wife

Back in Tilden, John was a young man without a wife who needed help with his child. It didn't take him long to satisfy this need. On December 23, 1880, he married pretty Almira Jane McFadden, a wise choice because he moved from one landowning family to another. The McFadden families were early settlers of the Tilden community and owned hundreds of acres of land.

Almira's father had been killed during the war, and she needed a husband to help manage the farm. She found the ideal match in John Wallace, a handsome young man with some family experience. The death of their loved ones had made this a promising match.

John Wallace was a very good fiddle player, and in rural Mississippi a local musician would have been very popular. "I think the girls would have liked handsome, talented John Wallace, just as they like musicians today," Julian told me. "He would have played often at barn dances, church socials and local parties." He also would have played at the White Springs Resort a short distance from Rosella Presley.

"It seems clear," Julian said, "that John had dalliances with other women, but he helped raise a passel of kids with Almira. Who knows what would have happened if he had not met Rosella down the road and started an affair with her? Again, we would not have had an Elvis Presley. This affair undoubtedly was the cause of a real bad falling out between John and his brother, and I don't think they ever reconciled."

Over twenty-three years, John and Almira Wallace raised nine children, all of them with the surname Wallace:

- Elnora, born September 1, 1882; Mackey Hargett's grandmother
- Bettie Lovie, born March 1885
- Robbie C., born August 1886
- Ausie Howard, born June 18, 1888
- John Kirby, born October 24, 1889
- Selma Ann, born November 1891
- Jessie Pearl, born April 21, 1895
- Willie Mae, born February 1898
- Archie Homer, born February 12, 1903

White Springs Resort

About two miles west of Tilden, on the banks of the Tombigbee River, the White Springs Resort catered to a wealthy clientele. Named for the four mineral springs that flowed from the hills into the river, it invited seekers of fun and health to bathe in and imbibe the healthy waters and indulge in a variety of entertainments.

The resort was a pearl of pleasure and opulence in an otherwise destitute region, a playground for the rich and a source of jobs for the poor. Spread over eighty acres, the resort featured two hotels, a dance hall and saloon, twenty-five rental cabins, a general store, numerous bathhouses along the river and a ferry to cross it.

Dances and political assemblies occurred frequently. "I believe, even without evidence, that John Wallace would have been a popular performer at these events," Julian said. "And he certainly would have had ample opportunities to meet other women. It's likely that he met Rosella Presley at White Springs."

Julian has always believed that Rosella and her sister Mary Jane, aka Rosalinda, had lived in a remote part of Itawamba and spent their days scratching out a living with little social interaction. "That turned out to be false," Julian told me. "The sisters had been provided a cabin by a man named William Marion Steele. It was located less than two miles from White Springs, the most popular resort in the region. They went to dances and parties at the resort and probably worked there. They certainly met wealthy men at White Springs."

Every Fourth of July, the resort sponsored an elaborate picnic and celebration. Some people made daytrips to White Springs, but many stayed for a week or more. The bubbling springs continually pumped life into the resort.

Today, not much remains of the resort, but several advertisements for it have survived. One of them, paid for by James M. Williams, ran in the *Fulton Southern Herald* on September 15, 1860.

James M. Williams, a farmer originally from Alabama, may have been the first person to operate the resort at White Springs. Two years later, he and his family were living in Tupelo. The building of the M&O railroad caused many people to move from Itawamba County to the Tupelo area. On the 1870 census, James was still living in Tupelo but working as a tinnier. The resort business may have been harder than he imagined.

White Springs Resort

> The subscriber takes this method of informing the public of the above-named springs and their well-known virtues need no further recommendation than can be given by the many hundreds who have tried their healing efficacy. The springs are situated on the Tombigbee River three miles south of Van Buren and eight miles north of Smithville in a pleasant and healthy locality where there are strong inducements for indulgence in field and river sports for the well, while ample preparations are made to promote the comfort and ease of the invalid; also, arrangements for bathing and a gymnasium for exercise and a number of suitable rooms for rent.

Julian found another ad that ran seventeen years later in the *Tupelo Journal*. Here is that opening ad abstracted from the *Tupelo Journal* by Martha Bone.

NEW HOTEL
AT
WHITE SPRINGS
IN ITAWAMBA COUNTY MISSISSIPPI

Seven miles north of Smithville, and 20 miles east of Tupelo and Verona, and 10 miles Southwest of Fulton.

The undersigned will open on the
FIRST DAY OF JUNE, 1877

The above hotel for the reception of boarders and visitors. The second ball of the season will be given on Wednesday July 4th.

The Proprietor announces to the invalid and pleasure- seeker that he has taken charge of the above noted watering place, and has thoroughly changed and refitted a new Hotel and Cabins for renters.

His rooms will be newly and neatly furnished, and his table supplied with everything that the adjacent can afford, also a meat market for renters.

A String Band has been engaged, and the Musical Department will be complete throughout the season. Game of all kinds plenty in the neighborhood, and fish innumerable in the river and lakes near the Springs.

Of the medicinal virtues of these Springs it is deemed unnecessary to say anything, as their properties have been analyzed and published and also tested by hundreds who visited them since their discovery thirty year ago. These Springs are renowned throughout North Mississippi and their healing properties are well known.

The Proprietor will spare no pains to make his guests and renters comfortable, and is determined that none shall leave dissatisfied. Renters will be furnished with neat and comfortable cabins, Board and rent will be furnished on the most reasonable terms. Give me a call if you are in pursuit of either health, sport, or fun. Rules of board and lodging, per day $2.00, per week $10.00, per month $30.00. Cabin rents 50 cts per day, $10.00 per month. Perfect satisfaction is guaranteed. Respectfully,

E. N. FEARS, PROPRIETOR
May 12, 1877

The apologetic tone of this ad suggests that the resort had been failing to live up to customer expectations and required a reboot, in today's terms. The proprietor, Elisha Fears, was a student in Alabama in 1860 and on the 1870 census was listed as a farmer in Smithville, Mississippi. On the next census in 1880, three years after posting his ad for the new hotel at White Springs, he was working as a clerk in a store in Smithville. His hotelier career was quite brief. Apparently, the resort business was harder than he had imagined.

White Springs Resort continued to operate, one way or another, for all of the twenty-eight years that the two Presley girls lived in the Tilden community. Julian told me, "I believe that John Wallace performed there as a musician for at least seventeen of those years."

Around 1890, John Wallace was thirty-seven years old. He had a dead wife, a dead son, and was remarried with five children. Instead of settling down, however, he began an affair with Rosella Presley. It would last for the rest of their lives.

Chapter 6
The Surprising Presley Girls

Julian's research into the pretty Presley sisters turned up surprising details that contradicted the popular notion that they were hardscrabble spinsters living a hard, sharecropping life in the wilderness of rural Mississippi with their grandmother. The truth is that Rosella and Rosalinda (aka Mary Jane) were having affairs with wealthy men and sometimes an irresistible hunk like John Wallace.

"Apparently, the concept of birth control was unknown to the sisters," Julian speculated. Rosella Elizabeth ended up with nine children who had assorted daddies, and Rosalinda had six. Large families could make sense in farm country. Once they had grown strong enough to work, children could do chores and earn money for the household. But younger offspring needed looking after until they could fend for themselves, so it made sense to have a grandma and a few older kids to do the child raising. A large crop of hungry children, though, could be expensive, and sharecropping contributed little cash, so the sisters needed to find supplemental income to support their growing households.

"I don't believe for a minute that the Presley sisters were hookers," Julian told me, "though to many in the Bible Belt their flexible morality would have caused a scandal if people found out about their behavior. Things that are called sexual escapades for a man are often considered harlotry for a woman. I think the Presley sisters were just hard pressed to make ends meet."

Rosella was born February 16, 1863, during the War for Southern Independence. Ten months later, her sister, Rosalinda, was born. Their father, Dunnan Presley, Jr. was a soldier and served under General Nathan Bedford Forrest.

An Unsettled Man

Dunnan Presley, Jr., born in Tennessee on July 1, 1827, was Elvis's great-great-grandfather who passed down the Presley name in an unconventional manner. Lineage in the US is usually conveyed to descendants based on the family name of one's father, but in the case of Dunnan's daughters by his second wife, who bore offspring with unidentified fathers, their children instead adopted their mother's surname—Presley. This is how Elvis's grandfather, Jessie Dee McDowell Presley, got his last name, otherwise his grandson would have been called Elvis Wallace.

Before Dunnan came to Mississippi and met Elvis's great-great-grandmother, he was married to Elizabeth Harrison and had three daughters and two sons. A year after his first child was born, he enlisted in a local militia called Company C, 5th Regiment, Tennessee Volunteers. He served in the War with Mexico (1846–1848) under General Winfield Scott. After serving for nearly nine months, he was discharged at Memphis and received 160 acres of land for his service. Oddly, he is absent from both the 1850 and 1860 census, and his whereabouts are unknown during that time. A marriage certificate, however, shows that he married Martha Jane Wesson in mid-August of 1861.

"I don't know why Dunnan came to Itawamba County without his family," Julian told me. "It appears, though, that Dunnan did not bother to divorce his first wife before marrying Martha Wesson. That may indicate that he just up and left."

With the Civil War in process, three months after his and Martha's daughter Rosella was born, Dunnan enlisted in Company E, Hamm's Regiment, Mississippi Cavalry and was later reported as a deserter, which sullied the Presley name.

"I believe Dunnan was not a deserter," Julian proclaimed. "He was serving under General Nathan Bedford Forrest, and no one deserted General Forrest and lived to tell about it. Undoubtedly, his deserter status was a misconception by careless researchers who didn't understand the Civil War."

Julian pointed out that General Forrest, who went on to become the first Grand Wizard of the Ku Klux Klan, surrendered in 1865 at Gainesville, Alabama. With the war over, all the troops simply headed home. Evidently, Dunnan went back to Tennessee instead, abandoning Martha and his two little girls in Itawamba County. He never returned. Finding that Dunnan was listed as a member of two different militia units led researchers to conclude that he must have been a deserter. The truth is quite different. When General Forrest was sent to northern Mississippi to set up an army unit with headquarters in Verona, he was not supplied any soldiers.

"Forrest had to recruit local militias—boys, old men, whoever he could get—to join the effort," Julian explained. "As militias were recruited, their names changed. The Itawamba County Cavalry might change to the First Mississippi Cavalry once General Forrest took it over. Dunnan was probably in the same unit all along, but because of a name change was thought to be in different units as a deserter."

If Dunnan Presley went back to his first wife, he did not stay with her. The record shows that he married a woman named Emily Pope in 1868 but had no children with her. In 1882, he was living in Arkansas with yet another wife, Harriet Troy, and had the last four of his eleven children with her. His last child was born when he was sixty-seven years old.

Elvis's namesake—his great-great-grandfather Presley—was a vigorous but very unsettled man.

A Broken Family

Dunnan Presley's Mississippi wife, Martha Jane Wesson, remarried in 1868, the same year that Dunnan married his fourth wife, but Martha died later that year. Her daughters, Rosella and Rosalinda, were just five years old when Martha died in childbirth along with infant Josephine. The sisters were suddenly living with their new stepfather, William Marion Steele, a local landowner.

The 1870 census shows them in a cabin on White Springs Road near Tilden, Mississippi, (GPS location: 34.17591, -88.36828). In 1871, perhaps overwhelmed by raising two young stepdaughters alone, William married a local woman, Sarah Brown, who became a surrogate mother for the girls.

This arrangement worked well for several years, at least until the sisters were approaching their teenage years. "I imagine that having these pretty teenagers flopping around the house, " Julain said, "probably half-naked much of the time, didn't go over very well with Sarah—especially if they were catching the eye of her husband, who as you recall was not related to them."

In 1875, maybe to keep peace with his pregnant wife, Steele sold eighty acres of his land to Millie Bowen Wesson, the maternal grandmother of Rosella and Mary Jane, who at fifty-seven also took custody of the girls. William's first surviving child, Joshua, was born this year. Fourteen months later, William and Sarah had another son, Vollie Joseph, and nearly two years after that Charles Warren was born. Over the next decade, William and Sarah would have four more children.

Rosella and Mary Jane almost certainly helped grandma sharecrop the land and probably found jobs at White Springs Resort. As teenagers, they could work in the laundry or the kitchen, tend the grounds, do hotel housekeeping—anything to make money for the family. "It makes sense that they worked at the resort since they lived so close," Julian explained. "And it would have been easy to meet wealthy men who were attracted to pretty young girls. The opportunity was certainly there." Unfortunately, neither the resort nor any records exist to confirm these ideas.

The 1880 census is the last time the name Rosalinda Presley can be found in the records. She appears on later reports, however, with other names—Mary Jane, Rose Mary, and Rosa Presley. Julian has not found any photograph of her.

On March 23, 1896, Grandma Wesson sold back the land on which they lived to William Marion Steele. She and Rosella's family moved next door to Joshua Steele, William's brother, near Fulton, Mississippi, and this is where Jessie Dee Presley, Elvis's grandfather, was born. By 1900, Rosella's sister had moved to Monroe County, Mississippi.

Many people have speculated about why Rosella never married. "During her lifetime, all the Southern states were struggling with the aftermath of the war," Julian reminded me. "Many young men had been killed, maimed or damaged mentally. There were few men left to marry."

In addition, day-to-day survival was difficult, particularly for women. There was no minimum wage, Social Security, Medicaid, welfare, food stamps or other safety nets. "Women worked in the home and on the farm," Julian explained. "They seldom traveled outside the local community. They tended to marry men they met at church or worked the fields with. It was common to marry cousins." Julian believes that staying unmarried may not have been Rosella's plan. "I think she just did what she had to do."

Certainly, bearing the children of wealthy men could provide the fathers with greater incentive to continue financial support for their children even if the men couldn't publicly own up to their roles for fear of scandal. "For this reason," Julian told me, "I think the daddies knew who their children were. Most of the children probably knew their daddies too. Unfortunately, for us to identify the daddies all these years later is a tough job."

One of Rosella's daughters, Doshie Presley Steele, told an interviewer, "I can't remember anyone ever talking about who our father was... It was a big mystery when we were children. My mother just didn't talk about it."

Julian's personal opinion was that Doshie's remark was probably a cover-up. "Almost certainly, the Presley kids knew. They lived in a small house in a small community. How could they not know who was visiting their mother? But I can understand not wanting to talk about the fathers who had virtually abandoned their children."

All in the Family

Rosella's life, and her sister's, were very different than I had imagined after reading the spare accounts in the traditional biographies. I never understood that the stepfather who was supposed to look after them had other unhealthy issues that undoubtedly affected the girls.

William Marion Steele was more than just Rosella's stepfather—he was the father of her first child, Walter G. Presley. Rosella got pregnant in March of 1878, shortly after her fifteenth birthday, and delivered little Walter as an early Christmas present on December 19 about nine months after William's second son with his wife Sarah had been born. This dramatic truth was proven by Julian's collection of family DNA, which contained samples of both Rosella's and William's family lines.

There is no doubt that Walter's mother was Rosella Presley, and his father was William Marion Steele. Julian's suspicions seem confirmed that William had been noticeably aroused by his young stepdaughter, Rosella, and that his infuriated new wife had insisted he jettison the nymphette from their home.

It's hard to imagine what Rosella must have been feeling. Her father had abandoned her when she was an infant, and then her second father had exiled her, at least until coming to her for the wrong kind of reunion. Could she have resisted William's advances? Was she now doomed to spend the rest of her life trying to prove herself worthy of a father's love?

No public records directly describe how the selfish actions of important men in her life had emotionally devastated Rosella. But the sequence of liaisons and childbearing over the course of her adult life provide tantalizing clues to the struggles she endured.

An Affair to Remember

Of the men who fathered children with Rosella, one of them, John Wallace, seemed to have a special place in her life. The affair that resulted in the birth of Jessie Dee McDowell Presley did not end there, and it continued even after Rosella had other children by other men and then moved away.

After Rosella's mother, Martha Jane Wesson, had passed away, Rosella and her stepfather/lover William Marion Steele managed to engineer a relationship with Rosella's fifteen-year-old daughter, Doshie. William's older brother, Joshua Steele, who was forty years older than Doshie, was needing company and Rosella was needing a place to live. Before long, young Doshie and Rosella moved from Tilden to the Clay community where Joshua lived. Doshie married the much older Joshua Steele, and Rosella had a comfortable place to live. Problem solved.

"You'd think that the distance to Clay would put an end to any burning embers between John Wallace and Rosella," Julian said. But interestingly, John Wallace showed up in the Clay community too. "It seems like John was kind of following Rosella around,"

Julian said. "It looked to me like there was still something going on there. Maybe a real love story. Not that it was keeping either of them from having sex with others, mind you."

The only known photograph of Rosella Presley about 4 years before she died.

During one of Julian's compulsive sessions of reading public records, he uncovered another possible chapter in this story: "In 1924, shortly before Rosella died, I found that she was living with her youngest son Joseph in a little house down a little old country road near Red Bay, Alabama. And guess who is living about a mile from Rosella? Yes, John Wallace. They're still close. In a different time, they might have spent their lives together. But then, they kind of did."

A Maze of DNA and Influence

Within the genetic maze of his ancestors lie the deep roots of Elvis Presley, the relatives with whom he shared DNA and who influenced him in unknown and unpredictable ways. He was a product of his ancestors—their habits, traditions, traits, lifestyles and values—all of which have rippled through generations of family. Just as our parents' genes are shared with us through the union of sperm and egg, our ancestors' beliefs and values are indelibly transmitted across the years through the telling of family stories and the imprinting of attitudes in a thousand different ways.

In his book *The Biology of Belief*, Dr. Bruce Lipton showed how genes carry no inevitability. We are not entrapped by our genetic make-up, not biologically or psychologically doomed by the shuffled genes that we're dealt. In fact, our beliefs have distinctly more power to control us, or break control over us, than our genes. It is the combination of genetics plus all that other non-genetic stuff we absorb from family members that make us who we are.

This book is about what Elvis was all the way back in time. He was the same as his eccentric and flawed ancestors but different as well. He reflected them in a unique way. Anyone who loved or admired the King must go back and see where he came from, and half of that story begins, as far as we know, with the Presley sisters and their broods.

Rosella's Children and Their Fathers

The following is a list of Rosella's children in their order of birth along with a biographical sketch. For the first time, the fathers of eleven of these children have been confirmed by Julian Riley, in

Five of Rosella's children at a family gathering. Fom the left: Doshie, Noah, Calhoun, Robbie, Joseph..

most cases by matching DNA against samples collected over the last ten years. Additional personal details will be provided later for Rosella's offspring who are in the direct ancestral line of Elvis Presley or have had a significant impact on his life.

Walter G. Presley, 1878—William Marion Steele

Walter Presley, Rosella's first child, was fathered by Rosella's stepfather. He was either born in 1878 (according to his draft registration), 1879 (as engraved on his tombstone) or 1880 (based on family records). He is missing from the 1880 census, and his personal story is sparse. He finally shows up in the 1900 census records living with Rosella next to his father's brother, Joshua Steele, in Pleasanton, Mississippi. A decade later, he was living near White Springs next door to his father, William Marion Steele, and was married to Samantha Brown, the niece of his father's wife. He is buried at Hopewell Cemetery in Itawamba County (GPS location 34.33055, -88.21699).

Essie Presley, 1882— Father Unknown

Essie Presley, born in 1882, was the third child born to the Presley sisters and Rosella's second child. She died at the age of six when Rosella was twenty-five years old. The cause and specific date of death and her burial place are unknown. Julian has not yet identified Essie's father.

Minnie Fee Doshie Presley, 1888—Tom Morris

Doshie, as she was usually called, was the last surviving widow of a Confederate War veteran in the State of Mississippi. She was born in the White Springs-Tilden community of Itawamba County. DNA has shown her father to be Tom Morris, a wealthy landowner in Itawamba County. The date of birth on her tombstone is June 22, 1886. However, social security records show her year of birth as 1889. In a newspaper article, Doshie said she was fifteen in 1903 when she married Joshua Steele, the brother of Rosella's stepfather. This would make her year of birth 1888.

Joshua Steele was about forty years older than Doshie and yet they had five children before his death in 1914. She never remarried. As in so many cases, Joshua's date of birth is in dispute. His tombstone states 1846, his death certificate says 1849 and a newspaper article lists it as 1844. Doshie is buried at Fairview Cemetery in Itawamba County (GPS location 34.45013, -88.17990).

Noah Persell Presley, 1887—Tom Morris

According to his WWI draft registration record, Noah Presley's birth date was August 29, 1887, but his tombstone indicates 1890 and his social security record shows 1891. What we know for sure is that after some DNA detective work, Julian has identified Noah's father as Tom Morris, a wealthy landowner and businessman in Itawamba County who also fathered Noah's older sister, Doshie. "I think that Rosella probably got to know Tom Morris at White Springs Resort," Julian told me. Tom Morris was also the father of John A. Jefferson Presley, the son of Rosella's sister Mary Jane (aka Rosalinda), making these two boys half-brothers as well as cousins.

On July 4, 1910, twenty-three-year-old Noah married Susan Griffin who was five years older than him. Susan was listed as "Miss" Susan Griffin on the marriage license, but she already had three sons with the surname Griffin—Sumter ("Sump"), James Whitford ("Whit") and Trannie Eckford ("Eack").

Though some have claimed that Noah may have fathered these boys, DNA has finally proven that their father was an Itawamba County man named James Madison Moore. Noah took Susan's sons into his household and reared them as his own, perhaps giving rise to the misconception that he had fathered them. Offspring of these three sons considered Noah to be their grandfather. Between 1912 and 1918, Noah and Susan would have six children.

By 1930, Noah was living in East Tupelo where he was affectionately known as "Paw Presley," "Papa" or "Daddy" within the family and "Mr. Noahie" by the community. He was mayor of East Tupelo for two years and owned a school bus. It was Noah who drove Gladys and Elvis Presley and others to visit Vernon Presley during his incarceration at Parchman Penitentiary. "Mr. Noahie" was looked upon as someone who would always help family and friends. During the depression, he made sure families had enough food. He is buried at Priceville Cemetery in Tupelo (GPS location is 34.26684, -88.65732). His epitaph reads: "Having finished life's duty, he now sweetly rests."

Jessie Dee McDowell Presley, 1897—John Wallace

Jessie Dee is recognized as the grandfather of Elvis Presley. He was born April 8, 1896, in Itawamba County, Mississippi. Jessie Dee and Minnie Mae Hood had five children. "I have tried to find a marriage license for Jessie and Minnie Mae, but I've had no success," Julian told me, "even though I've checked Itawamba and all the surrounding counties. It's possible that Minnie Mae, like Jessie's mother Rosella, never married—or that the marriage license was never filed with the county, which would mean there was no legal marriage."

Jessie Dee's son, Vernon Elvis Presley, is recognized as the father of Elvis Presley. Other children were son Vester Lee and daughters Delta Mae, Gladys Earline and Nashval Lorene. Jessie Dee was sometimes called "Dee" or "J. D.," which has confused many researchers because Jessie Dee had a second cousin named John Delton Presley. John Delton's 1954 divorce record in the Lee County Chancery Clerk's office, recorded in the name of Mr. and Mrs. J. D. Presley, is often mistaken as the divorce record of

Jessie Dee and Minnie Mae Hood Presley. In 1948, when Elvis was thirteen, his grandfather Jessie Dee married Vera Kinnaird.

Calhoun Presley, 1899—Robert A. "Bud" Steele

Calhoun Presley, a truck driver, was born May 9, 1899, in the Eastman Community of Itawamba County, Mississippi. In 1918, he lived in Cross County, Arkansas, where he registered for the World War I draft. He had two children with his wife, Mildred Clemmons, and four children with his second wife, Maud Mask.

Calhoun Presley with his wife Maud and their four children.

It took some detective work for Julian to find Calhoun's father. On a family heritage site, Julian discovered a woman who had claimed Calhoun Presley as her grandfather, a promising lead, but the woman did not respond to inquiries. Fortunately, a man named Ricky Simmons from Illinois contacted Julian about another matter under investigation, the moving of Elvis's birth house to a new location, a remarkable story that will be told later. Ricky's father and uncle were the men who moved the house up from the Presley property to Baker Street where it now resides.

Julian quickly learned that Ricky Simmons's mother and grandmother were descendants of William Marion Steele. Ricky believed a relative named Lisa in Missouri was from the Steele side of the family. At about this time, Julian found another relative of Ricky's, Tammy, who could only have been related through the Steele clan. "It looked like there was a man somewhere in Missouri or Arkansas who had been passing on his genes. Maybe he was the man I was looking for."

By coincidence, a restaurant building in Verona that Julian owned was being rented by a man named Chris Waddle, who was also a descendant of William Marion Steele. "So, I got Chris to let me analyze his DNA," Julian explained. "Ricky Simmons generously gave me access to his mother's DNA online. When we compared the DNA from all four folks (Ricky's mother, Chris Waddle, Lisa and Tammy) it all pointed to a common Steele ancestor."

Julian didn't think that forebear was William Marion Steele, because he was so much older than Rosella. "Yes, he had fathered Rosella's first child, Walter," Julian said, "but I think that was just an impulse. Besides, Calhoun was born twenty-one years after Walter. William Marion Steele was sixty years old by then."

Julian also concluded it couldn't be William's brother, Joshua, because he was married to Rosella's daughter. That would be just too weird. Was there another Steele brother who could have been the father?

"I was just getting to that," Julian explained. "William had another brother named Robert A. 'Bud' Steele. Bud was born in Marion County, Alabama, but lived in Tilden, Mississippi, with his brother William Marion Steele."

Bud Steele certainly knew Rosella, his brother's stepdaughter and one-time lover. In addition, according to public records, he also lived in Bounds Crossroads, Mississippi. And where do you suppose Rosella was living when Calhoun was born?

"She was in Bounds Crossroads," Julian told me with a grin. "Bud was the only Steele around those parts at that time.

He was living close to Rosella, was the right age—just ten years older than Rosella—and he matches up with all the other Steele DNA we have from descendants. He's Calhoun's daddy, there's no doubt in my mind."

Mack Presley, 1901—Father Unknown

Mack was born October 2, 1901, in the Eastman Community of Itawamba County, Mississippi. He was very tall and a good basketball player. Mack is believed to be buried in an unmarked grave at Mt. Pleasant Cemetery east of Tremont, Itawamba County (GPS location 34.22178, -88.21109). The cause and exact date of his death are unknown, but he died between 1917 and 1920. No DNA is available to identify his father directly, but Julian believes that Mack's father, as well as his young brother's, is Bud Steele, who also sired Calhoun Presley.

Half-brothers Calhoun (left) and Jessie Dee stand behind another half-brother, Mack. DNA has not yet identified Mack's father, but the three men shared a mother, Rosella.

After Calhoun was born in 1899, Bud moved seventy miles from Bounds Crossroads to Corinth in Alcorn County, Mississippi. Julian thinks things may have gotten too hot for him at Bounds Crossroads. Maybe his brother wasn't too happy about his dalliance with Rosella. Or maybe the neighbors were getting nosy. "At any rate,"

Julian told me, "Bud did come back to Bounds Crossroads, and in 1902 Mack Presley was born to Rosella. Another coincidence? I don't think so. I'm positive Bud Steele was Mack's father, but I don't have DNA proof yet."

Robbie Presley, 1903—Robert A. "Bud" Steele

Born March 1, 1903, Rosella's daughter Robbie was living with her husband Odis and son Lynn near Red Bay Alabama in 1930. Over the next five years she would have two daughters, Geraldine and Jewell Eveline. Robbie is buried at Mt. Pleasant Cemetery in Itawamba County, Mississippi, (GPS location 34.22178, -88.21109). Her epitaph reads: "Precious memories." Julian believes that Robert A. "Bud" Steele was the father of Robbie as well as her brothers Calhoun and Mack.

Joseph Warren Presley, 1907—Father Unknown

Joe was born January 6, 1907. According to census records from 1930, Joe and his family were living in Beat 5 of Tishomingo County, Mississippi. The day before Christmas in 1924, he married Delma Jackson. They had seven children:

- Bytha Mae (1927)
- Flavis Monroe (1929)
- Jettie Faye (1931)
- Lola Vae (1934)
- Vela Rae (1937)
- Grady Alvin (1941)
- Patsy Ruth (1943)

Joe died in 1979 and is buried at Ridge Cemetery in Itawamba County next to his wife (GPS location 34.45013, -88.17990). His epitaph reads: "Beyond the sunset" and "We will meet again. Love's remembrance lasts forever." Julian has had Joseph's DNA for a decade but is still searching for DNA that will help identify his father. He is not related to the Steeles.

Joseph Presley with his wife Delma and five of their children.

Mary Jane's (Rosalinda's) Children and Their Fathers

Here are Martha Jane's (Rosalinda's) children and their fathers.

Martha Jane Presley, 1880 —Father Unknown

Martha Jane's mother, Mary Jane, was just seventeen when Martha was born in 1880. "I believe that Mary Jane may have given birth to another child before this one," Julian told me, "but there is no child listed in the household on the 1880 census. If there was an earlier baby, maybe it did not survive." Martha Jane was named after Mary Jane's birth mother, Martha Jane Wesson. We have ten DNA samples related to Martha but are still lacking critical evidence to conclusively identify her father.

Martha Jane Presley's story is a Cinderella tale. By good fortune, her family had lived near the Hussey brothers. Tom Hussey and his younger sibling Charles had inherited several thousand acres of farmland and were among the wealthiest residents in the county. Martha Jane fell in love with her handsome prince, Charles, who was a director of Peoples Bank and Trust Company and had installed a telegraph line from Tupelo to his home in Richmond fifteen miles away so he could play the stock market. They were married and over the next eighteen years had eight children.

In this genetically convoluted family, Martha Jane's brother-in-law, Tom Hussey, was also the father of her brother and two sisters, though she may not have known. Tom Hussey was also the father of Rosella's daughter Essie, who was Martha Jane's niece. I haven't found any proper names for these complex relationships.

Martha Jane Presley is buried at Andrews Chapel Cemetery next to her husband Charles (GPS location 34.22678, -88.56241).

Ofelia Presley, 1883—Tom Morris

Born in 1883, when Mary Jane was twenty, Ofelia Presley was fathered by Tom Morris, a wealthy landowner who also was the father of other siblings.

John A. Jefferson Presley, 1887—Tom Morris

Born June 28, 1887, John was called "Paw John" by his family, according to his daughter, Carthy. To the rest of the community, he was "Big John" because he stood six and a half feet tall. He owned a store and blacksmith shop near Richmond, Mississippi. Neighbors could hear Big John pounding on an anvil before daylight on most days. He gave each of his ten children an acre of land to live on. He is buried at Andrews Chapel Cemetery (GPS location 34.22678, -88.56241). DNA has shown that his father was wealthy Mississippi landowner Tom Morris, who was also the father of Rosella's son Noah Presley, making Noah and Big John half-brothers as well as cousins.

John A. Jefferson Presley, at six and a half feet tall, towers over his wife, Minnie Raper Presley

Duskey Presley, 1888 —Tom Morris

Little is known about Duskey Presley except that she was born in May of 1888 and in 1913, at twenty-five, married William C. Pendergest. They had one son. Wealthy landowner and businessman Tom Morris was her father.

William David "Buck" Presley, Sr., 1893—Tom Morris

Born January 3, 1893, Buck Presley stood about six feet, three inches tall and liked to dip snuff. According to his obituary, he was a retired farmer, lifelong resident of Nettleton, Mississippi, and a devout Baptist. He is buried at Andrews Chapel Cemetery (GPS location 34.22678, -88.56241). His epitaph reads: "In my Father's house are many mansions." His father was Tom Morris, who also sired other siblings.

Thomas Eleanach Canan Presley, 1898—Tom Hussey

Thomas was born February 28, 1898. In 1919, he married Effie Curry and in 1920 their son Fleatus was born. His middle name Eleanach shows the Gaelic influence of his forebears. (See "Appendix F" page 277 for a list of his ancestors). By 1967, they were living at 135 South Canal Street in Tupelo. He was a farmer and a Baptist. He died of a heart attack in 1975, and his wife died six years later. They are both buried in unmarked graves at Andrews Chapel Cemetery (GPS location 34.22678, -88.56241).

Chapter 7

Jessie and Minnie

"Grandpa" Jessie Dee

After Elvis Presley became famous, Jessie Dee McDowell Presley publicly took credit for being the King's grandfather. Before then, he'd had little contact with either Elvis or his own son, Vernon, who was listed as "Father" on Elvis's birth certificate. This opportunism symbolizes, I think, the nature of the third son of Rosella Presley who over the years would easily distort the truth when it suited him.

As with many of Elvis's ancestors, the year of Jessie Dee's birth is in dispute. His draft registration lists it as April 9, 1897, which Julian believes is correct, but his death certificate and a marriage license for his second wife indicates his birth year as 1896. In either case, Jessie Dee was Rosella's fifth child. His father was John Wallace. He had eight siblings by an assortment of fathers, none of them married to his mother.

Jessie Dee was born on a farm owned by Joshua Steele in Itawamba County. His name was recorded as "Jessie Dee *McClowell* Presley," which most likely was a mistake. After diligently searching the records, Julian has found no one in Itawamba County with the name McClowell.

"I do not believe that Rosella Presley, who couldn't read or write, was making up names," Julian told me. "But if the person writing down that name by hand made a small 'd' instead of a capital 'D,' that small 'd' could be mistaken as 'cl.' McDowell would then become Mcclowell, a tiny error resulting in a nonexistent name."

This small mistake, repeated over and over, undoubtedly caused personal problems for Jessie Dee, confounded researchers for decades and led to many false conclusions and errors in Elvis biographies.

Julian has found no information about Jessie Dee's formal education, but the boy worked hard to provide for the family, which never owned a home and relied on outside support from friends and the fathers of Rosella's children.

When he was fifteen, Jessie Dec and Minnie Mae Hood began living together, a relationship that produced five children between 1914 and 1925. Minnie Mae was about seven years older than Jessie, just as Gladys Presley years later was several years older than their son, Vernon, who is generally regarded as the father of Elvis Presley.

Julian has searched all the adjoining counties in Mississippi but has found no marriage license for Jessie Dee and Minnie Mae. When their son, Vernon, was born in 1916, Jessie's home address was Route 2, Fulton, Itawamba County, Mississippi (GPS location 34.34881, -88.34749).

In mid-1918, Jessie Dee registered for the World War I draft. The registration described him as tall and slender with blue eyes and black hair. He signed his name, so we assume he could read and write. A photograph of Jessie Dee in a uniform indicates that he was drafted or possibly joined the military, perhaps the National Guard.

Around 1924, after being discharged from the military, Jessie Dee and his family followed his brother, Noah Presley, in a move from the Fulton area to East Tupelo where Jessie found work as a farmer and carpenter. "I believe they moved in the spring of that year," Julian explained, "because Jessie purchased some Lee County property from S. H. Wells for $1,100.00 on March 29, 1924."

About three years later, in 1927, Jessie Dee bought property from Hazzie and Addie Long on Old Saltillo Road in East Tupelo. Hazzie was the brother of a man named Sam Long who you may recall had married Tee Hussey, the woman who received a large parcel of land as a wedding present from her father, Tom Hussey. And Tom, as described earlier, was the wealthy, unmarried father of Jessie Dee's sister, Effie, and two of his first cousins through Mary Jane Presley. Clearly, these people all knew each other.

Jessie worked hard and played hard but was considered very demanding by family members. He seems to have been quite vain and selfish. He loved fine clothes, and he saved up twenty-four dollars over many months to buy a tailor-made brown suit with pearl buttons. According to townsfolk, he would strut around town with his head in the air and a cane in his hand. He hated poverty and didn't want people to know he was poor.

He demanded that Minnie Mae account for all the food put on the table but kept his whiskey locked up. He was hard on his children, particularly Vernon. Jessie would not approve of anything Vernon did, and Vernon resisted doing anything that pleased Jessie. Jessie kicked Vernon out of the house at sixteen, and their relationship remained bitter all their lives.

Jessie paid off his property loan on April 17, 1934. He owned the property on Old Saltillo Road until Elvis bought him a house in Kentucky years later.

Julian told me, "I've found many photographs of Presley and Hood family gatherings in Itawamba County, but I haven't found even one picture of Jessie Dee or Vernon at any of these events. And I haven't found a single picture of Jessie Dee and

Minnie Mae together. Lots of pictures of Noah Presley, yes, and of Minnie Mae—they are at the gatherings—but not Jessie Dee and Vernon." It seems that the family, especially Vernon, did not like Jessie Dee, or that he did not like them.

Jessie's half-brother, Calhoun, had this to say about his sibling: "For most of his life, Jessie drifted from one job to another all over Mississippi, Kentucky and Missouri. He was a sharecropper in the summer and a lumberjack in the winter … He was an honest man, but he enjoyed drinking whiskey and was often involved in drunken bar brawls."

Julian told me, "It's surprising that Vernon and Gladys named one of their babies after Jessie, although it wasn't the baby who lived."

When Vernon was charged with forging a check along with Lether Gable and Travis Smith, who was Gladys's brother, Jessie Dee filed bail for Travis but refused to bail out Vernon, who remained in jail awaiting trial.

Repeating the abandonment pattern of his grandfather, Dunnan Presley, Jessie abandoned his family to work in the shipyards on the Mississippi gulf coast. He moved around a lot and finally settled in Louisville, Kentucky, working as a night watchman at the Pepsi-Cola plant. For Vernon Presley and his siblings, it was as if they didn't have a father.

In *Elvis and Gladys,* author Elaine Dundy incorrectly wrote that Jessie Dee had filed for a divorce in 1946 and falsely claimed that Minnie had deserted him. The judge granted the divorce in Lee County, Dundy claimed. But this has no basis in fact. No marriage license exists, and the research on which Dundy based her report was flawed.

"There was a divorce in Lee County for J. D. Presley," Julian told me, "but that divorce was for Jessie's second cousin, John Delton Presley, who had the same initials—J. D." Unfortunately, this error has gained a life of its own. When searching the internet, I found this same mistake repeated over twenty times almost word for word from Dundy's book, *Elvis and Gladys*. Unfortunately, the fake fact has become an accepted truth.

In December of 1948, when Elvis was almost fourteen, Jessie Dee married Vera Kinnaird, a woman he had met at the Pepsi-Cola plant. It was the second marriage for her. They would have no children together.

Julian found their 1948 marriage license and discovered two obvious lies Jessie had made on the document. The first lie was listing the name of Jessie's father as "John Pressley" when his father was actually John Wallace, as Julian had discovered. Secondly, Jessie lied about his mother's name, stating it was "Rosie Wesson." His mother, Rosella, was a Presley, not a Wesson. It was his great-grandmother Millie who was a Wesson.

Jessie Dee told the truth about his father's first name, John, but not his last name, hoping to look more "decent" in her eyes. And he did the same thing with his mother's name, using a common variant of her actual first name but exchanging her last name for his great-grandmother's.

There were no computers in those days to instantly flag the deceit. "There never was a John Presley in Itawamba County," Julian told me. "I know because I checked the records." These lies have caused researchers and biographers to make numerous errors documenting the roots of Elvis Presley, many of them now part of the historical record.

Why would Jessie Dee McDowell Presley lie about family names on his marriage license? "To save face," Julian explained. "I believe he lied about the names because he didn't want his new wife to figure out he was the illegitimate son of John Wallace and Rosella Presley."

The lies were then made even more indelible after Jessie Dee died. When providing information for his death certificate, his wife repeated the erroneous information, listing John Presley as Jessie's father and Rosie Wesson as his mother. Apparently, Vera still believed the lies.

Around 1958, Jessie attempted to capitalize on the fame of his grandson, Elvis, by making a record on which he sang the songs "Swinging in the Orchard," "Stop Kicking My Dog Around" and "The Billy Goat Song." Julian Riley explained to me, "I think these were probably songs he learned from his fiddle-playing father, John Wallace."

"I don't think Jessie and Vernon ever reconciled their differences," Julian told me. "But once, in 1959, Vernon visited his father in Kentucky to introduce him to his new wife, Dee Stanley."

Jessie Dee died of heart disease in 1973 at Methodist Hospital in Louisville, Kentucky. He is buried at Louisville Memorial Gardens (GPS location 38.18876, -85.81876).

Vernon did not attend the funeral. Elvis sent flowers. Vera got married again.

"Grandma" Minnie Mae

Minnie Mae Hood's family came to the Itawamba County town of Fulton in the 1830s from across the eastern border in Alabama. Her grandfather Joshua built a cabin when they arrived, and it's likely Minnie Mae was born there on June 17, 1890, to Joshua's son, William H. "Buck" Hood, and his wife, Mary Louisa. Many Hood relatives still live in the area. A number of ancestors are buried in a cemetery across the road from the Mt. Pleasant Baptist Church northeast of Fulton, Mississippi (GPS 34.22178, -88.21109).

We don't know how Minnie met Jessie Dee, a handsome young man who was seven years younger. Their first child, Vester, was born a year later, contradicting the widespread belief that Vernon was the firstborn son. Vernon was born two years later in 1916 followed by sisters Delta Mae, Gladys Earline and Nashval Lorene. Having found no marriage license for Jessie Dee and Minnie Mae after an extensive search, Julian has concluded they were never officially married.

The marriage was troubled almost from the start. Family and friends have reported that Jessie was sometimes mean, often drunk and always self-centered. Minnie Mae was thought of as a "harsh woman" who used a stern countenance and brusque manner to help her survive hard times and a difficult marriage. "I have not found a photo of her with a smile," Julian told me. "I wonder if she knew how."

Minnie Mae was not afraid of her husband and frequently let him know her disappointment with his behavior. The corrosive relationship slowly collapsed over time until Jessie finally abandoned the family. "Some biographers have politely called it an unofficial separation," Julian explained, "but I think the marriage was simply shattered. She thought she'd gotten a raw deal in life—and in fact she had. Jessie just wanted to be anywhere but home."

Elvis truly loved his Grandma Minnie, and the two had a special bond. Despite her stern exterior, she was fiercely loyal to her family. "Elvis probably acquired much of his loyalty to his mom and dad—and to his friends and cousins—from Minnie Mae," Julian concluded.

Jessie wandered for a time before settling in Louisville and remarrying. Minnie Mae moved in with Elvis and his parents, finding a measure of happiness there. From that point on, she lived with Vernon, Gladys and Elvis in all their homes, including Graceland, outliving them all. "In a life full of hardship, probably the hardest thing that Minnie Mae had to endure was losing all the people she was close to," Julian said.

On Minnie Mae's grave, which lies to the left of Elvis's, the following words are inscribed:

> "Her children shall rise up and call her blessed. Her husband also and he praiseth her." Proverbs 31:24

She was a gracious lady, our precious mother, and a virtuous woman.

In simplicity she taught us, with God-given wisdom she guided us through hardships and heartaches and taught us to look to God for our strength.

She was love in motion and with a quiet, sweet, gentle, and humble spirit.

She was our close and trusted friend and a friend to all who knew her and she was loved by many.

A flower that never faded.

She was the queen of our home. We love you Mom and we deeply miss you.

Nash, Delta, Gladys, Vester .... and in memory of Vernon and Elvis

Jessie and Minnie's Children

Before Jessie Dee abandoned his family, he and Minnie Mae had five children. Like Jessie's mother, Rosella, Minnie Mae gave birth without the formality of a marriage. Many researchers and fans want Jessie and Minnie Mae to have been husband and wife, but there is no documentary evidence that they were married or divorced.

Because rumors of a divorce decree persist—probably based on Elaine Dundy's book, which has scattered a lot of false information into the wind—I asked Julian what he thought.

After a pause, Julian answered, "It's not inconceivable that when Jessie was thinking about marrying another woman, he started worrying that his relationship with Minnie Mae could be construed as a common law marriage. He might have even sought legal counsel. But no divorce decree was ever granted in Kentucky or Mississippi or I would have found it."

Mosy likely, then, all five of Jessie and Minnie Mae's children were illegitimate. At least the offspring knew who their parents were, though they could never be sure there were no other siblings out there.

Here is a list of Jessie Dee's children and a biographical sketch of each.

Vester Presley, 1914

Contrary to numerous books and websites, Vester Lee Presley was the first child born to Jessie Dee and Minnie Mae. He was born on September 11, 1914, and was the only paternal uncle of Elvis Presley. After moving to Memphis, Vester often returned to visit relatives in the Lee and Itawamba counties of Mississippi. On these trips, he would sometimes bring his mother, Minnie Mae, so she could visit relatives and friends.

Vester worked for years as a gate guard at Graceland, and his friendly manner made him popular with Elvis fans. It also helped earn him a reputation for flirting with the young women who came to the gate.

Nine months after Elvis was born to Gladys Love Smith, Vester Presley married Gladys Smith's younger sister, Clettes. Thus, two brothers, Vester and Vernon Presley, were married to two sisters, Gladys and Clettes Smith. Five years later, Vester and Clettes had a daughter, Patsy. The two Presley-Smith marriages made Patsy and Elvis double first cousins.

In 1978, Vester published a memoir entitled *A Presley Speaks.* He died January 17, 1997, at the age of eighty-two. He is buried at Forest Hill Home & Memorial Park – Midtown, Memphis, Tennessee (GPS location 35.09920, -90.01732).

Vernon Presley, 1916

Often referred to as Jessie Dee's firstborn son, Vernon Elvis Presley was actually Jessie's second child. He was born on April

10, 1916, north of Fulton in Itawamba County (GPS location 34.34881, -88.34749). The state of Mississippi erected a historical marker on the site in 2009, and the property is now owned by Mackey Hargett, Vernon's first cousin. When Vernon was about seven years old, Jessie Dee moved the family from this location to East Tupelo, Mississippi.

Much has been written about Vernon's incarceration at the Mississippi State Penitentiary, often called Parchman Prison. The incident began when Vernon decided to sell a stolen hog to Orville Bean, a dairy farmer who was also Vernon's landlord. He did not have a hog to sell, so Vernon decided to steal one from his father, Jessie Dee, wrongly assuming the crime would not be discovered. Most likely, Orville had paid a substandard price for the hog suspecting it was stolen property. Unhappy with the amount Orville had paid by check, Vernon, with assistance from two friends, Lether Gable and Gladys Presley's brother, Travis, attempted to right the wrong by forging a check with a higher amount. Vernon took fifteen dollars as his share of the proceeds.

Unfortunately, Jessie Dee discovered Vernon had stolen one of his hogs, and the forgery was quickly detected. The three perpetrators were arrested on November 16, 1937. Livid that his son had stolen from him, Jessie Dee chose to bail out Travis, Gladys's brother, but refused to put up bail for Vernon to teach him a lesson. This act appears to have driven a permanent wedge between father and son. Vernon would never again live in East Tupelo so long as his father resided there.

Vernon's plea of not guilty was made too late for his case to be tried in the court's fall term. Without bail, he spent six months in the county jail before his trial began on Monday, May 23, 1938. During this long stretch, he changed his plea to guilty and in late 1937 sat with his family for a photograph.

Elvis Presley and his parents had a family portrait taken in the Tupelo county jail.

Decades later, the photo turned up in a collection of photographs held by the Official Elvis Presley Fan Club in Leicester, England. The blank, gray background of the photo is most likely a concrete wall in the brand-new Lee County jail in Tupelo. For the family, this photograph could be considered both a Christmas picture and a birthday photo—Elvis would turn three in January. The expressions of Vernon and Gladys betray the precarious future they are awaiting. He was convicted about five months later and given a three-year sentence with no credit for time spent awaiting trial.

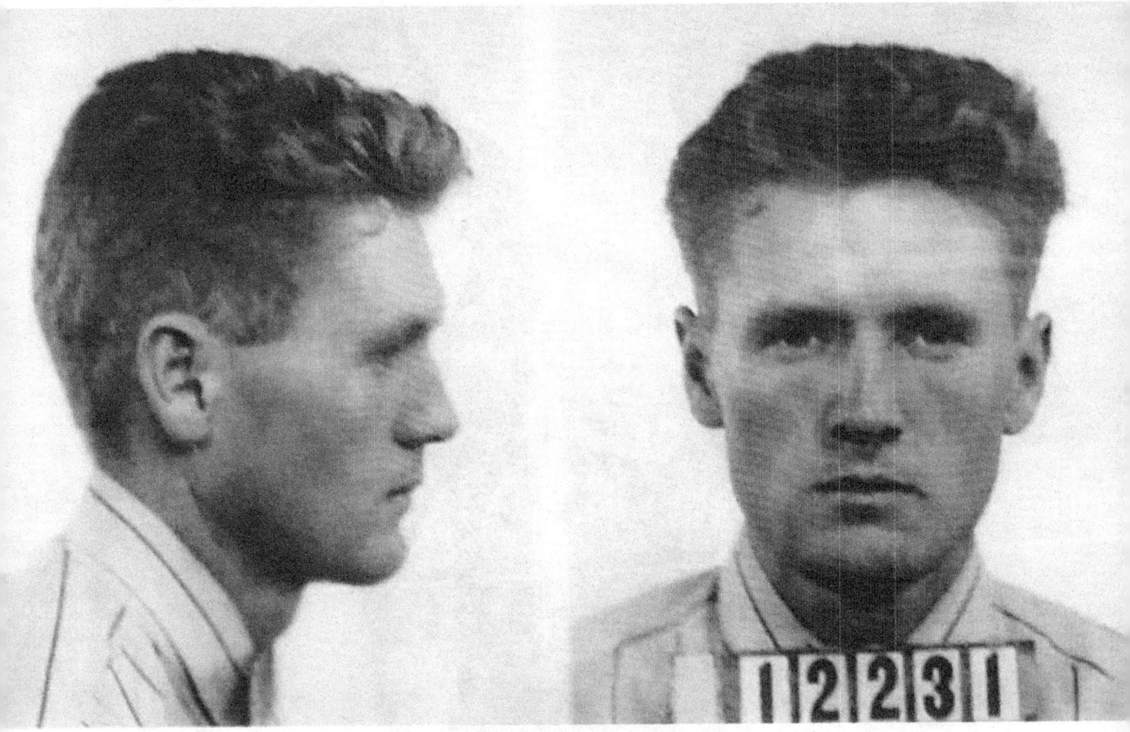

Julian Riley's research uncovered a document never before made public and worth adding to the historic record. Vernon was received at Parchman on June 1, 1938, and was assigned prisoner number 12231. Vernon's mug shot shows his hair cut very short on the sides. The twenty-two-year-old is described as "five-feet, ten-and-one-half inches tall weighing 147 pounds." Interestingly, the document reveals that Vernon had a fifth-grade education. This is the only definitive source we have found about Vernon's education. The document goes on to describe an "oval face, concave nose, arched eyebrows, small mouth with good teeth, medium complexion, slender build, sandy hair, blue eyes and a shoe size of nine." He had nine brown moles on his chest and an irregular scar on his right inner wrist. Vernon specified no religious affiliation.

Finally, the document bears this statement: "The superintendent or anyone whom he might designate is hereby authorized to open and examine mail, packages or any article sent me." Signed "Vernon Elvis Presley" (prisoner's signature).

It is unclear exactly how long Vernon spent at Parchman. Julian believes he was released February 6, 1939, which would put Vernon in prison for about fifteen months. It is clear from Orville Bean's letter to the governor, which appealed for an early release, that Vernon was still in prison on December 1938.

Vernon's cousin, Noah Presley, made many trips in his school bus transporting Elvis, Gladys and other friends and family to visit Vernon at Parchman. While Vernon was in jail, Gladys lost the small house she and Elvis were living in, and for a time they stayed with relatives. Much more will be revealed about Vernon throughout this book.

Vernon outlived both Gladys and Elvis but in later years developed diabetes and suffered from heart problems. He died in 1979 and was buried on the grounds of Graceland in Memphis (GPS location 35.04531, -90.02297).

Delta Mae Presley (1919)

"Aunt Delta," born June 19, 1919, had no children with her husband, Pat Biggs. The date of their marriage is not known. Her husband died in 1967. After Elvis bought Graceland, Delta lived there until her death in 1993. She is buried at Forest Hill Home & Memorial Park – Midtown, Memphis, Tennessee (GPS location 35.09920, -90.01732).

Gladys Erlene Presley (1923)

Not much is known about Elvis's Aunt Gladys, other than she was known as "Little Gladys." She moved to Florida sometime between 1945 and 1951 and is buried at Roselawn Cemetery in Tallahassee, Florida (GPS location 30.48662, -84.26570).

Rev. Nashval Lorene Presley (1925)

"Nash" was born on December 14, 1925, and became a licensed and ordained Assembly of God minister. She married William Earl Pritchett, who was three years older than her and had worked with Vester as a security guard at Graceland. Pritchett children include Jesse Earl, Jerry Wayne, Donna Kay and Karen Sue.

Elvis had bought land for his aunt's church in Walls, Mississippi, put a double-wide trailer on it and Nash commuted there from Memphis. According to Nash's daughter, Donna, Elvis then called her mother into his room at Graceland and asked if his aunt had a piano for the church. The answer was no.

"Do you want one?" Elvis asked. "How about the one in the music room?" She accepted the offer. The beautiful, gold grand piano had been given to Elvis by Priscilla, and he no longer wanted it.

The instrument had to be moved, of course. Nash's husband, Earl, took the legs off the piano, wrapped it in moving blankets, rounded up a front-end loader, and with the piano in the bucket headed out of Graceland's front gate, down Elvis Presley Blvd., then drove about twenty-five miles to the church in Walls.

But the piano would not fit through the door of the church. Nash suggested taking out a wall, but Earl pointed out that the piano was so big there'd be no room for people in the sanctuary. So, he loaded up the piano in the bucket again, drove it to the gates of Graceland and up the driveway.

Later that night, Nash explained the problem to Elvis and asked if she could trade it in. He told her it was hers now and she could "burn it in the front yard" if she wanted. Nash went to a music store and traded it for a small Spinet—not a great business deal, but good for the church. The gold piano eventually ended up at the Hard Rock Café in Tampa, Florida.

Nash and her husband moved permanently to Wynne, Arkansas, six months before her death on April 25, 1994. She is buried at Crosslawn Cemetery in Wynne, Arkansas (GPS location 35.26734, -90.79135).

Mackey Hargett's Secrets

Mackey Hargett, the man who had pointed Julian's research toward the pivotal John Wallace, had a lot more to offer than that simple tip. As his relationship with Julian deepened, stories emerged that would have been lost to history had Mackey's name not been passed on to Julian after a lecture.

Discovering a Famous Relative

Mackey's grandmother, it turned out, was Elnora Wallace Yarber. At first, this meant nothing to Julian until he figured out that Elnora was the oldest daughter of John Wallace and his wife Almira. Put another way, Mackey's grandmother was the half-sister of Jessie Dee Presley and an aunt of Vernon Elvis Presley. But no one seemed to know this. Elnora and her descendants had been lost in the chaos of Presley family ties.

Mackey's grandmother had told him that John Wallace fully acknowledged Jessie Dee as his son. When Jessie would go to his mother, Rosella, for money, she'd send him to his father, John Wallace, who would help him out.

In 1956, as Elvis was quickly becoming famous around the world, Grandma Elnora explained to thirteen-year-old Mackey that the heartthrob all the girls were screaming over was his second cousin. She took time to explain the family history so he could accept the truth.

Elvis's grandfather, Jessie Dee, she clarified, was Grandma Elnora's half-brother—they had the same father but different mothers. Elnora had eventually spun off on her own and married Joseph Yarber, having seven children with him, one of which was Lillian, the granddaughter of John Wallace.

Lillian, who was born in Itawamba County, fell in love with Tearsie Hargett when she was in her thirties. In 1943, they had a son, Mackey, before Tearsie joined the army and left to fight in World War II. Lillian was living in East Tupelo on the Old Saltillo Road near the area where Vernon and Gladys had lived. At the time, though, it's unlikely she knew that Vernon and Elvis were her cousins.

Lillian's boyfriend, Tearsie Hargett, was a projectionist at the Lyric Theater on Broadway Street, one of the two movie houses that Elvis visited frequently. It's fun to imagine that at least once, Lillian, Tearsie and young Elvis all visited the Lyric at the same time.

In the early 1940s, while World War II was underway, Lillian and Tearsie married. Mackey, their only child, was born August 23, 1943, when Elvis was eight. Less than a year later, Tearsie was killed fighting in France with the 3rd Armored Tank Division under General George Patton. Mackey never knew his father and grew up as an only child.

For the next ten years, Lillian remained single, and Mackey went to school near his grandparents in Belmont, Mississippi. Then, in 1953, Lillian married Garland Nevels, who was helping build Highway 25 from Fulton to Belmont. The newly formed family soon moved to Brookhaven where Mackey went to high school, but he frequently visited Belmont to pump his grandmother for more information about the family. Learning that he had an unknown cousin who was becoming famous was exciting to Mackey, a young boy in an obscure region of Mississippi.

Mackey at Graceland

In 1960, Mackey turned seventeen and got his driver's license. At his insistence, he and his mother made the two-hour car trip to Graceland, where Elvis had lived for just two years. The gatekeeper stopped them as they turned into the driveway, but after Lillian explained they were Elvis's cousins, they were allowed to drive right up to the front door of the mansion. Things were different in those days.

Mackey Hargett with his second cousin, Elvis Presley.

Elvis was not home, but Vernon came out to greet them. We don't know the details of this initial meeting of first cousins, but we know Vernon gave them a personal tour of Graceland and gave Mackey his telephone number so he could make sure Elvis would be there before making another trip.

Over the next eighteen years, Mackey would visit Graceland many times. He would call, and even if Elvis were out of town, Vernon would invite him to drive up and enjoy Graceland hospitality, but Mackey was not allowed to bring other visitors except for his mother. Never did Vernon refuse Mackey's request to visit Graceland, but sometimes a trip had to be rescheduled.

Elvis's mother, Gladys, had died in August of 1958 and Vernon had remarried. His new wife, Dee Stanley, and her three sons, lived at Graceland until December 1961, so Mackey met them all and shared rare pictures with Julian of Dee and her boys Billy, Ricky and David. He took pictures of the boys in the swimming pool with Vernon and an interesting photo of their bicycles next to Elvis's motorcycle—moments in time at Graceland.

On some trips, Mackey stayed with Vernon's brother, Vester, and his family at 1111 Car Avenue in Memphis. In a long conversation with Julian, Mackey reminisced about going with Vester to collect eggs at the chicken house behind Graceland.

Elvis loved animals. The Graceland menagerie over time had peacocks strutting the grounds, sixteen horses, a raft of ducks and two Great Danes given to Elvis by Priscilla. A squirrel monkey was given to Elvis on Christmas 1966 by the Lewis family, who lived near Graceland. A mischievous chimpanzee named Scatter often hung out with company dressed in human clothes. "Elvis trained Scatter to do nasty things," Elvis's aunt Lois wrote in her autobiography, *The Forgotten Family of Elvis Presley*. "If you were a girl, don't show up with a skirt on. That monkey would pull it up every time."

Elvis with his pet monkey, Scatter (left) and a wallaby sent by Australian fans.

Elvis kept a few donkeys on the property too. Until the fences around Graceland were completed, the donkeys were kept in an empty swimming pool to prevent escape. Twice, Australian fans sent Elvis wallabies, soft and cuddly relatives of kangaroos, but Elvis donated them to the Memphis Zoo. A talking Mynah bird, which had learned typical phone conversation from household members, was kept in the kitchen. It would occasionally blurt out, "Elvis isn't here right now... Elvis is in a meeting... Elvis can't come to the phone... Elvis is asleep... Sorry, Elvis is busy."

On one visit to Graceland, Mackey was photographed standing next to beautiful movie starlet Anita Wood and Vernon's sister, Nashval. Lillian had her picture taken with Vester and everyone remarked at the family resemblance of Lillian to Nash.

Meeting Cousin Elvis

Not until 1963 did Mackey finally meet his famous cousin. As he was sitting in the living room of the Graceland mansion, Vernon called for him to come into the kitchen. He arrived to find that Elvis had just descended the back staircase.

Vernon said, "Elvis, this is a cousin of yours on the Wallace side of the family."

When Mackey related this story to Julian, it confirmed that the family considered John Wallace to be the patriarch of the Presley line, even though Julian could not prove it with DNA. "I also knew by the way Mackey told me this story," Julian explained, "that Vernon's introduction, linking him to Elvis, was a very important and exciting moment for that young visitor from the hills of Itawamba County."

After some conversation in the kitchen, Vernon gave Elvis a gift—a pearl-handled pistol—which Elvis stuck into his belt. Mackey felt privileged to witness the exchange and noted how much pleasure Elvis seemed to get from receiving the gun.

For the rest of the day, Mackey was allowed to hang out with family and other friends of Elvis. He felt genuinely accepted into the clan.

Later that evening, a dark-haired girlfriend of Elvis descended the main staircase to join the group on the main floor. Later, Mackey would learn this was Priscilla Beaulieu, the woman who would later marry Elvis.

The group, which included cousins Billy Smith and Gene Smith, departed the mansion and went to the Memphis fairgrounds by special arrangement after it had closed for the night, the pearl-handled pistol still stuck into Elvis's belt. Elvis loved to sing while wandering the grounds and particularly liked the bumper cars. Mackey was allowed to photograph anything and anyone he wanted. He knew this was special because the family usually did not allow any photographs to be made.

A flash photo taken at night at the fairgrounds. To the left is Red West. The young woman behind Elvis is his girlfriend Priscilla Beaulieu.

Mackey was amazed at Elvis's collection of automobiles. Animals, guns and cars seemed to be Elvis's *thing*. To Julian, Mackey lamented that before Elvis had died, Vernon sold most of Elvis's vehicles.

Mackey recalled that some evenings he would be invited with Elvis's friends to the skating rink or a movie house for a late-night show.

A Tragedy

On one tragic Saturday night while Mackey was in Memphis, he was hanging out with brothers Billy and Bobby Smith, two of Elvis's first cousins who were the sons of Gladys Presley's brother, Travis. Billy wanted to visit his girlfriend, so Mackey drove him to her house and returned to Graceland. Bobby was hungry and wanted to get some snacks from a store across the street. As Mackey was leading the way across Highway 51 traffic, he heard car tires screeching.

Bobby had been struck and thrown onto the hood of a vehicle. An ambulance arrived and Mackey accompanied Bobby to a Memphis hospital. When other family members arrived,

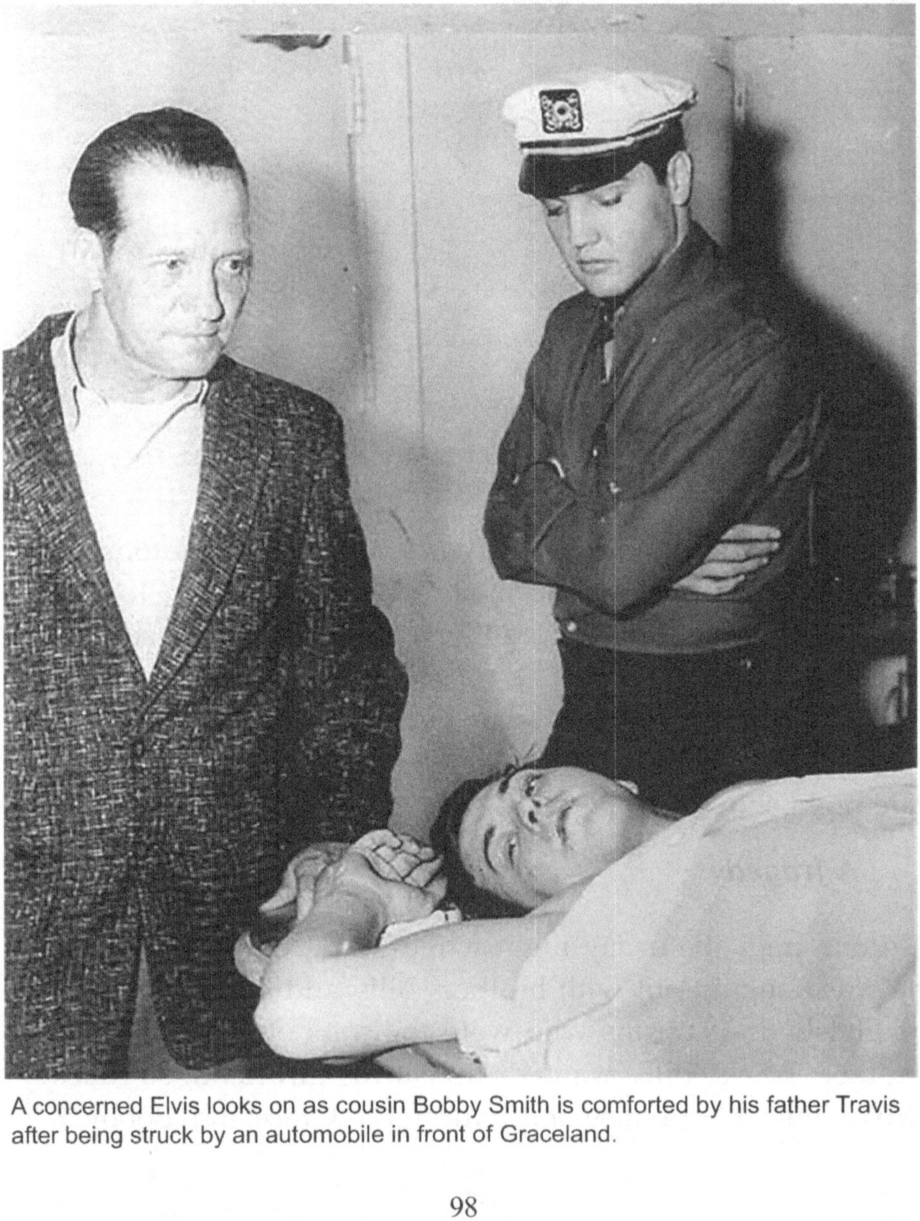

A concerned Elvis looks on as cousin Bobby Smith is comforted by his father Travis after being struck by an automobile in front of Graceland.

they wanted to know why Bobby's brother was not there, so Mackey drove back to the home of Billy's girlfriend and brought him to the hospital.

Mackey captured a rare photo of the aftermath in the ER. In the picture, Bobby is lying on a gurney as Elvis and Bobby's father, Travis Smith, look on—a remarkable glimpse into this personal tragedy. Bobby survived the accident, but the long-term effects of his leg injuries plagued him for the rest of his life.

Married, with Children

On February 4, 1966, Mackey married Sherrie Moore and over the next six years had three children—Anna, Matthew and Joel. While he was raising a family, his trips to Graceland were limited to about twice per year. Most of the time, Elvis was not at Graceland, so Mackey would stay with Vernon or Vester. Sometimes he just drove to Memphis for the day and returned the same evening.

In mid-1971, Mackey took his daughter, Anna, to Memphis where she had her picture taken with Vernon and Dee. The following year, Mackey and Sherrie were divorced and Mackey remarried. Over the following years, Mackey visited Vernon and his second wife Dee at their homes on Hermitage and Dolan Drive. The Dolan Drive home backed up to the Graceland property and had a backyard gate that opened onto the grounds of the mansion.

In 1974, on one of his last trips to Memphis, Mackey discovered that Vernon and Dee had separated. Vernon had purchased Dee's interest in the Dolan Drive house and was living with a girlfriend, Sandi Miller, at 1293 Old Hickory Road. Sandi took the last photo of Mackey and Vernon together at this home.

Chapter 8
A Cherokee Princess

The Legend of Morning White Dove

One of the most colorful legends of Elvis's family story is that his lineage through Gladys, his mother, goes back to a Cherokee "princess" named Morning White Dove, aka Morning Dove White. Sometimes her first name is spelled "Mourning." Nearly all Elvis family trees in books and on the internet trace the King's heritage back to this Cherokee woman, and most fans and family members have believed the tale to be true. Some sincere believers have created portraits of what Morning White Dove looked like to illustrate the tale online.

A fictitious sketch of Morning White Dove used on the GENi family tree site.

The legend of Morning White Dove begins when a full-blooded Cherokee Indian princess married a white man, William A. Mansell, in the early nineteenth century. According to the legend, Morning White Dove and William Mansell moved to the

Alabama frontier where they prospered, becoming landowners and leading members of the community. Her knowledge of native herbal medicine helped many homesteaders living in a strange new world. Four generations later, a direct ancestor of the Cherokee woman and her white mate gave birth to a child who would become one of the most famous popular entertainers in the world—Elvis Presley.

The legend of Morning White Dove was given wings when stated as fact in the popular biography *Elvis and Gladys*. Offering no conditions for her assertion, author Elaine Dundy wrote: "The earliest female that can be traced with certainty in Elvis' maternal line was his great-great-great-grandmother, Morning Dove White [various authors have interchanged the last two parts of this name]. A full-blooded Cherokee Indian, she was born in about 1800 and is buried in Hamilton, Alabama."

The Native American woman in this photo has been falsely identified as "Morning White Dove" but is actually Princess Eat No Meat from Oregon.

The accompanying photo, identified as "Morning White Dove," has appeared all over the internet. Unfortunately, this is not Morning White Dove. In fact, there are no known pictures of her. The photo shown here is a portrait of Princess Eat No Meat, who is not related to Elvis Presley and did not live in the area around Mississippi. She was from the Umatilla tribe in Oregon, and this photo, taken by Major Lee Moorhouse in 1900, is listed in the National Anthropological Archives of the Smithsonian.

Even well-known scholars have been seduced by the lure of Elvis legends, and their academic credentials sometimes give undeserved credibility to preposterous lies. In his book about famous Scots from Ulster (of which Elvis is one) historian Alister McReynolds claimed that Walter Mansell, an ancestor of Elvis's adored mother Gladys Love Mansell Smith, married "Morning White Dove" in the early 1700s.

McReynolds was wrong on all counts. It was not Walter Mansell but rather William A. Mansell who had a relationship with a woman referred to as Morning White Dove. It was also not in the early 1700s; it was in the early 1800s. In addition, there are no records establishing a marriage between these individuals. And finally, there was never a man named Walter Mansell in the area; there was a family member named David Walter Mansell, but he was not born until 1882. By then, Morning White Dove had been dead for many years.

This was sloppy and misleading scholarship. Obviously, McReynolds did no primary research to establish the facts. In his book, entitled *Kith and Kin: The Continuing Legacy of the Scots-Irish in America,* McReynolds also claimed that the man who would have been Elvis's "great grandfather, six or seven times over, married a full-blooded Cherokee woman." The author believed Elvis's "clean, strong jawline came from that heritage."

As we will demonstrate, the woman in question was certainly not a Cherokee. And one's jawline cannot be used as evidence of one's lineage, otherwise Ancestry.com would be out of business.

McReynolds stated that Mansell had "emigrated to North America a few years beforehand." In truth, there were at least seven generations of Mansells born in North America before William A. Mansell. David Mansell emigrated to North America from Wales nearly two centuries before Morning White Dove created so much confusion.

All these ancestors and dates are documented in Julian's online family tree, and the Mansell bloodline is detailed in Appendix B of this book. A simple inquiry from Mr. McReynolds could have prevented so much misinformation from polluting the public record.

We shouldn't be too hard on this historian, however, because most of the members of the Elvis Presley family seem to believe the legend of the Cherokee princess. Even Elvis claims that he was part Cherokee. Much of this mythic content came from the lips of friends and family members who, believing the family stories passed down for years, passed them on in their interviews with researchers and biographers.

So, what is the truth about Morning White Dove, and can we really know it after all these years?

Truth Teller

Julian Riley is the man to ask about Morning White Dove, so I asked him. Julian's credentials, as described earlier, have made him an expert on the Indians of the region around Mississippi. He has been collecting Indian artifacts for nearly sixty years. I've accused him of being a relic himself. The Chickasaw Indians in Oklahoma now possess a large collection of artifacts discovered by Julian, and much of what they know today about their homeland in Mississippi is the result of Julian going into the field, studying maps, digging holes, finding important artifacts and doing research.

Julian has made important historical discoveries and written numerous papers about the Indians of the region. "Not just the Chickasaws," Julian told me, "but also the Choctaws, Cherokees and Seminoles, which were all part of the so-called Five Civilized Tribes. I'm very familiar with these tribes because they were all fighting each other—and intermarrying, as well."

Birth of a Legend

About the legend of Morning White Dove, Julian was blunt. "That's one of the most ridiculous stories I've ever heard!" The first published mention of this "fiction," he told me, was in Elaine Dundy's book *Elvis and Gladys*, which was based on an interview by Tupelo resident Roy Turner with a relative of Doll Mansell Smith, the mother of Gladys Presley, whose bloodline can be traced back to a woman everyone calls Morning White Dove or some variation of it. But the interview subject was not a primary source—he was merely reporting family traditions that had been passed down to him through the generations. As most researchers will tell you, family stories are among the least reliable source of accurate information.

"Roy is a friend of mine and did the best he could, I suppose," Julian said, "but he lacked the research tools we have today... and the internet. The book's author, however, never seemed to question the integrity of the stories passed on to her. She just wrote them up and printed them."

Julian said that the story of Morning White Dove in the book was a textbook example of somebody writing about something they knew nothing about. Neither Roy nor Elaine Dundy had studied the history and traditions of the Indians of the south.

"For example," he explained, "a Cherokee wouldn't name a child Morning White Dove. That's a name out of a movie—a Gene Autry western, maybe. Indians would have given their children names in their own language, not names like 'Morning,' which was popular among the English. And they usually used one-word names."

In Julian's online Elvis Presley family tree, I found eleven additional women with that first name as follows:

- Mary Ann Morning Rebecca Carroll (1844)
- Morning Flowers (1773)
- Morning P. Franks (1793)
- Morning Kimbrough (1689)
- Eliza Ann Morning Mansell (1825)
- Morning Mansell (1798)
- Morning Dizenie Mansell (1826)
- Morning Melton (1731)
- Morning Caldonia Anilla Palmer (1900)
- Morning Peacock (unknown)
- Morning Pierce (1690)

In this list, the woman named Morning Flowers was the mother of William A. Mansell, the man whose legend claims married Morning White Dove. Researchers who bothered to unearth this fact immediately became excited and started looking for Indians earlier in the Mansell bloodline. But the story of Morning Flowers gives yet more credibility to Julian's arguments.

Flowers, it was discovered, was simply the woman's family name, and her mother gave her the common English first name of Morning. On several census reports, Morning Flowers, born in 1773 in South Carolina, is listed as a "free white woman." If she had been an Indian, this certainly would have been stated.

Bigamist, Deserter or Family Man?

"Even more importantly," Julian explained, "William A. Mansell didn't marry that woman. Not only is there no marriage certificate anywhere—I've looked—but William was already married to another woman!"

William A. Mansell was born in Martin, North Carolina, in 1791 and died in Hamilton, Alabama, at the age of seventy-four. Mansell family members were early settlers of Alabama. The family was large and well-to-do.

In 1808, when he was seventeen, William A. Mansell married Jane Ellender Egar in Jackson County, Tennessee. Over the next fourteen years, they had six children. A son, also named William A., was born first in 1809, and then came Benjamin, Hannah, Simeon, Martha and finally Lumin in 1822.

During the time William A. Mansell and Jane were raising their family, William fought with Andrew Jackson in the wars with the Creek Indians in Alabama. He fought with Old Hickory at the Battle of Horseshoe Bend, and later in Florida. As payment for his military service, William and a war buddy named Moses Purser were given land grants in Marion County, Alabama. Moses Purser moved to Marion County with his wife, Maphy, to claim his allotment.

"It turns out that Maphy Arnett had been previously married to a man named Mr. White, first name unknown," Julian explained. "Maphy had given Mr. White a daughter, and they named the little girl Morning. If you search names, you'll find that 'Morning' was a common female name at that time, particularly among people from the British Isles."

Sometime in the 1820s, probably after his son Lumin was born, William also moved his family to Marion County. It is unlikely that William A. Mansell had two wives—Jane and Morning White—living in the same county at the same time.

We do not know exactly when or how William met Morning White, but it is likely that when William spent time visiting Moses Purser he became attracted to his friend's eighteen-year-old stepdaughter. "William and Morning just settled down and started having babies," Julian conjectured. The couple never married but had four children. They would have been very surprised that their relationship would give rise decades later to the fantasy that Elvis was part Cherokee.

"Sometime later," Julian said, "someone just added the name 'Dove' to Morning White, probably to make her sound more Indian. And then author Elaine Dundy wrongly decided that the woman's name was actually Morning Dove and that the 'White' was tagged on to distinguish her as friendly to 'white' Americans rather than 'red' Englishmen." All of this, of course, was nonsense.

We know that on the 1840 census, William A. Mansell is found living in Marion County, Alabama, with a wife listed as thirty to forty years old, an accurate range for Morning White, not Jane (Egar) Mansell. Two sons and two daughters are found living in the Mansell household with ages appropriate for Morning White's children.

Besides having six children with his wife Jane, William had four children with the woman legend calls Morning White Dove. A daughter, Morning Dizenie, was born in 1826, followed by John B., James Jordan and Pheby. John B. Mansell, whose mother was Morning White, established the lineage that would eventually produce Elvis Presley.

"William Mansell may have betrayed his wedding vows," Julian suggested, "but he was not a bigamist—I'm sure of that. We will probably never know if he abandoned his first family or found a way to be present in both."

After the death of Morning White, the census records suggest that William somehow restored his relationship with his first family because Jane and four of his six children are living with him in the same household. This may have been a more difficult assignment for William than fighting in the wars against the Creek.

Nineteenth Century Prejudice

"It never made sense that William married Morning White Dove," Julian told me. He was not finished stating his case. "Anyone knowledgeable about Indians in the southern states would know that."

"How would they know?" I asked, establishing that I was among those not knowledgeable about Indians in the South.

Julian replied, "In that time, even more than today, there was a real stigma regarding Whites marrying Indians. Just like in the south, there was a stigma against marrying Blacks. You might sleep with an Indian woman, even have kids with her, but you wouldn't marry her and advertise it. You could be run out of town if you did. Probably, William Mansell, like most European Americans of the time, viewed Indians in general as second-class individuals."

The biggest argument against the Cherokee princess myth, however, is that there are no Cherokees in that part of Alabama. "There are Chickasaws there," Julian explained. "But the Cherokees are over in the Carolinas and Georgia. She could have been a Creek, but William and Moses Purser had just got over fighting a bloody war with the Creek Indians."

Inventing a Legend

"I'm trying to think of how we could provide more real evidence of who this woman was," I told Julian.

"Or who she *wasn't!*" Julian said. "Well, I did just that. It's what I do. I dig holes for Indian artifacts and dig deep into the records to get accurate information. Sometimes I have to go direct to the source, if I can find it."

Julian explained how he had spoken with his friend, Roy Turner, who had done most of the interviews that provided fodder for *Elvis and Gladys*. Roy had told him that the story about Morning White Dove being Cherokee and marrying William Mansell had come from a man in Hamilton, Alabama named Joel Palmer, a direct descendant of Morning White Dove.

According to Julian's *Roots of Elvis* family tree, Morning White's daughter, Morning Dizenie Mansell, married a man named Russell P. Palmer in 1843, establishing the bloodline that would produce Joel Palmer several generations later, and finally Elvis Presley. All the descendants of Dizenie and Russell would have Indian DNA if there was any to inherit.

"It turns out that Joel Palmer was still alive," Julian explained. "I found out he was in a nursing home in Hamilton, Alabama, so I grabbed a camcorder and a friend, Dr. Taylor, and made the hour-long drive to see Joel."

Other members of the Palmer family already had sent in their DNA to get analyzed. Some of these descendants attended Julian's interview. "It was so interesting," Julian said. "They knew what I was looking for, and they started right off making excuses about what DNA information was already out there."

Finally, Joel responded to Julian's question about why he believed he was part Indian. "Well, my grandparents were quite dark, their skin was dark," he explained. "We all thought he might have been part Indian."

Julian turned to me as he related this story. "That was it!" he said. "There was nothing more to it than that. His grandpa had dark skin so they thought he might be part Indian."

Julian had checked with the source of the legend, and the source had nothing to back it up. But the legend inadvertently spawned by that simple but unsupported family story had been endorsed by a popular biography of Elvis. It had then spread like a virus through the Elvisphere, boosted by careless authorities who should have known better and exaggerated by fans who loved the exotic story. Until now, it has been considered part of the Elvis canon.

"What about DNA?" I asked. "Palmer's DNA could scientifically prove whether the Palmers had any Indian blood. If they didn't have any, then Morning White Dove couldn't be Indian, and neither could Elvis."

"Exactly," Julian said. "So, I asked Joel Palmer if he'd give me a DNA sample. He said, 'sure, no problem.' He gave me a sample and we tested it—and there was no Indian heritage in his sample. None at all. I also found out that the other DNA samples the family had tested also showed there was no Indian blood. So, I think we've finally put this nonsense to rest."

"Well, maybe," I said. "In these times, there are facts… and there are *alternative* facts."

Julian nodded. "Yeah, I'm sure one of these days somebody will come up to me and say, 'You know, I watched Elvis play a half-Indian in *Flaming Star*, and I'm sure he's really part Indian. Just look at him! That jawline and those high cheekbones. I don't care what your DNA says.'"

There are so few known facts about Morning White that she has become a kind of mystical figure, which means many people may not want to abandon the "Cherokee princess" they have come to love and admire. She was mostly a blank slate, so she can be whatever an admirer wants her to be. She was not an Indian, of course, but she was a mysterious frontier woman who captivated the heart of William Mansell and gave the world the immense gift of Elvis Presley.

Chapter 9

From Morning White to Elvis Presley

Generation One

Morning White Dove was a real person, though she was not an Indian, and her last name certainly was not Dove. From this point on, we will call this matriarch of the Elvis Presley bloodline simply Morning White. The streaming of genes through five generations from Morning White to Elvis has produced a fascinating story with still more tantalizing surprises that have been hiding behind the Elvis myths and PR propaganda.

No matter how William A. Mansell and Morning White met, they spent more than ten years together and had four children. The nature of their personal relationship and William's continuing connection if any to his wife and previous children are unknown—probably *unknowable,* considering the two centuries that separate us from them. But from records and stories Julian has excavated from the dustbin of history, we can assemble an accurate chronicle of the Mansell family, which is just as important to the making of Elvis Presley as John Wallace and the two Presley sisters, Rosella and Mary Jane.

Children of William Mansell and Morning White

We have precious few facts about Morning White, but we know affirmatively that she had four children with William Mansell.

Morning Dizenie Mansell

Morning Dizenie jump-started the Palmer branch of the family tree when she married Russell Palmer and gave him twelve children. She was the great-grandmother of Joel Palmer, who sparked the legend of Morning White Dove.

John B. Mansell (Great-Great-Grandfather of Elvis)

John B. Mansell is the undisputed great-great-grandfather of Elvis Presley. He was born in 1828 in Marion County, Alabama, but had difficulty staying in one place for long. He fathered as many as nineteen children with at least two women. Julian has confirmed much of this story, but some of it may never be proved.

John Mansell squandered his portion of the family farm. On the 1840 census, John was living in Marion County, Alabama, with parents William and Morning White, one brother and two sisters.

By 1850, John was married to Elizabeth Sarah Gilmore, who everyone called "Betsy," and their two children, William M. and Edy. Julian has been unable to find the family on the 1860 census but believes they were living in Monroe County, Mississippi. In 1880, he moved north of Oxford, Mississippi.

James Jordan Mansell

James was born in 1832 and in 1850 was living in western Marion County, Alabama, next door to Spencer Brown, who married James's sister, Pheby. In 1860, there were two Mansell children in the James Jordan household who do not appear to be his children—nine-year-old Susan and seven-year-old Simuel

Mansell. James was killed in the American Civil War when he was thirty-two.

Pheby Mansell

Pheby was born in 1835 and married Spencer Brown, a neighbor of her brother James Jordan Mansell. In 1900, she was living with her son in Marion County, Alabama. She died in 1914 at the age of seventy-eight.

The Gilmore Bloodline Merges

The Gilmore bloodline directly connected to Elvis when John B. married Betsy Gilmore and they had a son, White Mansell, Elvis's great-grandfather. Betsy was a descendant of John Gilmore, who was born in 1700 in Ulster, Ireland, and emigrated to North America. He died in Augusta, Virginia, in 1759. The Gilmores have been a subject of intense research for Julian because Gilmore genes must be found in anyone claiming to be directly related to Elvis Presley.

On the 1870 census, John B. Mansell was living around Abbeville, Mississippi, with Amanda Bennett and four children, so sometime before 1870 John divorced Betsy and married Amanda.

During the eight years between 1859 and 1867, however, John B. found a way to have seven children with both wives at the same time. To clarify John's egalitarian approach to establishing a blended family, here is a list of his conjugal output.

- 1859, Nancy, with Betsy Gilmore
- 1859, James C., with Amanda Bennett
- 1860, George, with Betsy Gilmore
- 1861, John, Jr., with Amanda Bennett
- 1862, Lucinda, with Betsy Gilmore
- 1865, Caroline, with Betsy Gilmore
- 1867, J. Laspen, with Amanda Bennett

An Unidentified Father

In *Elvis and Gladys,* author Elaine Dundy claimed that John B. Mansell fathered two children with Rebecca Gilmore Mansell, who was not only the sister of John's first wife, Betsy Gilmore, but also was the mother of a child with John's half-brother, William M. Mansell. The two children in question are Rebecca's daughters Dukie Elizabeth, born in 1874, and Lucinda ("Lou"), born in 1876. Both were born after Rebecca and her husband were divorced and William had remarried.

This matter takes on greater importance because John B. Mansell is the direct genetic connection between Morning White and Elvis Presley, and the Gilmore family line plays a big part in the unfolding lineage.

Julian does not have the necessary DNA samples to confirm that John B. had an affair with his wife's sister, Rebecca. "It seems unlikely to me, however, that John is the daddy of Rebecca's girls," Julian confessed. "In 1874, John is forty-six and living in Abbeville, Mississippi. It's doubtful that he'd ride a horse almost a hundred miles to have sex with his sister-in-law when he has a younger wife, Amanda, in Abbeville. That's a great distance to travel in those days and would take three or four days one way. Plus, Rebecca was sharing a house with John's son, White Mansell, which would make having a sexual relationship a bit awkward."

Abel White Semial Mansell (called "White" by friends and family in a nod to "Mr. White," the father of Morning White) was John's third child. According to Julian, the father of Rebecca's two children most likely would be someone who lived near White and his aunt. A candidate would be John's oldest son, William M. Mansell, who was not only White's half-brother but was living next door to him.

Did Rebecca have an affair with her good-looking nephew, William M. Mansell, who was only three years younger than her? We may never know.

On the 1880 census, John was still living in the Abbeville area. Julian believes he died around 1885 and may be buried at Abbeville Cemetery in an unmarked grave near other family members (GPS location 34.51671, -89.50227).

Generation Two

White Mansell

The second generation of Elvis's maternal bloodline begins with Abel White Semial Mansell, known as "White." The son of John B. Mansell and Betsy Gilmore was born on October 25, 1849, in Hamilton, Alabama, the same town where Julian interviewed Joel Palmer 150 years later about so-called Morning White Dove. Julian has not found White on a census before 1870, but on the 1860 census report he located a man named Simuel Mansell living with James Jordan Mansell in western Marion County, Alabama.

"I think this is White Mansell, and that his given name, Semial, was simply misspelled as Simuel on the census report," Julian told me. "There is additional convincing evidence for this. James Jordan was White Mansell's uncle."

The reasons why eleven-year-old White was living with his uncle, and where his parents were at this time, remain a mystery.

The Tackett Bloodline Merges

By 1870, White Mansell was living in Saltillo, Mississippi, next door to Abner H. Tackett. If he had not moved there, we would not have had an Elvis Presley. White Mansell was married to Martha Tackett and had not yet started a family. Martha would become the great-grandmother of Elvis Presley.

In 1880, White Mansell was living in District 2, Beat 2, in Lee County with a very large family. In the household were: his wife, Martha; three daughters including Octavia Luvenia; one son; his mother, Betsy; two sisters; his aunt; and two cousins. The Tackett bloodline merges with Elvis Presley's lineage when Martha Tackett gives birth to Octavia, Elvis's grandmother.

The aunt living in White Mansell's household was Rebecca, the sister of White's mother, not Martha Taylor, the wife of his Uncle James Jordan Mansell. White's father, John B. Mansell, was living in Lafayette County, Mississippi, with his new wife, Amanda, and their family.

At the turn of the twentieth century, White Mansell lived on the Hussey farm north of the Andrews Chapel Cemetery in Richmond, Mississippi (GPS location 34.22944, -88.56133). At that time, many of the families related to Elvis were living and working on the Hussey farm—families with names like Smith, Mansell, Tackett, Presley, Loyd, Richards, Helms and Hussey.

White Mansell was listed as Mansell White on the 1900 census. "All these name changes and misspellings on official documents make researching the family a very tough job," Julian told me. "Before the internet, I would spend hours in government buildings and libraries reeling through blurry microfiche records to find tiny details that could help me solve a mystery. Fortunately, most information is now on the internet so I can do a lot of work at home."

By 1910, White had moved to the Hoyles community in Pontotoc County. His daughter Octavia "Doll" and her husband Bob Smith were living in White's household, and this is where Gladys Smith, mother of Elvis Presley, was born in 1912.

According to the 1920 census, White was still living in Pontotoc County Mississippi, but the census taker recorded his name as Sim W. Mansell, "Probably just to frustrate me," Julian said. He believes White Mansell may be buried in an unmarked grave next to his second wife, Sarah, at Andrews Chapel Cemetery, Lee County, Mississippi (GPS location 34.22678, -88.56241. Martha is buried at Carolina Cemetery next to the

Carolina Methodist Church in Booneville, Mississippi (GPS location 34.68173, -88.60520).

White and Martha had eight children. All of them except Octavia were great-aunts or great-uncles of Elvis.

- 1872, Mary Melissa
- 1875, Ida Bell
- 1876, Octavia Luvenia "Doll"
- 1878, Ada Josephine
- 1882, Sim E.
- 1890, Argus L.
- 1892, John Hugh
- 1892, Elmer L.

Octavia Luvenia "Doll" Mansell

Octavia, the great-grandmother of Elvis Presley, was the third child of White and Martha Tackett Mansell. The 1880 census lists her as "Lucy," one of her nicknames along with "Loo." This, of course, makes her hard to find in the records. Julian has identified her most likely birth year as 1876.

Octavia was the third child of White Mansell and his favorite. She was as spoiled as she was beautiful and, despite a lifetime battle with tuberculosis, loved to show off her slim figure and porcelain-like features at square dances in one of the large buildings on the Hussey farm. John King, who was married to her sister Ida, told his family that Octavia "was about the prettiest woman I ever laid eyes on!" But another woman who was raised on the Hussey farm claimed that "Doll Mansell was a … flirt!" You can fill in the redacted words.

Those who knew Octavia called her "Doll," which was a fitting description for her prettiness. The nickname suggested a China doll, perhaps, or even a broken doll.

In 1901, Octavia married her cousin, Hallie Jefferson Smith. She was still single and at risk of being an "old maid," so she was ready for a husband. Hal's mother was Octavia's biological aunt, Anna Lillian Mansell, one of the many children of John B. Mansell, Elvis's great-great-grandfather. In addition, Aunt Anna's mother, Betsy Mansell, was Octavia's grandmother as well as a Gilmore.

Throughout the various bloodlines of Elvis Presley, we find repeated patterns of behavior—illegitimate children with unknown daddies and intermarriages between family lines and relatives. "All the shenanigans that went on for decades between kin make an interesting melodrama but a researcher's nightmare," Julian told me. "The old joke that 'I am my own grandpa' has sometimes seemed prophetic."

Anna had married Mileage Obadiah Smith in 1874 after having a child out of wedlock. As we've seen, illegitimate children were a common crop in the county. Anna was sassy and often pompous, stiff but energetic, truly the engine of the family. Like Jessie Dee's dressing up like a dandy in public, Anna almost never left home without a little black hat perched on her head.

Obadiah was Anna's opposite in almost every way, and domineering Anna ruled the roost. During the American Civil War, Obadiah joined the 4th Georgia in 1863, but apparently the discipline of military service did not stick. By all accounts, he was illiterate and lazy, and some have speculated that he suffered from "shell shock" (PTSD) from the war. He struggled to make a living and never managed to own a house; the family always boarded with family members or others.

After about twenty years of living in poverty with an unmotivated husband, Anna finally walked out. Before long, she had a child with a man whom Julian has not identified.

When Hal Smith could no longer resist Doll's obvious charms and advances, he proudly married the prettiest girl in the area. After a year of marriage, however, Hal brought his wife back to her father, White Mansell. Julian explained why.

"Hal, a smart farmer and practical man, told his father-in-law, 'Here, you can have her, I don't want her anymore. She's lazy and she won't work. She won't keep house.' Well, Doll is supposed to be the prettiest girl around but her husband is returning her to her father. How does Doll feel about this? Pretty darn humiliated, I'd guess—her feelings were hurt. She probably sought revenge."

Hal decided to marry another local girl, Mary Jerusha Plunkett, who was not nearly as pretty as Doll. They set the wedding date for September 6, 1903. Julian speculated: "What better way for Doll to inflict pain on her former husband than to marry his older brother, Bob Smith."

So, Doll landed another cousin as her next husband, a good-looking, gentle farmer who had been following her around most of his life but never had done anything about it. "Doll didn't love Bob Smith," Julian explained, "didn't care about him really, but Bob didn't care. Suddenly he was married to the prettiest girl in the area, and he was over the moon. And he was good to her—worked himself practically to death for her."

They lived and worked on the Hussey farm like most of their relatives and friends. Their first daughter, Effie, was born July 21, 1904, and died when she was fourteen months old. Finding Effie's gravestone in the Andrews Chapel Cemetery near the Hussey farm was pivotal in motivating Julian to launch his Elvis research project (See "Chapter 4: Ground Zero" page 41).

Three daughters—Lillian Panther (1906), Linnie Lavelle (1908) and Retha (1909–1910)—were born prior to the turn of the decade, and then the Smiths suddenly left the Hussey farm and moved out of the county. In 1910, the census shows Doll living in Pontotoc County, Mississippi, with her husband and three children. April 15 was Census Day in 1910, so the Bob Smith family, along with youngest daughter Retha, would have been residing in Pontotoc before that date. Retha must have been born before April 15, 1910.

"It bothered me for a while," Julian said. "Why would they just up and leave the Hussey farm where they'd been for so long? Why take the whole family over to the next county?"

Admitting he was missing one critical DNA sample to prove his theory, he revealed the best answer he had come up with. "One word—jealousy."

I begged for more than that single word, and Julian obliged.

"Two things we know, "he explained. "First, Doll was not madly in love with Bob Smith, might even have been bored with him. And second, Doll was beautiful and alluring, probably the dream girl of a lot of farm hands in the area."

"Sounds like you're suggesting an affair."

Love Is All There Is

"It turns out there was a man about Doll's age named James Alford Love who had the opportunity. He lived over on Eggville Road, not that far away from the Hussey farm. If he was coming over to the farm and sleeping with Doll when Bob was working his ass off, and Bob found out, that would be a great reason for Bob to move his wife out of harm's way."

"So, they go to Pontotoc?"

"Yes, because Doll's father had previously moved there."

Julian had not made up this character named James Alford Love (aka James Alfred Love in some records). This figure had left a footprint on Mississippi history. Four years older than Doll, he was born in 1872 to Larkin and Sarah Love. He was married to Bell Powell and had at least four children—Elodie (1898), Maude Lillian (1901), Henry (1905) and Audie (1910). His family had been close to the Mansels for years, in fact, there was a family connection. James Alford's aunt, Mary Love, had married Thomas Newton Smith, the older brother Bob Smith's father. More than likely, James Alford Smith and "Doll" had known each other for many years, perhaps had gone to school together.

"Most likely," Julian conjectured, "Alford Love is the father of Gladys, Elvis's mother."

I recalled that Doll had tuberculosis. Since none of her family members reported getting TB, which is highly infectious, she probably had a latent infection and lived a normal life. It is also possible that she was misdiagnosed with TB by a country doctor without the knowledge and technology to distinguish it from bacterial pneumonia, or even from sarcoidosis, an inflammatory disease. None of her children or her husband ever contracted TB, so misdiagnosis is not unlikely. Certainly, she was able to have numerous children, so we know she was capable of having sexual relations.

"You seem focused on Gladys as the possible daughter of Doll's dalliance," I said.

"Because Gladys gives us a pretty good clue," he replied. "It's in her name—Gladys *Love* Smith. Ever wonder why 'Love' is her middle name?"

The most well-known explanation for Gladys's middle name came from Elaine Dundy, the influential author of *Elvis and Gladys*, a biography once considered authoritative and mined for so-called "facts" by countless other authors. Dundy wrote: "Up around Saltillo way near the Mansell clan lived a Steven S. Smith and his wife Mary and their children Elizabeth, Ann, Wesley . . . Pelham, and Leila Love. This youngest daughter, born in 1870, would give Elvis's mother her Bible and her middle name."

A major problem with this uncorroborated story is that census records show that Leila was indeed the daughter of Steven S. Smith, but her middle initial is consistently shown as "D." Apparently, her middle name was not "Love," as Dundy claims. Thus, Leila could not have given her middle name to Gladys, though she may have pledged her "love" in an inscription in the Bible she purportedly gave to Gladys.

Perhaps Dundy confused the girl's heartfelt writing as a middle name: "From Leila, Love." Or maybe the story was just another unsubstantiated family legend.

Did naming Gladys "Love" expose her biological father and his wife's conjectured indiscretion to the world? Well, the small communities in which they lived probably knew about Doll's affair with Alford Love already, perhaps before Bob did. If there was no secret to keep, permitting Doll to use the name "Love" for her daughter would be an easy way for Bob to keep the peace. Today, that middle name resonates like a clanging bell announcing Doll's attempt to straighten out history.

This line of reasoning, however, caused me to think about James Alford's daughter, Maude Lillian, who was born in 1901. I recalled that Doll's first surviving daughter, born five years later, was given the name Lillian. Since names are often given to honor loved ones past and present, is it possible that Maude Lillian was…?

This is why DNA is such a valuable tool—it can clear up sticky problems. The trouble is, we need the appropriate biological samples before we can make sense of them. If you have information or evidence that could help us resolve this mystery, please contact us at elvis@calumeteditions.com.

Doll survived until two years after Elvis was born, but we have uncovered no stories about Doll visiting her infant grandson. According to mortuary records, when Doll died in 1937, just fifteen dollars was spent on her funeral. The average amount spent on a funeral in that region was close to eighty dollars. The only message on her casket was "County," which credited Lee County with providing the casket.

Elvis's grandmother and grandfather are buried next to each other in unmarked graves at New Spring Hill Cemetery near Saltillo, Mississippi (GPS location 34.33639, -88.60719). After extensive research, we have located with 99 percent certainty where these graves are located in the cemetery. If you go to New

Spring Hill Cemetery, look for a grave marker for Chester and Anna Mae Robbins. In the photo below, Julian Riley is standing next to the unmarked graves directly in front of the Robbins plot.

Julian Riley stands next to the unmarked graves of Robert "Bob" Smith and Octavia "Doll" Mansell Smith.

Robert Lee "Bob" Smith

Bob Smith is credited with being the maternal grandfather of Elvis Presley because he was married to Octavia "Doll" Smith, who gave birth to Elvis's mother, Gladys. Julian Riley has cast doubt on Bob's paternity of Gladys, however, and, as previouisly mentioned, has proposed that James Alford Love may have been Elvis's biological grandfather. If this were true, Elvis's family tree would acquire many new branches, and some old branches would be pruned away.

Bob Smith and Doll Mansell were cousins, probably first cousins. Marriage between first cousins would provide a genetic intensification and a doubling of the risk of birth defects. Yet, cousin marriage was common in insulated communities of the agrarian South. It is illegal for first cousins to marry in twenty-four states, but that means it is legal in twenty-six.

Health records are not available for the children of Bob and Doll, so we don't know whether their relatedness caused any health or mental problems, but probably not. Their children tended to have lifelong problems with the use of alcohol, but this is likely due to their upbringing and community tolerance for alcohol consumption rather than cousin marriage.

Bob seems to have been a modest, hardworking sharecropper and occasional moonshiner. He lacked neither the skills nor the luck to be a successful farmer. Tupelo Alderman John Marcy described the poverty in which his family lived in these words: "They were so poor they wore hog rings [C- or D-shaped fasteners] in their shoes—wore 'em on every toe to keep the soles of their shoes on."

After he moved the family to Pontotoc County in 1910, his failure to support the family through honest farming led him into part-time moonshining. He had a knack for making—and drinking—good moonshine, which was illegal in Mississippi even before Prohibition. His secret to making pure, blistering, mule-kick "white lightning" was attention to the complicated distillation process, which most moonshiners never took the time to get right. But there were often consequences for this illicit career. Alderman John Marcy, said, "Sometimes they [the Smith family] were asked to move on."

Bob Smith died unexpectedly in 1932 after moving the remnants of his family back to Lee County. He had never stopped loving his wife, and everyone had expected the tubercular Doll to pass away first. Bob died of pneumonia before he could sell his last batch of moonshine, and his family was left penniless. He was buried in an unmarked grave in the New Spring Hill

Cemetery in Saltillo, Mississippi, where Doll also lies in obscurity (GPS location 34.33639, -88.60719).

The Myth of the Jewish Elvis

When Martha Tackett married White Mansell and provided Tackett ancestors for Elvis Presley, she inadvertently created the makings of an enduring myth. Gladys Presley and Elvis earnestly believed that they were part Jewish because of Martha. Elvis believed it so strongly he had a Star of David placed in the upper left corner of his mother's tombstone at Graceland. The Jewish symbol, representing an assumed bloodline of the family, oddly coexists with a Christian cross in the upper right corner honoring their practiced religion.

Gladys Love Presley's tombstone at Graceland. Elvis had a Star of David placed in the upper left corner.

Elvis was often photographed with a necklace featuring a Chai, the Jewish symbol for "life." Elvis's birth house contained a gold Jewish menorah with nine Hannukah candles. Elvis belonged to the Jewish Community Center in Memphis and gave money to various Jewish organizations, including $150,000 to the Memphis Hebrew Academy.

For years, the family believed that Jewish heritage had been delivered through the Tackett bloodline. So deep was this conviction that family members reported it as fact to Tupelo resident Roy Turner when he interviewed them for author Elaine Dundy's book *Elvis and Gladys*.

If a belief is repeated often enough, it becomes indistinguishable from truth. The unchallenged Jewish myth found its way into print, and Dundy's book developed a reputation as an authoritative biography of Elvis's early years. Like the legend of Morning White Dove, which has been debunked in these pages, the surprising Jewish connection was cited so frequently by other authors and researchers that it became a cornerstone of the Elvis canon.

In *Elvis and Gladys,* Dundy wrote about the marriage of White Mansell to Martha Tackett: "She was the daughter of Abner and Nancy J. Burdine Tackett and though Abner was to marry several times after, Nancy is of particular interest to us. According to Elvis's third cousin, Oscar Tackett [who shared the same ancestors, Abner and Nancy], Nancy was Jewish." The only proof that author Dundy offers is this: "Again, names often tell a story and two of Martha's brothers were given Jewish names, Sidney and Jerome." This is not what Julian and I consider to be conclusive proof.

With those brief words, Elaine Dundy unknowingly perpetrated a fraud. Yes, a woman named Nancy Burdine was born in 1826. Both she and Abner, who was twenty-three years older, lived in Kentucky, but there are no public records showing a marriage, a Tackett son credited to her, or any Jewish heritage, so this is either pure conjecture or a family tale. Some researchers have speculated that she was an immigrant from Lithuania but have not supplied their evidence. With so little to go on, it seems premature for Dundy to make such a bold claim without significant caveats.

We know a bit more about Abner Hampton Tackett. It is true that he had several wives. We know from records that he married Celia Butler in 1827. His second wife was Elizabeth Willett, marriage date unknown, and in 1873 he married Elizabeth's sister, Sarah.

"Maybe Nancy Burdine was a lover, not a wife, which is why there are no records," I said to Julian.

"Well," Julian said thoughtfully, "I considered that. So, just to be sure, I decided to get some DNA to get to the bottom of it. So, I went to Roy Turner, who lives in Tupelo," Julian explained, "and asked him where he got his information. He said Oscar Tackett's the one who had told him the Tackett's had Jewish blood."

Unfortunately, Oscar had died. "Fortunately, I know Oscar's son, Lowery Tackett, quite well," Julian said. "I got in my car and drove over to the Home Depot where Lowery works and had a nice chat with him. He had absolutely no idea why his daddy told Roy Turner he was part Jewish. 'We never had any Jewish blood in us,' he told me."

Julian asked Lowery to give him a DNA sample, which he did. "I looked at the results when they came back," Julian said. "Not a drop of Jewish blood in there."

According to Jewish law, which confers Jewish lineage by way of the mother, "Jewish blood" would have passed through to Elvis from a female ancestor. If Lowery Tackett had no Jewish blood, then his great-grandmother, who we believe was actually Celia Butler, had no Jewish ancestry or she would have passed it on to Lowery. Of all Elvis's ancestors, only Elvis's great-great-grandmother could have passed Jewish blood to Elvis, but she had no Jewish blood to share, so Elvis was not even technically a Jew.

When he was a teenager in Memphis in 1953, Elvis and his family rented the first floor of a small house at 462 Alabama Avenue for fifty dollars per month. Rabbi Alfred Fruchter and his wife Jeanette occupied the upstairs. The landlord was a widow named Mrs. Dubrovner whose husband had been a kosher butcher. On Saturdays, Elvis often helped the Fruchters as a "Shabbos Goy," a gentile who performs work that religious law prohibits Jews from doing on the Sabbath, such as turning lights off and on.

The Fruchters never suspected Elvis might be Jewish, their son told an interviewer, or "they would never have asked him to be a Shabbos Goy." Until her death, Jeanette Fruchter often talked about "the nicest boy you could ever hope to meet."

Gladys Love Smith and Her Siblings

Despite battling illness most of her life, Octavia Luvenia "Doll" Mansell Smith gave her husband, Bob Smith, nine children. Julian Riley has cast some doubt about this, speculating that at least one of them may have been fathered by James Alford Love. Regardless, the Smith children all battled alcohol and other serious problems. In the order of birth, these are Doll's children and a brief account of their lives.

Effie Smith (1904)

Effie Smith was born ten months after Bob and Doll were married on July 1, 1904, in Lee County. Undoubtedly, there was a bit of father's disappointment that a girl had been born—a boy eventually would have been able to do more of the hard sharecropping work on the Hussey farm where they lived and worked. But Bob was a kind and loving man. With grief, he and Doll buried Effie fourteen months later in Andrews Church Cemetery next to the farm (GPS location 34.22678, -88.56241).

Lillian Panther Smith (1906)

Before Doll's infant Effie died, she became pregnant again and gave birth Jan 2, 1906, to Lillian Panther Smith. Another girl! Maybe next time God would give Bob and Doll a boy. At twenty, Lillian married Charlie Mann and had twin daughters who did not survive. The next year, she and Charlie had a son who died eight years later. Over the next twelve years, however, they would have one daughter and five sons. "Maybe she was trying to make up for the dearth of males in Bob and Doll's household," Julian told me.

Following the two infants who did not survive, all of Lillian and Charlie's children were Elvis's first cousins. They are:

- Garland (1927)
- Flora (1928)
- Charles (1930)
- Robert Melvin (1931)
- Billy Lee (1934)
- Bobbie Jane (1938)
- Kenneth Wayne (1940)

Census records show that in 1940 Lillian and Charlie were living near Richmond in Lee County. After Charlie died in 1957, she married James Fortenberry, who was with her until he died December 11, 1971. Lillian lived another eleven years. She died at the age of eighty-four in Memphis, and her funeral was held on March 16, 1990. She is buried at Forest Hill Home & Memorial Park – Midtown (GPS location 35.09920, -90.01732).

Linnie Lavelle Smith (1908)

On February 14, 1908, another daughter, Linnie Lavelle Smith, was born. Bob was now outnumbered three-to-one by females. When Linnie turned seventeen, it appeared that Bob and Doll were anxious for their daughter to get married. Julian's efforts uncovered an interesting note written to the Circuit Court of Lee

County on Valentine's Day, 1925. It said: "Please let Eddie Smith have marriage license for himself and Miss Luvell Smith. You have our full permission."

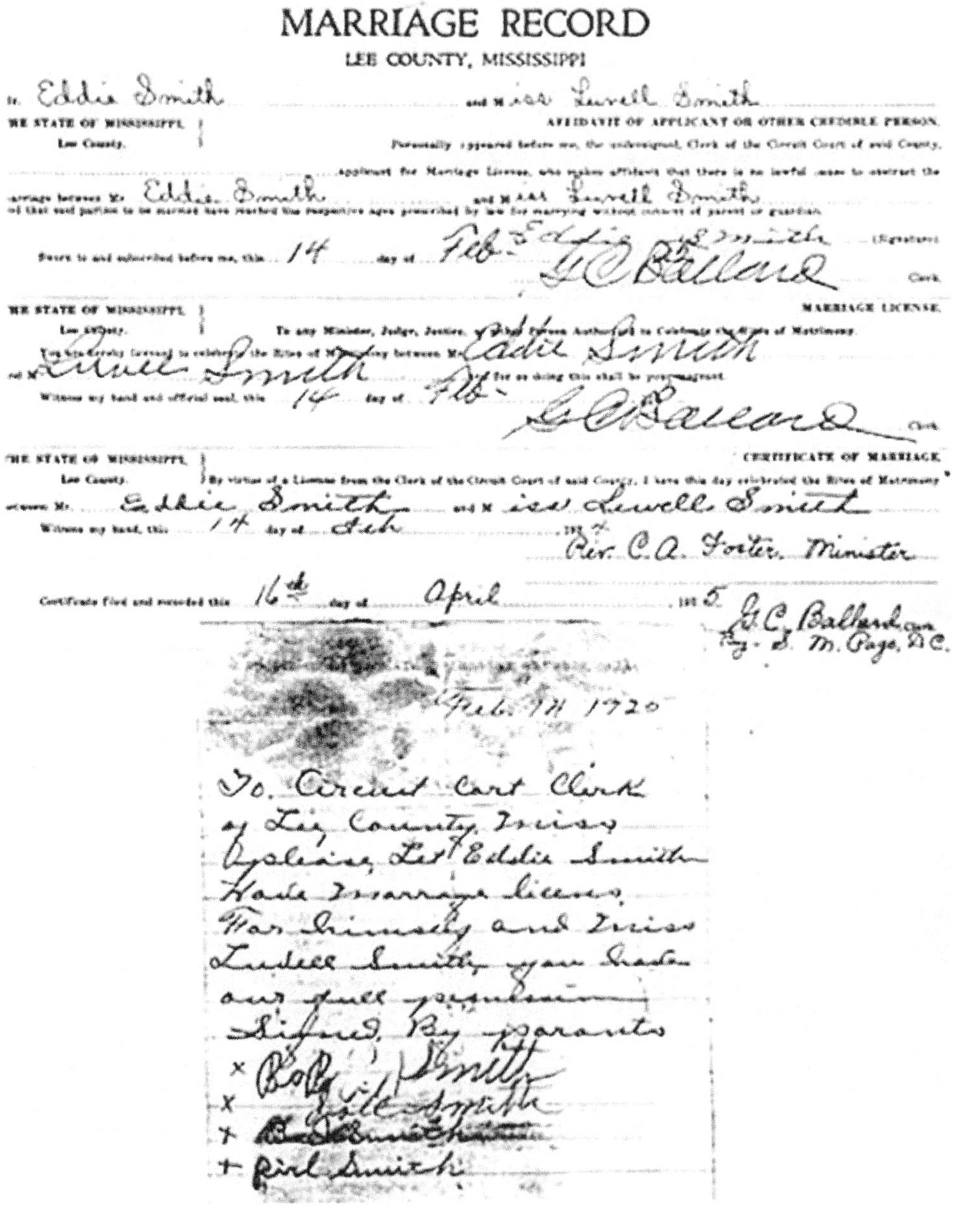
MARRIAGE RECORD

LEE COUNTY, MISSISSIPPI

Eddie Smith and Miss Luvell Smith

THE STATE OF MISSISSIPPI, Lee County. AFFIDAVIT OF APPLICANT OR OTHER CREDIBLE PERSON.

Personally appeared before me, the undersigned, Clerk of the Circuit Court of said County, applicant for Marriage License, who makes affidavit that there is no lawful cause to obstruct the marriage between Mr. Eddie Smith and Miss Luvell Smith

Sworn to and subscribed before me, this 14 day of Feb.

G C Ballard, Clerk

THE STATE OF MISSISSIPPI, Lee County. MARRIAGE LICENSE.

To any Minister, Judge, Justice, or Other Person Authorized to Celebrate the Rites of Matrimony

Eddie Smith

Luvell Smith

Witness my hand and official seal, this 14 day of Feb.

G C Ballard, Clerk

THE STATE OF MISSISSIPPI, Lee County. CERTIFICATE OF MARRIAGE.

By virtue of a License from the Clerk of the Circuit Court of said County, I have this day celebrated the Rites of Matrimony between Mr. Eddie Smith and Miss Luvell Smith

Witness my hand, this 14 day of Feb

Rev. C.A. Foster, Minister

Certificate filed and recorded this 16th day of April

G.C. Ballard
By S. M. Page, D.C.

Feb. 14 1925

To. Circuit Cort Clerk
of Lee County Miss
please Let Eddie Smith
Have marriage licens
For himself and Miss
Luvell Smith you have
our full permission
Signed By parants
x Bob Smith
x Lola Smith
+ [illegible]
+ Pirl Smith

A handwritten note to the Circuit Court giving permission for Linnie Lavelle Smith and Eddie Smith to marry.

The document was signed by the couple's parents: "Bob Smith, doll Smith, Bud Smith, pirl Smith." Pearl's name is misspelled phonetically, and her name and Doll's are not capitalized. It appears that someone else wrote the note and the parents just signed it. "I was thrilled to find such a document signed by Elvis Presley's maternal grandparents," Julian said.

Linnie married William E. "Eddie" Smith on February 14, 1925. William was the second cousin of Julian Riley's mother, which shows how closely the Riley clan is entangled with this story. Linnie Lavelle died April 9, 1979, at the age of seventy-one. She is buried in Memphis at Forest Hill Home & Memorial Park – Midtown (GPS location 35.09920, -90.01732).

Linnie and William had five children:

- Lee Edward, Sr. (1926)
- Annie Laverne (1928)
- Robert Melton (1930)
- Carroll Junior (1932). Carroll bore a resemblance to Elvis and was part of the King's world, serving as a guard at Graceland. He suffered from PTSD and alcoholism after service in the Korean War and died of alcohol poisoning at his uncle Travis's home in February 1961.

On July 4, 1956, Carroll Junior Smith was seated next to Elvis on a train between Chattanooga and Memphis.

- Tony Eugene "Gene" (1934). Gene grew up with Elvis and for the early years of Elvis's career was an omnipresent member of the Memphis Mafia. He died in 1977.

"Gene" Smith and Elvis grew up together and were first cousins.

Retha Smith (c. 1910)

Yet another daughter was born to Bob and Doll in 1910. The exact date of her birth is not known, but it was before the family moved to Pontotoc County and the census taker visited on April 15, 1910. As a young girl, Retha attended a small school called Patterson near Eggville, Mississippi. The school no longer exists today. By 1927, Retha had withdrawn from school to "work at home," a common occurrence for girls in that era.

One of the most interesting notes found during Julian's research was written to the Circuit Clerk of Lee County, Mr. G. C. Ballard. The note reads: "Mr. Ballard you let Purvie Loyd have married license for Rether Smith." It was signed "Bob Smith, doll Smith," but the name Doll is not capitalized. It's unclear if Bob and Doll wrote the note themselves or had someone write the note and they just signed it.

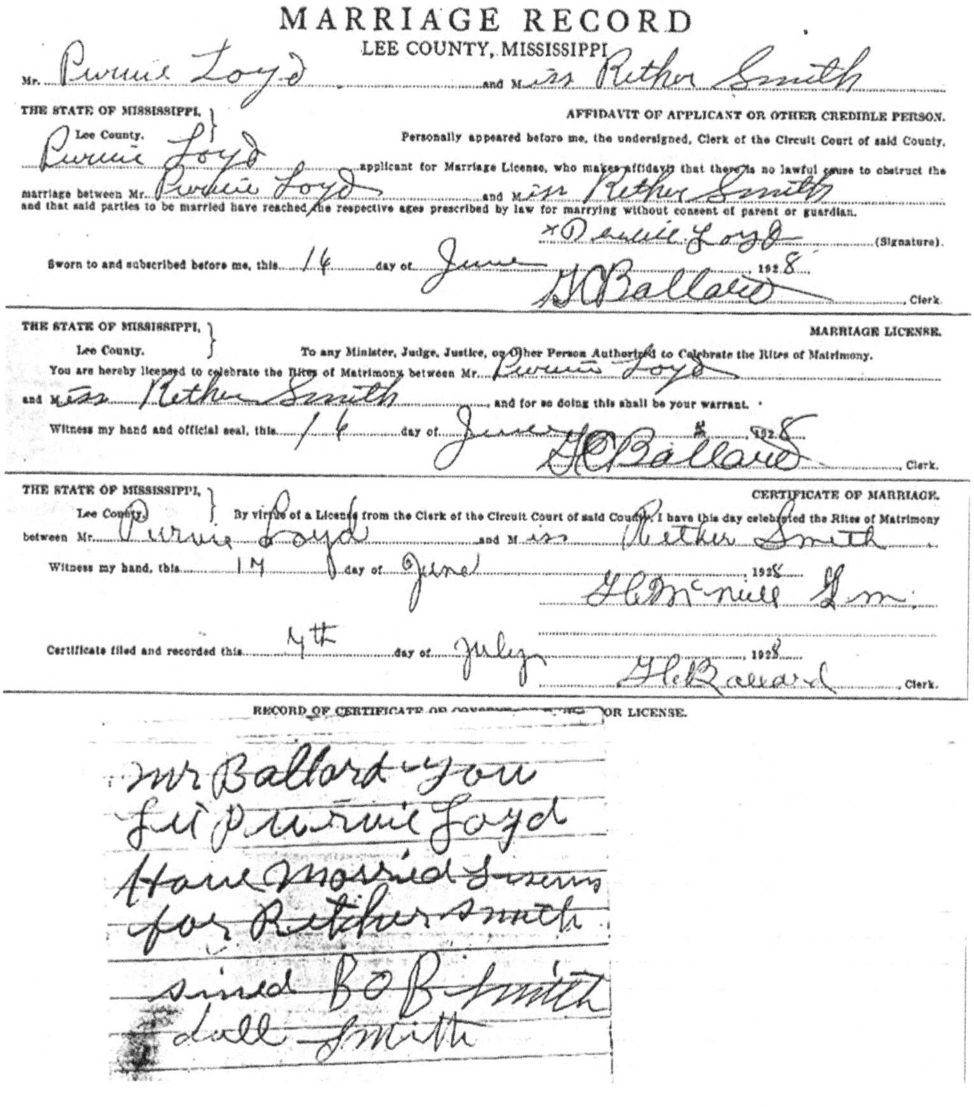

MARRIAGE RECORD

LEE COUNTY, MISSISSIPPI

Mr. Purvie Loyd and Miss Rether Smith

THE STATE OF MISSISSIPPI, Lee County. } AFFIDAVIT OF APPLICANT OR OTHER CREDIBLE PERSON.

Personally appeared before me, the undersigned, Clerk of the Circuit Court of said County, Purvie Loyd applicant for Marriage License, who makes affidavit that there is no lawful cause to obstruct the marriage between Mr. Purvie Loyd and Miss Rether Smith and that said parties to be married have reached the respective ages prescribed by law for marrying without consent of parent or guardian.

x Purvie Loyd (Signature).

Sworn to and subscribed before me, this 16 day of June 1928

G C Ballard Clerk.

THE STATE OF MISSISSIPPI, Lee County. } MARRIAGE LICENSE.

To any Minister, Judge, Justice, or Other Person Authorized to Celebrate the Rites of Matrimony.

You are hereby licensed to celebrate the Rites of Matrimony between Mr. Purvie Loyd and Miss Rether Smith, and for so doing this shall be your warrant.

Witness my hand and official seal, this 16 day of June 1928

G C Ballard Clerk.

THE STATE OF MISSISSIPPI, Lee County. } CERTIFICATE OF MARRIAGE.

By virtue of a License from the Clerk of the Circuit Court of said County, I have this day celebrated the Rites of Matrimony between Mr. Purvie Loyd and Miss Rether Smith

Witness my hand, this 17 day of June 1928

G C McNeill G.m.

Certificate filed and recorded this 4th day of July 1928

G C Ballard Clerk.

RECORD OF CERTIFICATE OR ... OR LICENSE.

Mr Ballard you
let Purvie Loyd
Have married license
for Rether smith
sined BOB Smith
doll Smith

The request to allow their daughter's marriage was granted and Retha married Purvie Loyd June 17, 1928. They had one child, a son named Robert Harold Loyd, a first cousin of Elvis.

Apparently, though, the marriage was not such a good idea. The couple divorced several years later and Retha married Walton G. Riley, a distant relative of Julian's, who outlived his wife by forty-six years. Retha died in an accidental stove explosion in 1941 at the age of thirty-one and is buried in an unmarked grave at New Spring Hill Cemetery near Saltillo, Mississippi (GPS location 34.33639, -88.60719).

Gladys Love (1912)

Gladys, the mother of Elvis, was born near the Hoyle community in Pontotoc County, Mississippi, on April 25, 1912. As a young girl she attended the small Patterson school near Eggville in Lee County. The schoolhouse no longer exists.

As a young girl, Gladys was listless and lazy, according to her big sister Lillian: "Hog-lazy—that's what we called her. We'd be shaking out the beds and you'd turn around and there'd be Gladys lying across one asleep." But she was certainly a likable kid with a winning personality. A neighbor, Vera Turner, said "she had the sweetest disposition of all the Smith girls." She was not rowdy or demanding like the others, just pleasant to be around, a manner probably honed by the need to continually court the generosity of others for survival. She was not good at "book learning," but she excelled at basketball and was such an aggressive forward on the girl's team that only coach Mary Harville could guard her.

By the age of fifteen, Gladys had also withdrawn from school to "work at home." After Bob Smith, the man most people believed was her father, had passed away, Gladys moved to East Tupelo with her mother to take a factory job. Gladys met Vernon Presley and on June 17, 1933, they were married in Verona just four miles south of East Tupelo. Through the years, Gladys's closest friends included Annie Cloyd Presley (wife of Sales Presley, a cousin of Elvis), Christine Houston Presley (wife of Noah Presley, Elvis's uncle) and Zora Mears Riley (Julian Riley's aunt by marriage).

On January 8, 1935, Gladys gave birth to twin boys. The first, Jesse Garon, died shortly after birth, according to the doctor. The second son, Elvis Aron, survived and the rest is history.

Gladys died August 14, 1958, in Memphis. She was initially buried at Forest Hill Home & Memorial Park – Midtown in Memphis (GPS location 35.09920, -90.01732). On August 26,1977, her body was moved into the mausoleum where her son, Elvis, had been entombed. On October 2, 1977, both the bodies of Gladys and Elvis were moved by Paul McCarver to the grounds of the Graceland where they lie today. Her epitaphs read: "Sunshine of our home" and "Not mine but Thy will be done."

Travis James (1914)

As a child, Travis was enrolled in school at Patterson—a small school near Eggville in Lee County that his sister Gladys also attended. A school record from 1927 shows that Travis's school attendance was very irregular. Travis married Lorraine Ivy in 1937. Five years later, his younger brother Johney would marry Lorraine's sister, Lois Ivy, making their children double-first cousins. Travis and Johney did not like each other and frequently had bloody arguments.

In 1938, Travis pled guilty with Vernon Presley and Lether Gable to forgery of a small check and was sentenced to three years at the Mississippi State Penitentiary in Parchman. Jessie Dee Presley, Vernon's father, put up bail for Travis to keep him out of jail pending trial and sentencing, but did not bail out his son. Travis served his entire three-year sentence at Parchman Prison. According to family stories, Travis battled drinking problems throughout his life and moved from job to job.

Prison records state that Travis had no education and could not read or write. His teeth were "bad," and he was five-feet, seven-and-one-half inches tall. His body showed evidence of a hard life. He wore a tattoo, "NBB," on his right forearm. At that time in Mississippi, the mark defiantly communicated a willingness to fight, take pain and dish it out. He had a number of scars, including a cut scar on his left thigh.

Travis and Ivy had two sons, Billy and Bobby. Billy Smith served as a loyal member of Elvis's "Memphis Mafia" for many years. Bobby helped out until an accident shattered his legs, (See "Chapter 7: Jessie and Minnie: Mackey Hargett's Secrets" page 91). The injuries plagued Bobby until at twenty-seven he committed suicide by drinking rat poison. Travis Smith and his family moved to Memphis in November 1948, around the time that Vernon, Gladys and Elvis moved there. After Elvis Presley became famous, Travis worked for many years as a gate guard at Graceland with his brother-in-law, Vester Presley. At last, he was enjoying stable employment thanks to Elvis. Travis died in 1973 and is buried at Forest Hill Home & Memorial Park – Midtown in Memphis (GPS location 35.09920, -90.01732).

Travis Smith and his family: wife Lorraine Ivy Smith; sons Billy (left) and Bobby.

Tracy (1917)

Tracy was born June 19, 1917. Like other siblings, he attended the Patterson school near Eggville, Mississippi. The building does not exist today. In 1927, Tracy was listed on the school record as enrolled but with irregular attendance. A childhood disease had caused a hearing loss, which interrupted his learning to speak. He lived the life of a hobo and some thought he was mentally handicapped. He never married and died at the age of forty-nine on June 28, 1966. He is buried in Memphis at Forest Hill Home & Memorial Park – Midtown (GPS location 35.09920, -90.01732).

Clettes (1919)

Clettes was born on September 14, 1919, in Lee County. As a young girl, Clettes was listed on the Patterson school record as "withdrawn from school for unknown causes." Patterson was a small school near Eggville, Mississippi, that no longer exists. Eight months after Elvis was born to her sister, Gladys, Clettes married Vester Presley, the brother of Gladys's husband Vernon. These marriages made their children double-first cousins. Clettes and Vester Presley had one child, Patsy Presley, who worked for many years as secretary to Elvis.

With a little make-up and a matching beehive hair-do, Patsy Presley (left) looked very much like Priscilla Presley.

Clettes was known to family members as a hard drinker, a profane "loudmouth" and a woman who had a ribald sense of humor matched by her bawdy personal conduct. She is buried in Memphis at Forest Hill Home & Memorial Park – Midtown (GPS location 35.09920, -90.01732).

Johney Lee (1922)

The youngest offspring in the Smith household, Johney was born on April 19, 1922. As a young man, he developed an alcohol problem that plagued him for the rest of his life. In her autobiography, *The Forgotten Family*, Johney's wife, Lois, accuses him of abducting her and forcing her into a marriage.

Johney was drafted into the US Navy during WWII and after basic training went on the run for two months rather than face the risks of battle. Eventually, he was caught and served two months in a military prison and then was assigned to duty in Oxnard, California. His wife wrote, "I prayed that the navy would make a man out of Johney, and he would stop drinking."

Johney Lee Smith, Gladys Presley's brother.

Unfortunately, it didn't. When he was finally assigned to duty overseas, he didn't get on the ship, deciding that incarceration a second time for being AWOL was safer, which proved true. Enemy forces destroyed his assigned ship.

After the war, Johney's allergy to work and careless infidelity created a series of family crises and thrust the family into perpetual poverty. Lois elaborated on Johney's episodes of rage and spousal abuse. "Once, Johney beat me so hard in the head," she wrote, "I had to have surgery. I was scared of him. Johney had a lot of anger inside of him, and his drinking made everything worse." A close friend of hers, Mary Stonebreaker, told me that Johney would often rap Lois's knuckles so hard when she was disobedient that her joints had to be surgically replaced.

Elvis bought Johney and Lois a little house over a hundred miles away from Tupelo near Arkabutla Lake, Mississippi. It was the nicest place they had ever lived because of Johney's inability to hold a job. Lois's friend, Mary, told me, "I think he chose a place that far away so it would be hard for them to come back and visit."

Despite their wretched existence, Johney and Lois had five children:

- Jackie (1944)
- Nick (1947)
- Janet (1949)
- Brenda (1950)
- Tony Lee (1952)

Johney and Lois finally divorced in 1963, and Johney died five years later at forty-six after having another daughter, Ginger, with a woman known to us only as "Jen." Lois passed away in 2010 at the age of eighty-four. Johney is buried in Memphis at Forest Hill Home & Memorial Park – Midtown (GPS location 35.09920, -90.01732).

Chapter 10
Gladys's Journey

To many diehard Elvis fans, Gladys Presley, the mother of the King of Rock and Roll, is revered as a kind of Madonna, the mother of Christ and a symbol of innocence, purity, virginity, chastity, love, royalty and immortality. To Elvis, who cherished his mother, the love and attention with which she enveloped him undoubtedly made her an object worthy of such high honor and a loving son's zealous devotion. It is not difficult to forgive Elvis for overlooking the imperfections of the mother he adored and for excusing her adolescent behavior, about which he must have known considering the legion of relatives around him with similar conduct and undisciplined tongues.

Unfortunately, the Madonna, a metaphor used by numerous writers to suggest the depth of fan sentiment for Gladys, represents a collection of qualities no human could possess, not even Gladys Love Smith. According to Roman Catholic belief, Mother Mary was conceived without sin, a phenomenon called the Immaculate Conception. Somehow, according to this doctrine, her conception was untainted by the impurity of sexual intercourse, which would have caused Mary to spiritually inherit the sins of her parents just as infants physically inherit their parents' genes. Christian teaching also insists that Mary conceived the child Jesus without having sexual union with a man, thus preventing Jesus, her son, from the stain of original sin.

Her virginity prior to giving birth is a hallmark of Christianity. Mary, we are told, lived a selfless life of obedience to God and service to her only son, Christ the King.

That both Jesus, the King of kings, and Elvis, the King of rock and roll, are referred to with royal titles may be the only commonality between the Madonna, a queen mother, and Gladys Presley, another queen mother. No doubt Gladys became a loving and lovable mother, otherwise Elvis would not have loved her so deeply.

In the poverty-stricken world of early 1900s Mississippi, life was hard, moments of pleasure were rare, morality was elastic and survival was a daily struggle. Christianity nominally prevailed country culture, but its tenets were easily ignored or adapted to current situations.

Into this sod stew of life, Gladys was born not through Immaculate Conception but most likely through her mother's adultery—an act that was certainly not Gladys's fault, but in those times blameworthy to anyone who knew the "sin" of Doll Mansell. And so, the affair between Doll Mansell and James Alford Love, if true, became a closely guarded secret. The need to keep personal matters secret seems to have been ingrained into Gladys, which could account for the difficulty researchers have had in unearthing some fundamental truths.

The reality of her mother's affair awaits the final proof of DNA, but there is considerable circumstantial evidence as mentioned above—Alford's last name being used as an honorific after Gladys's first name (Gladys "Love" Smith); Alford Love's easy access to Doll Mansell prior to Gladys's birth.

In 1930, when Gladys was around eighteen or nineteen years old, newly analyzed records showed that she was living with her remaining family members along the road from Tupelo to Eggville. Astoundingly, their dilapidated house was on a farm owned by James Alford Love. If our theory is correct and Love is Gladys's biological father, Alford Love was now living next door to his daughter (in country parlance, however, this could be a half-mile away). Julian discovered the location of Love's house, which had been demolished and replaced by a manufactured home (GPS location 34.33427, -88.55188).

A manufactured home owned by Danny Page now sits on the site of James Alford Love's farmhouse in Eggville, Mississippi.

As Julian and I were exploring the Eggville area with local resident Rhonda Grammer, we stopped for pizza at Hardin's Country Store in Eggville. Rhonda spotted a local acquaintance, Danny Page, and struck up a conversation. By coincidence, Danny was the man who had bought the old Alford Love place and tore down the rotting house. He was now living in the manufactured home I had photographed just fifteen minutes earlier.

Danny, now in his sixties, was a trove of information about the people and places in the Eggville area. He knew Love family members and also the Harris family in which Clarence Clinton "Pid" Harris, a young man of Gladys's age, was a son. Pid had become Gladys's boyfriend, and another local resident had told Julian that their relationship had become intimate. So we asked Danny if he had known Pid.

"I knew his father pretty well," Danny told us, "but Pid himself, just a little bit."

We asked Danny if he could tell us what he knew about Pid Harris. "Well, he was different," Danny answered. "That's all I can say." And that's all we could extract from him—Pid was different. "I know the Harris kin around here, and they know me too," Danny explained.

One local resident told us that Gladys had become pregnant by a man named Harris. If that happened, we suspect the father was Pid Harris, but we have no DNA confirmation yet. When the relationship with Pid abruptly ended, she fell in with a married farmer who was working the local Burke farm. Her lover abandoned the relationship, it seems, because of a guilty conscience. If Gladys was pregnant and starting to show, however, that revelation may have scared off the farmer.

Rex Stanford, one of Gladys's suitors.

On the other side of the Alford Love house in 1930 lived a young man named Rex Stanford and his family. Rex, a good-looking fellow, predictably fell madly in love with beautiful Gladys Smith. He desperately wanted to marry her but lacked the nerve to ask for her hand.

At fifteen, Gladys was a chubby but charismatic young lady, but by 1930 the chubbiness had melted away revealing a beautiful and curvaceous woman. Like Elvis's paternal great-great-grandmother, Rosella, Gladys had caught the eyes of many eligible (and likely some ineligible) males in the area. She had also provided some excitement because of her buck dancing skills at various local events.

Buck dancing, based on various European and African dance traditions, is an American folk dance that sprouted in the southern Appalachians. In this precursor to clogging and tap dancing, a solo dancer accompanied by a fiddle player would show off flatfooted, high stepping moves while keeping a straight torso, similar to Irish step dancing. Look up "shuffle dancing" on YouTube for video of a modern-day version.

Typically, only men did buck dancing, so when a young girl like Gladys performed these energetic moves it must have stirred up a lot of testosterone. Gladys was no one-trick pony, though—she could also do the Charleston and loved dancing to Jimmie Rodgers' "Corinne, Corinna." According to author Patricia Jobe Pierce, "People thought of her as a 'joyous and pretty' young girl."

"It's likely that Gladys was evaluating her marriage prospects with increasing desperation," Julian told me. "Her older sisters had all gotten married, and Gladys was probably worried about being left an old maid." Her second sister, Linnie Lavalle, who was only four years older than Gladys, had married William Smith (no relation) in 1925. Gladys's oldest sister, Lillian, had married Charlie Mann after a proper courtship in 1926. And then Retha, only two years older than Gladys, had run off in 1928 and married Perry Loyd, a field hand who had recently arrived in the area. And now, if Gladys were pregnant, well…

Rumors buzz through the Mississippi countryside like black flies, and there are numerous stories of Gladys having a child, perhaps more than one, before she married Vernon. We have not confirmed these speculations, but in the 1930s it was rare in the fertile fields of Tupelo for a young woman to not marry or at least get pregnant before twenty-one, which was Gladys's age when she wed Vernon Presley. Vernon's grandmother, we should remember, had borne nine children without the benefit of marriage, and her parents most likely had not wed. Rosella chose to raise all her children, but many other pregnant girls simply gave their babies to other family members to be raised.

Facing Poverty

In October of 1932, Doll's husband, Bob Smith, suddenly developed pneumonia, grew blind almost overnight and died. He was wrapped in a winding sheet provided by family friend Lily Mae Irwin and buried with no ceremony in an unmarked grave at New Spring Hill Cemetery (GPS location 34.33639, -88.60719). His family was left with no savings or income.

Gladys and other girls from the Eggville area were most likely being bused into Tupelo to work in the textile industry before Gladys and her financially strapped family moved to East Tupelo. Gladys eventually took a job sewing clothes at the Tupelo Garment Company at 495 Green Street about two blocks from Reed Manufacturing. Like Gladys, over 80 percent of the work force for these enterprises lived outside Tupelo.

Julian's Uncle Alwyn Westmoreland, who worked for Doty Brothers Motor Company (located next to Reed Manufacturing and two blocks from the garment factory), drove one of these buses. He lived in Richmond, so all he had to do was stop and pick up the girls on his way to work each morning. Garment factory wages were low but provided needed cash for families, like the Smiths, that had no other source of income during the depression.

Julian's mother, Jewell Westmoreland, and his aunt, Mittie Westmoreland Hussey, both quit school early and took jobs at Reed Manufacturing, often riding Alwyn's bus to their jobs. The money they earned helped Julian's grandfather save his farm from foreclosure.

Uncle Alwyn's bus. Julian's mother, Jewell, is standing on the far right of the photo.

About this time, Gladys Smith met Faye Harris working at the garment factory, and they became close friends. Faye lived on Adams Street in East Tupelo. Having a friend nearby was a big reason the Smith family moved to a house at the corner of Berry and Adams Streets across from Faye Harris. This intersection was only two blocks from where Gladys would give birth to Elvis.

East Tupelo was also a logical place to live because two of Gladys's uncles, Sims and Gains Mansell, lived in the area. The Mansell brothers were the first preachers to serve at the Assembly of God church that Elvis attended after it was built in 1938.

Jessie Dee and his family were living in a four-room house on Old Saltillo Road down the street, and while the Smiths didn't know them well, the Presleys must have seemed quite well-to-do by comparison. Jessie Dee had a job, the Presleys owned their home and uncle Noah owned a grocery store.

Gladys's First Proposal

After the Smiths moved to East Tupelo, Rex Stanford finally worked up the nerve to propose marriage to Gladys, who put him off by saying she had to think about it. But after Rex's proposal, two important things occurred that changed the future history of popular music in America.

First, Rex Stanford received a draft notice. Rather than wait for induction into the army, he joined the National Guard, which allowed for a short six months of active duty stateside instead of war duty overseas for an undetermined period of time. This relieved Gladys from having to make a quick decision about his proposal. Rex, however, continued to hope for a future with Gladys when he returned six months later.

Second, after Rex left for Guard training, Gladys met the Presley family at the neighborhood First Assembly of God church, a charismatic fundamentalist sect of Christianity. The church services in 1932 were joyful and exuberant, the congregants often emotional and physically active. At this church, the guitar-wielding preacher would often prowl the platform seeking inspiration and then break into song, rapturously urging the believers to join in. The Bible-thumping sermons stirred up a maelstrom of guilt and shame, holy visions and hellish nightmares, tears and laughter, heavenly bliss and otherworldly delirium. The congregation loved the cathartic experience.

Casting aside her interrupted relationship with Rex, Gladys began dating Vester Presley, a randy young man with an eye for pretty girls. At this same time, Gladys's more libertine sister, Clettes, was hooked up with Vester's brother, Vernon. At some point, Gladys impulsively decided that the cute, blond, seventeen-year-old Vernon was more to her liking than Vester even though she was four years older than Vernon. The sisters swapped boyfriends, and Vester apparently approved the switch—he married Clettes in September of 1935.

Faye Harris told interviewer Jerry Hopkins, "[Vernon] and Gladys started going together, going to the roller rink in town or having picnics over at the fish hatchery. The hatchery was one of the nicest places we had in those days, with trees to sit under and a nice lake to look at."

We cannot possibly know Gladys's emotional condition when she decided to pursue young Vernon, but the couple eloped two months later and were married June 17, 1933. When Rex Stanford returned to Tupelo, his beloved Gladys was a married woman. Rex eventually would overcome his heartbreak, marry another Lee County woman and become Julian Riley's father-in-law upon the marriage of his daughter Linda. Roots run deep in Lee County.

Elvis's Birthplace

Vernon's family had lived on a dairy farm owned by Orville Bean, and in 1934 Vernon was still working there. One day, after learning his wife was pregnant, Vernon drummed up the courage to ask Orville for a loan to build a home for his expanding family.

Orville, who knew Vernon's family, loaned the young man 180 dollars, enough to buy a house "kit" from Leake and Goodlett, a Tupelo firm that sold all the precut materials as a package. A variety of simple house designs were available with slight variations to suit personal tastes: front door to the right or left of the window; fireplace in the center of the house or on the back wall; and larger windows available for one side of the dwelling or the other. It is likely that many, perhaps most, of the shotgun shacks in Tupelo were built from kits, which is why the structures are nearly identical.

Julian Riley's grandfather, Noonan, loaned Jessie D. Presley money to buy his four-bedroom house on Old Saltillo Road.

Vernon, with help from his father, built the dwelling next to

Jessie Dee's more spacious home. Jessie had borrowed money from Julian Riley's grandfather, Noonan, to acquire the four-room house, which was packed with kin—Jessie and Minnie Mae, of course, but also Vernon's brother Vester and sisters Delta, "Little" Gladys and Nashval. Vernon and his father, who had never gotten along, were suddenly next-door neighbors on Old Saltillo Road, a main artery that transported locals between Tupelo and Birmingham, Alabama.

Jessie Dee and Minnie Mae lived in this house with four of Vernon's siblings. Elvis's birth house was built next door.

In June 1956, the *Tupelo Daily Journal* misidentified a photo of Jessie Dee's house by writing this caption: "Home Sweet Home. This is the song Elvis would have sung about this house in East Tupelo where he was born."

Vernon's house next door had no indoor plumbing and no electricity. Actually, the house was connected to a rudimentary electrical grid, but the cost of electricity made it too expensive for the Presleys to use. Elvis would live there for three years.

The original birth house of Elvis Presley was built next door to his grandparents' larger house on Old Saltillo Road.

The home, similar to others in mill villages, was called a "shotgun" shack by locals. Folklore says this term refers to a type of long and narrow construction in which you could stand in the front door, fire a shotgun, and the pellets would go out the back door without hitting anything.

The building today referred to as the "birthplace" of Elvis is not the dwelling in which Elvis was born. Julian and I have finally unearthed the true, hidden story of Elvis's true birthplace.

While Vernon was incarcerated at Parchman Prison, Gladys could not afford to make loan payments on their home. The property reverted to Orville Bean, who had financed the construction. After the Presleys had moved out, Orville rented it to other families, but over time the building deteriorated badly.

Sometime before 1956, Orville simply demolished it, which was cheaper than fixing it up. Suddenly, Elvis's birthplace no longer existed—but then, no one cared, because at that time Elvis was just a skinny East Tupelo kid whom few people could remember.

After 1956, however, Elvis was one of the most famous entertainers in the country, and even Tupelo's city fathers knew he could help put Tupelo on the map for tourism. On September 26th of that year, Elvis returned to Tupelo to perform triumphant "Homecoming" concerts at the Mississippi-Alabama Fair and Dairy Show in Tupelo, the same venue where he had placed fifth in a music contest at the age of ten. After receiving the keys to the city, Elvis gave the mayor a contribution to purchase fifteen acres of land "to build a park for the kids of East Tupelo." It was no coincidence that the land, recently listed for sale, was where Elvis was born.

On September 26, 1956, Elvis performed a "Homecoming" concert in Tupelo and was given the keys to the city by the mayor.

Elvis returned the following year for another show. This time he donated approximately $14,000 for a youth recreation center to be built on the birthplace land, the funds coming from a special trust he had set up for that purpose. In 1958, Mayor James Ballard sent out letters requesting donations for the project. In his letter, Ballard wrote that the city intended to buy a parcel of land on which one small house resided. We believe that house was Jessie Dee's former home. The reference in the letter to a single small house on the desired land, which could only be Jessie Dee's house, confirms that Orville Bean had previously torn down Elvis's birth home or it would also have been present.

Despite Elvis's contributions and other public donations, progress on development stalled, according to researcher Roy Turner, until a frustrated Elvis called Mayor Ballard and "told him if dirt wasn't moving by the end of the month there was going to be hell to pay." Excavation equipment showed up almost overnight, leveling a steep hill on the property to provide the flat land required for Elvis Presley Park and the massive quantity of dirt needed for work on nearby East Main Street. Soon after, the Elvis Presley Youth Center was erected. It is now the Elvis Presley Birthplace Museum.

A local girl sits on a steep hill that was present on the birthplace property prior to excavation for road construction.

A sign announces the site of the coming Elvis Presley Youth Recreation Center. In this promotional photo, a covered wagon with live horses announces the upcoming release of Jailhouse Rock. The picture was taken prior to Park excavation—notice the hill that is still present behind the Youth Recreation Center sign.

A major problem loomed, however. Jessie Dee's house, which didn't fit into the park's plan, was still on the property. And there was no birth house. The first issue was resolved when the city hired house movers Richard and Ernest Simmons to remove Jessie's four-room home. We don't know if the movers bought the house or it was bartered for their efforts, but the dwelling ended up on Baker Street. Richard Simmons told Julian that he moved his family into the house and made substantial improvements over time. He lived there for eleven years before selling it to another party.

"I'm amazed that no one considered the historical value of Jessie's house," Julian told me. "Elvis probably spent a lot more time in that house than in his own place. And so many close relatives of Elvis lived there. That house may have been more of an influence on Elvis's growing up than the birth house. I'm just glad it wasn't torn down."

Jessie Dee and Minnie Mae's home was moved from the birthplace property to Baker Street. It has been modernized and enlarged.

The Simmons brothers also helped resolve the second issue—the missing birth house. The city had found a nearby shotgun house that was strikingly similar to Elvis's birthplace. The house was owned by Gus Croft, a fifty-year-old employee of Star Grocery, and his wife Mary Francis. Somehow, they had been raising a family of six in that tiny, two-room shack. The Simmons brothers moved the Croft house to its current location (GPS location 34.25998, -88.68006). Old Saltillo Road was later renamed Elvis Presley Drive.

The Croft house was not immediately restored, however. I spoke with Richard Simmons' son, Ricky Simmons, in December of 2021, and he remembered sneaking into the dilapidated building as a boy and smoking cigarettes with his friends. "It was pretty rundown then," he told me. It would not be until 1971, more than a decade after the house was relocated, that the East Heights Garden Club, along with the Tupelo Park and Recreation Department, would finally restore the outside and interior of the house and add period-appropriate furnishings, though not the original ones.

This dwelling in Tupelo is called Elvis's birthplace according to the sign, but it is not the original birthplace.

We must rely on Vernon Presley's memory to detect the differences between Gus Croft's home and the original birth house. Vernon stated that on the original structure, the two windows on one side were larger than the windows on the other side. The replica building has windows of the same size on both sides. Vernon also drew a simple floor plan of the original house that clearly shows the fireplace on the back wall.

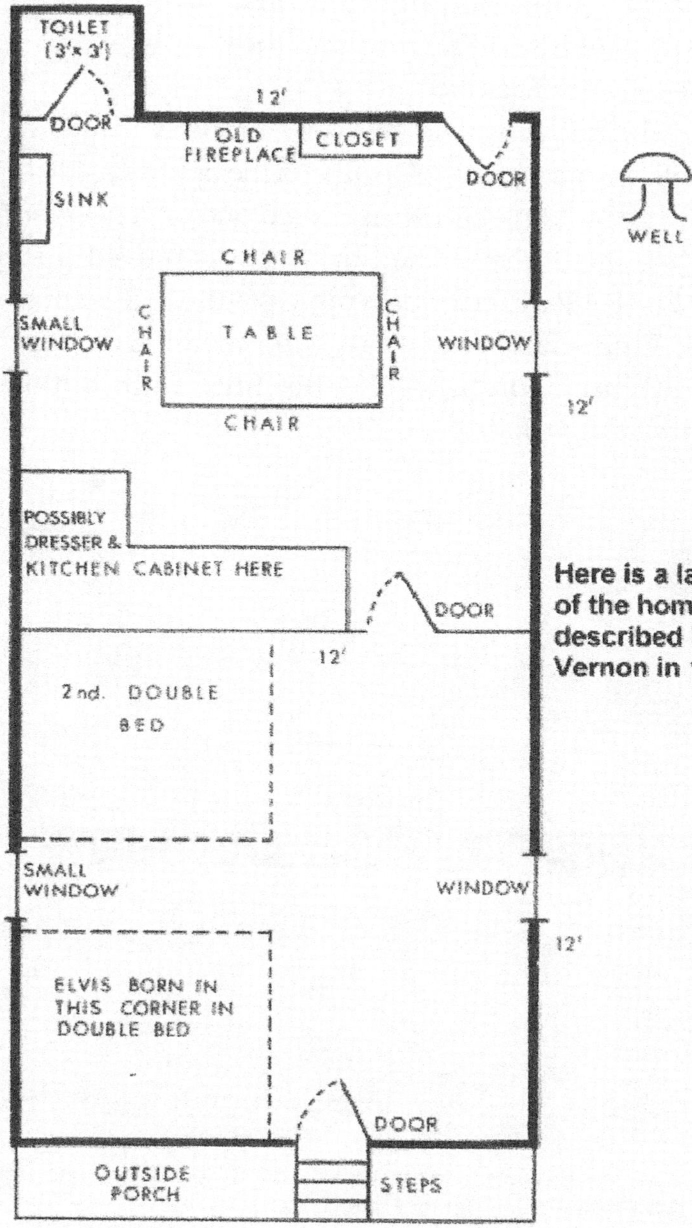

Here is a layout of the home as described by Vernon in 1964.

Vernon Presley's floorplan sketch of the original birth house has been tidied up for readability, but it shows the fireplace on the back wall (top of drawing.)

Since Vernon and Jessie Dee would have built the fireplace, Vernon probably got that part right. Yet on the replica house, the chimney is in the middle of the roof, and the back wall reveals no signs of a pre-existent fireplace.

The church that now sits on park property south of the birthplace replica was originally located on the opposite side of Old Saltillo Road. The building had been moved once to a new location and turned into apartments. The building was moved a second time to Elvis Presley Park, creating a more picturesque setting.

In 1964, Elvis closed out the youth center trust fund by writing a last check for $2,803.17, his final contribution for development of the property.

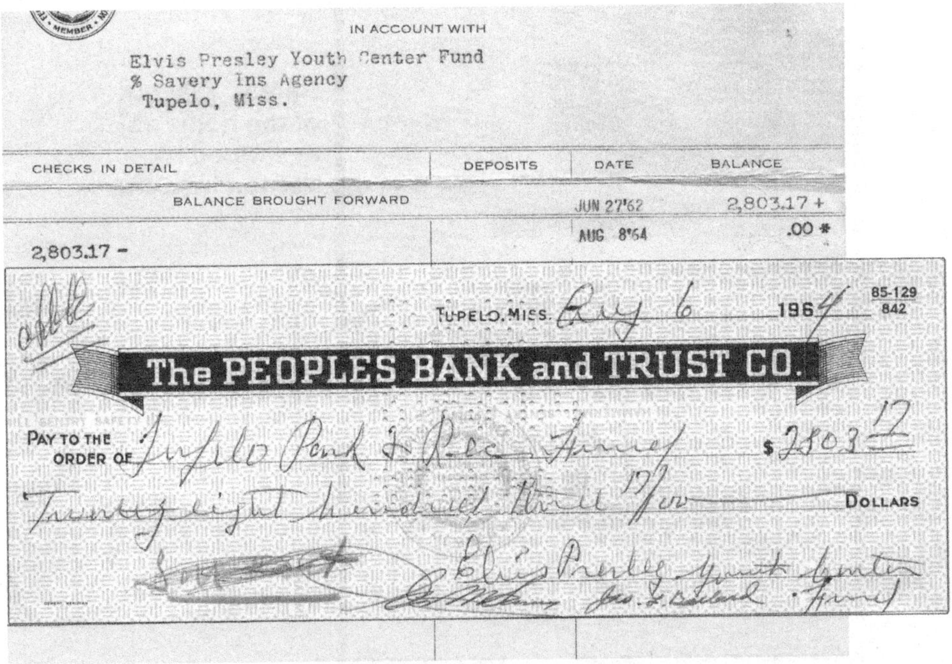
IN ACCOUNT WITH

Elvis Presley Youth Center Fund
% Savery Ins Agency
Tupelo, Miss.

CHECKS IN DETAIL	DEPOSITS	DATE	BALANCE
BALANCE BROUGHT FORWARD		JUN 27'62	2,803.17 +
2,803.17 -		AUG 8'64	.00 *

TUPELO, MISS. Aug 6 1964 85-129 / 842

The PEOPLES BANK and TRUST CO.

PAY TO THE ORDER OF ... $2803 17

... DOLLARS

Elvis Presley Youth Center Fund

This is the last check that Elvis wrote to the Tupelo Park & Recreation Fund, which closed out the Elvis Presley Youth Center Fund.

I do not fault the city for making improvements to the historic site, but it is misleading to conceal the fact that a house promoted as the Birthplace of Elvis Presley is really a Disneyland replica of it. The sign next to it promotes this falsehood:

BIRTHPLACE OF
ELVIS PRESLEY

Elvis Aaron Presley was born
Jan. 8, 1935, in this house built
by his father. Presley's career
as a singer and entertainer
redefined American popular
music. He died Aug. 16, 1977,
at Memphis, Tennessee.

I am sure that few pilgrims would travel to Tupelo to tour the home in which Gus Croft raised his children, but it wouldn't hurt to provide a simple explanation for Elvis fans—a footnote, even—that the house is a replica. This is an iconic example of the distortions that have eroded the true story of Elvis Presley. Many errors have occurred because of sloppy research or faulty memories, but this sleight-of-hand was deliberate.

Twins

The story of Elvis's birth has been retold many times with little respect for the facts. It has been repeated endlessly that around the fifth or sixth month of Gladys's difficult pregnancy she knew her rapidly expanding baby bump contained twins. The traditional version states that her new husband, Vernon, was the father—a reasonable conclusion since Vernon and Gladys were newlyweds. Alternative theories suggest that Gladys, already disappointed in her choice of mate after a few months of marriage, had sought solace from another man who sired the twins.

Dr. William Robert Hunt.

Regardless, the birth event finally occurred and Dr. William Robert Hunt, the doctor hired by the Tupelo Garment Factory to care for employees, arrived to deliver the babies. Since then, as Julian told me, "Almost every woman in East Tupelo has remembered being in the house for Elvis's birth." Perhaps they all came by to provide encouragement—there is no way of knowing. The simple facts of the birth were provided in writing by Dr. Hunt. For every year of his practice, Dr. Hunt wrote down the facts of each birth he attended in his Physician's Record.

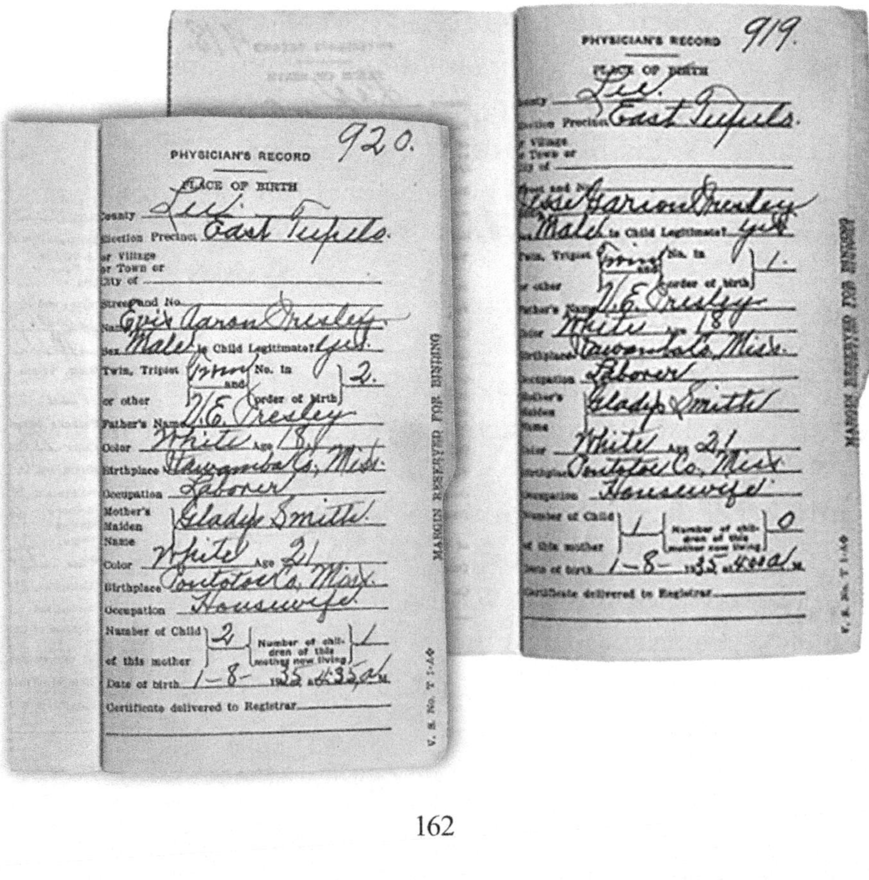

PHYSICIAN'S RECORD 920.

PLACE OF BIRTH
County Lee
Election Precinct East Tupelo
or Village or Town or City of
Street and No.
Name Evis Aaron Presley
Sex Male Is Child Legitimate? Yes
Twin, Triplet or other Twin No. in order of birth 2
Father's Name V.E. Presley
Color White Age 18
Birthplace Itawamba Co. Miss.
Occupation Laborer
Mother's Maiden Name Gladys Smith
Color White Age 21
Birthplace Pontotoc Co. Miss.
Occupation Housewife
Number of Child of this mother 2 Number of children of this mother now living 1
Date of birth 1-8-35 4:35 a.m.
Certificate delivered to Registrar
MARGIN RESERVED FOR BINDING
V. S. No. T 1-40

PHYSICIAN'S RECORD 919.

PLACE OF BIRTH
County Lee
Election Precinct East Tupelo
or Village or Town or City of
Name Jesse Garion Presley
Male Is Child Legitimate? Yes
Twin, Triplet or other Twin No. in order of birth 1
Father's Name V.E. Presley
Color White Age 18
Birthplace Itawamba Co. Miss.
Occupation Laborer
Mother's Maiden Name Gladys Smith
Color White Age 21
Birthplace Pontotoc Co. Miss.
Occupation Housewife
Number of Child of this mother 1 Number of children of this mother now living 0
Date of birth 1-8-35 4:00 a.m.
Certificate delivered to Registrar
MARGIN RESERVED FOR BINDING
V. S. No. T 1-40

On the night of January 7, 1935, his notes show that he attended Gladys Presley at her home on Old Saltillo Road in East Tupelo. At four o'clock the next morning, he delivered a stillborn infant. Thirty-five minutes later, a surviving infant, Elvis Aaron Presley, was born. Apparently, Dr. Hunt misspelled Elvis's middle name.

After Gladys gave birth to twins at her home, she and Elvis were taken to the Tupelo Hospital, which was originally a YMCA. The car in front was Dr. Hunt's automobile.

A simple explanation offered for burying Jessie in an unmarked grave is that the family could not afford a tombstone. But after Elvis became wealthy, why would the family continue to leave the gravesite unmarked? Gladys certainly would have known where her child was buried. However, cemeteries change over time. Tombstones are added, trees grow up and some are removed, bushes appear... After Gladys died in 1958, Vernon and Elvis may not have been able to find the grave.

Julian Riley interviewed a man who seemed to remember the location of Jesse's grave. Freddy Brown is the son of Marshall and Vona Mae Brown, the couple that drove Gladys and Vernon to be married in Verona. Freddy is related to Elvis on both the Smith and Presley sides of the family. Freddy told Julian that he remembered visiting Jesse's burial site when attending funerals of other family members but could no longer remember the precise location.

Julian and I remain puzzled by the appearance of the large angel statue, described earlier, that appeared suddenly next to the family plot of Sales Presley. (See "Chapter 1: The Riley Factor: The Angel" page 10). Could this statue be a commemoration of baby Jesse installed by an impassioned Elvis fan? Could it be marking the unmarked grave itself? Would the grave, if found, contain the body of an infant… or be an empty tomb? The mystery continues.

Twin Toes

A seldom-reported anomaly of Elvis's birth has introduced a compelling twist to the question of who his father was. Elvis, it turns out, was born with webbed toes on his right foot. He often referred to them as "twin toes," a phrase he believed referred to him being a twin. Actually, the term "twin toes" merely refers to the joining of two toes by a webbing of the skin between them. Usually, it is the second and third toes that are joined. The medical term is syndactyly.

We know that Elvis had this condition because Lamar Fike, an original Memphis Mafia member, wrote in *Elvis: Truth, Myth and Beyond* that Elvis told him about his twin toes. Elvis's ex-girlfriend, *Hee Haw* star and former Miss Tennessee Linda Thompson, said in a recently unearthed interview that "he had twin toes, which meant that his second toes from the big toe and the third toe were conjoined up to what would be the knuckle. And I used to tease him a lot about having webbed toes. That's something most people don't know."

Elvis's "twin toes" are clearly visible on his right foot. The second and third toes are joined higher than normal from the base.

Another girlfriend, Ginger Alden, who was with him the day he died, wrote in her memoir that while she was having a conversation with Elvis, he "pulled off one of his socks to show me his right foot. His second and third toes were joined together at the bottom, a physical attribute he called 'twin toes.'"

Syndactyly occurs when a natural process of fetal development is halted. During the earliest stages of development, all of us have webbed feet—even webbed hands! But at about six to eight weeks, a process called apoptosis is supposed to occur. A special enzyme is released that gently dissolves the soft tissue connecting the toes and fingers, leaving twenty distinct and wiggling digits. In some cases, though, that process is halted, and the child may be born with full or partial webbing between the toes or fingers.

This condition occurs in about one in every 3,000 births. Since the population of Tupelo in 1950 was 11,527, there statistically should be about four individuals with twin toes present in town. We know of at least eight—Elvis, Lawrence Riley and Lawrence's offspring and other close kin. Lawrence is Julian Riley's uncle.

Children are more likely to be born with webbed toes if there is a family history of the condition. For this reason, when exploring the possibility of who really fathered Elvis, as we do in this book, it can be useful to look for twin toes as evidence. While the lack of this condition cannot rule out a candidate, the presence of twin toes can point out likely suspects.

The obscure topic of twin toes is relevant because our investigation into the paternal bloodline of Elvis has led us to identify Lawrence David Riley, Jr. as Elvis's most likely father. There is considerable other circumstantial evidence for this, as presented throughout the book, but one important marker is the fact that Lawrence Riley had twin toes just as Elvis did. And Lawrence's offspring had this condition as well. Clearly, this was an inherited trait of the Rileys. Unfortunately, we are still missing one critical DNA sample to determine if Elvis was a Riley too.

A Close Companion

Like most of the Smith family members and their offspring, Gladys was no stranger to alcohol. After the difficult birth of her twins, which resulted in the hospitalization of both Gladys and baby Elvis, alcohol became a close companion.

Priscilla recalled her mother-in-law as "a surreptitious drinker and alcoholic." Elvis's cousin Billy Smith told author

Alana Nash, "As a teenager, I could tell when she was inebriated. But she stayed in her room. She was not one to openly drink, not even with family. I guess because she didn't want to be like the rest of them."

Nash also reported that Lamar Fike, a longtime member of the Memphis Mafia, had told her: "Right before we left for the service [US Army bootcamp], Gladys was getting bloated. The menopause was driving her absolutely screwloose, and she'd take those amphetamines, and she'd wash 'em down with beer." The last days of loneliness following Elvis's induction into the army were the end of a life filled with hardship.

Gladys Presley (front) on March 24, 1958, as Elvis left for the US Army reception station at Fort Chaffee, Arkansas. She would die less than four months later. On the left is Patsy Presley next to her mother, Clettes Smith Presley.

Looking at photos of Gladys in chronological order, one can easily see the rapid erosion of her health. The pretty girl that Vernon married quickly becomes bloated. Dark smudges appear beneath her increasingly dull, sad eyes. I cannot look at these pictures without mourning her. I want to give her a hug and call a doctor.

Many authors have blamed her alcohol abuse on the unrelieved grief of losing a child. Reportedly, she also had a miscarriage in 1942, which could have compounded her sense of loss. But I think her sorrow and depression was the result of much more than that. In an interview, her sister Lillian said, "After Elvis became famous, Gladys was never happy another day. She never had peace no more." As Elvis's fame grew, so did her worries about Elvis's safety and her unhappiness with her marriage.

The Garage

When Elvis was a toddler, probably around 1937, Vernon worked part-time at a garage owned by Troy Keith. Troy's brothers "Dutch" and Clem also worked there. The Keiths had grown up near Gladys in the Eggville area, so she would have known them before they all moved to Tupelo.

Vernon often brought little Elvis with him to play while he worked at the Keith garage. As related to Julian by local sources, on one occasion Elvis burned his leg on a hot stove, and Vernon worried that Gladys would angrily accuse him of failing to look after her precious son.

The same sources also revealed a darker side of the story. One of Troy Keith's brothers (probably "Dutch," as he had numerous wives) sometimes used Vernon's presence in the garage as an opportunity to take a break and visit Gladys at her home. Apparently, all the Keiths and some of their friends knew about this affair. Tantalizing as this tale is, neighborhood accounts of these misadventures remain the only evidence we have that Gladys may have been unhappy enough with Vernon to risk intimacy with "Dutch" Keith.

The Petition

When Elvis was about three, Vernon was convicted of forging a check and incarcerated at Parchman Prison. Without his income, Gladys was unable to keep the family home. She and Elvis moved in with Elvis's grandparents, Jessie Dee and Minnie Mae, for a short time, but the relationship between Gladys and Jessie had always been fragile and the arrangement did not work out. The solution was to move again, this time into the family home of Gladys's cousin, Frank Richards, on Maple Street. Gladys took a low-paying job at the Mid-South Laundry.

Somehow, Gladys found the energy to organize a community petition to get Vernon released from prison. The petition, probably typed at Chancery Clerk Byron Long's office in Tupelo where he signed it, was addressed to Mississippi Governor Hugh L. White. It read as follows:

> We, the undersigned do most respectfully petition your Excellency to grant Vernon Presley, who plead guilty at the May Term, 1938, of the Circuit Court of Lee County, Mississippi, on a charge of Forgery and sentenced to the State Penitentiary for a term of three years, a full and complete pardon and assign as reasons therefore the following:
>
> First: The only connection this man had with the offense committed was to accept $15.00 not to tell on the other parties connected with the crime but immediately told the truth when asked about it.

Two: This is a young man, twenty-three years of age, has a wife and one child dependent upon him for support and maintenance; and has never been charged with any other offense.

Third: We believe this man has been sufficiently punished and that he ought to be granted a suspension of sentence and a full and complete pardon.

Gladys went first to her closest friends, the most likely to show support, and asked them to sign the petition. The third and fourth signatures were by L. D. Riley and Zora Riley. "L. D." are the initials of Lawrence David Riley, Sr., the used car salesman who became a close friend of Gladys and married one of her other friends, Zora Mears, who then became Julian's aunt. We believe this is more evidence that Julian's Uncle Lawrence Riley was close to Gladys.

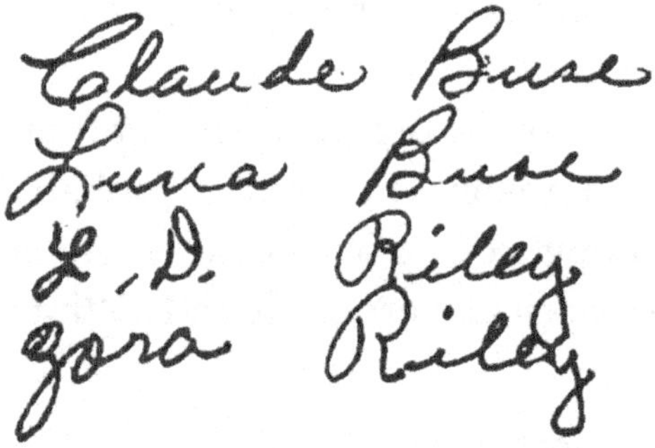

The third and fourth signatures on Gladys's petition n were those of Lawrence David Riley, Sr., and his wife, Zora Riley.

I suggested to Julian that it seemed odd for a close girlfriend of Gladys to marry the man who had fathered children with Gladys. Had Lawrence slept with Gladys, one of Zora's closest friends?

Julian was unsurprised by my question. He explained, "Lawrence was actually married twice before he married Zora. In 1932, he married Evelyn Martin—he was a month shy of turning twenty-two. But it didn't last long. And then he married Octavia Edwards, but I don't know exactly when that was. He didn't marry Zora until July 18, 1937, which is two-and-a-half years after Elvis was born and well over three years after Lawrence would have gotten Gladys pregnant."

It was possible that Julian's uncle, suffering from an unhappy marriage, had sought consolation from pretty Gladys in the spring of 1934, which probably was between his first two marriages. I'd like to think he did not cheat on his wife. After all, later in life he became a Baptist minister and evangelist. Interestingly, in a handwritten letter to Carmen Montez described in my earlier book *Letters from Elvis*, the performer not only confessed that Vernon was not his father but claimed that his father was a part-time evangelist.

In 1933, Lawrence's marriage to Evelyn resulted in a son, Lawrence David Riley, Jr. His marriage to Zora produced six children who could be unknown half-siblings of Elvis:

- Charles Edward (1938)
- Kenneth Wayne (1939)
- Winnie Katherine (1943)
- Norman Zealous "Butch" (1945)
- Betty Ann (1951)
- Norma Sue (1956)

Solving the identity of Elvis's biological father would require obtaining the DNA of a sibling or offspring of Elvis, so you can see the difficulty. There is only one known offspring, Lisa Marie, and one brother, who was listed as stillborn.

We have analyzed contributed DNA from over a dozen individuals who believed they were illegitimate children of Elvis, always hoping they were right. Unfortunately, we found none of these candidates related to Elvis, and so the mystery persists.

Vernon Released from Prison

On February 6, 1939, Governor Hugh White responded to Gladys's petition for Vernon's early release by suspending the last six months of his sentence on condition of continued good behavior. Vernon's co-conspirators, Gladys's brother Travis Smith and friend Lether Gable, served their full three-year terms at Parchman.

While Vernon had been in prison, little Elvis had received all of Gladys's affection. According to author Patricia Jobe Pierce in *The Ultimate Elvis,* "A role reversal was taking place. It disturbed friends whenever they heard Elvis coo to his mother, 'There, there, my little baby,' or prattle on with her in baby talk ... Elvis had become the parent and Gladys the child."

Once home from prison, Vernon found that he had been replaced as the dominant male figure in Gladys's life. On many nights, it was Elvis who shared Gladys's bed and Vernon slept on the floor without protest.

Starting School at Ledyard

Biographers have stated that in the fall of 1941 Gladys enrolled Elvis into the first grade at the East Tupelo Consolidated School, but this is incorrect. According to Julian, he started school at the Ledyard Primary School in South Tupelo.

"I had a hard time reconciling that Elvis went to school in East Tupelo when his family was then living in South Tupelo," Julian explained. "Friends and family members of the Presleys have described how Gladys would walk Elvis to school every day. They talked about how Elvis would sit on the porch and watch his mother come home from work. Well, Elvis attending Ledyard school would explain all these stories."

The family was living on Maple Street, and the Ledyard School was across the street from them. The Tupelo Garment

Factory where Gladys worked was just three blocks away at 248 South Green Street (GPS location 34.25376, -88.70677).

Hooligans

Eugene "Ed" Christian, a local historian and childhood friend of Elvis, wrote down these stories for Julian, who had never heard them before.

> My first recollection of Elvis was when he and his mother moved to Maple Street in Old South Tupelo sometime during World War II. I remember that Elvis was at first somewhat shy around me and my friends, but he soon blended in. Most of the time, Elvis seemed sad, but he was happy to have new friends and to be a member of our little gang. We were not a bunch of hooligans, but we were perhaps a little mischievous, not so much as to harm anyone. My Great Aunt Perl called Jackie Stevens, James Harold Loyd, Jerald Tackett, Jackie Clark and myself, and Elvis, the "Wild Bunch." Sadly, all but I have passed away.
>
> I remember the corncob wars we had with rival groups, not like enemies—more like friendly competitors, although at times the wars could get heated, especially if someone slipped in a slingshot. In one of these wars, Elvis was hit in the back of the head leaving a good size knot. He never cared much for corncob wars after that.
>
> He always enjoyed our "chicken raids." On South Green Street, just south of the King's Creek Bridge, there was a large, abandoned cattle barn, a grain silo, four or five one-room shacks and wild

chickens. It was these chickens we would chase and sometimes catch. I remember us taking them down to King's Creek and trying to roast them over an open fire.

I remember the time we laid in wait on top of the old livery stable on North Spring Street for Tupelo police officer Ed Conn to walk by. When he did, we would drop balloons filled with water in front of him. One time, however, Elvis dropped a balloon too late, hitting Officer Conn. We got down quickly from that building and ran. At that time, Officer Conn was in his sixties, and there was no way he could catch us.

I remember the time Elvis and I borrowed Fred Ingellis's guitar. We wanted to serenade a couple of very cute sisters, and they invited us in. Elvis leaned the guitar against a post on the front porch and forgot that it was there until a clap of thunder reminded us. Apparently, it had been raining for some time because the guitar was filled with water and was ruined. Elvis promised Mr. Ingellis he would pay for the guitar, but he never did.

Jap Town

Vernon was away from home during these precarious months because he had been sent back to prison—not to be incarcerated, but to help build one. The US had entered World War II in December of 1941, and the Works Progress Administration (WPA) had decided to construct a POW camp in Como Mississippi. Inappropriately called Jap Town, it housed only German POWs.

Prisoners in a World War II POW camp in Mississippi.

Vernon had been reclassified by the Selective Service as IIA, which meant he was ineligible to be drafted because of occupation. Presumably, his carpentry experience was needed for the Jap Town project.

Shortly before Jap Town was completed, Vernon received his dismissal slip and asked a fellow worker, Bill Parham, if he had been let go too.

"No," Bill told him. "No slip."

Vernon must have shaken his head in dismay. Why was he always the first to be fired?

The war, however, had created an economic boom, and Vernon found well-paying work in Memphis, earning more money than ever but returning home only on weekends. Then he learned about an even better opportunity down on the Gulf of Mexico.

Chapter 11
Bringing Up Elvis

The Shipyard

Until May of 1943, Vernon had been working out of town with few opportunities to come home and see his family. By the age of eight, Elvis was becoming a little man and would soon have an abundance of life experiences that would shape him forever. In May, the Presleys moved temporarily to Moss Point, Mississippi, where Vernon and his cousin, Sales Presley, worked in the shipyard. Some biographers and Elvis encyclopedias say this temporary move occurred in the summer of 1941, but records show this is incorrect.

Vernon had been eager to leave Tupelo because he and his father, Jessie Dee, were at each other's throats all the time. This would be the first time that Gladys and Elvis would leave Tupelo. In Moss Point, Sales and Annie Presley, along with Gladys, Vernon and Elvis, were packed into a one-room, screen-walled shack in the stinking humidity of the Gulf. They had planned to be there all summer but lasted only five weeks, returning to Tupelo in June. They despised the pervasive stench, Gladys and Elvis did not like the seafood (Elvis would never eat fish after this) and the suffocating heat was unbearable for Annie, who was pregnant. Homesick, everyone wanted to return to the pleasant living conditions of Tupelo, and when Vernon learned that Jessie Dee had left town to work in the shipyard, he agreed. For the first time since November of 1937, Vernon was going home to East Tupelo.

Though Jessie Dee had started earning money in the shipyard, he refused to send any of it home to Minnie Mae. With no income, she couldn't make the house payments and lost her home to the bank. Vernon ironically moved his family and Minnie Mae into a house across the street from the Croft house, which would eventually be moved down the street to Elvis Presley Park and be resurrected as the replica birth house. (See "Chapter 10: Gladys's Journey: Elvis's Birthplace" page 151).

Jessie Dee never returned to Minnie Mae, but at least he had stayed home and supported his children until they were grown, unlike some of his ancestors.

Back in East Tupelo

For one week at the end of June, Vernon worked at Dunn Construction in Millington, Tennessee, before taking a job at L. P. McCarty and Sons in July. Few people owned cars during World War II, and tires and gasoline were in short supply, so every day Vernon walked a mile across the levee from East Tupelo to his job in Tupelo and then back home at night. He loaded the delivery truck with food and tobacco products for delivery to customers throughout northeast Mississippi. He managed to stay employed at McCarty for five years and worked alongside his cousin, Sales Presley, until the family moved to Memphis.

He was earning far less money at McCarty than he did at the shipyard where he had earned $353 over five weeks, an average of about seventy dollars per week. McCarthy paid him just twenty-four dollars per week—$1,233 for an entire year—but he greatly favored working at McCarty compared to the exhausting and sweaty work at the shipyard.

McCarty and Sons was the first business in Tupelo to have a computer. Marcus Posey of Verona worked in the computer department and was the only person Julian could find who remembered Vernon working for the grocery wholesaler. He told Julian that Vernon and Sales had donated their blood when Marcus's grandmother, Rosie Young Estes, was hospitalized and needed a transfusion of a rare type. Vernon, he recalled, used to smoke his cigarettes down to the nub and eventually had skin cancer removed from his lip. He was sure Elvis must have visited Vernon and Sales at work occasionally but had no specific memories of the boy.

With Vernon's steady paycheck and Gladys also employed, Vernon's family seemed to be on the verge of prosperity. The Presley family moved to a house at 904 Kelly Street in East Tupelo across the street from close friends of Gladys, the Clark family. They were just a couple houses away from Vernon's Uncle Noah and his family. Marshall Brown was across the street and Faye Harris less than a block away on Adams Street. Living so close to many of her friends must have been a happy time for Gladys and her family.

The Kelly house eventually was bought by Julian, who put the pieces in a trailer that now resides on his property.

In September of 1943, Elvis started the third grade at East Tupelo Consolidated School, later renamed Lawhon School, with Mrs. Harvey as teacher. He had a little girlfriend at the school, Elois Bedford Sandifur, who remembered that their fourth-grade teacher was Mrs. Dillard.

On August 18, 1945, Vernon purchased a house on Berry Street in East Tupelo from Orville Bean, the victim of the forged check that had sent Vernon to Parchman Prison. Orville, however, had helped get Vernon released early, so apparently the men had reconciled their differences. In truth, Orville was probably kinder to Vernon than Jessie Dee.

In this photo (circa 1945) from the left: Elvis Presley; Evon Farrar, now Mrs. Bobby Richey; James Farrar, Fourth District Justice of the Peace. Middle row: Guy Harris, captain of the Tupelo Police; LaVerne Farrar; Bobbie Spencer. At the bottom is Odell Clark. DNA has confirmed that Bobbie Spencer was the secret daughter of Elvis's Uncle Noah Presley; her sister, Dorothy (not in the picture), was the illegitimate daughter of one of Noah Presley's stepsons. Photo: courtesy of Guy Harris and Wanda Powell Heagy.

Orville's daughter, Mrs. Oleta Grimes, was Elvis's fifth-grade teacher at East Tupelo Consolidated School. She encouraged the budding singer in his music and occasionally sent over food to Vernon and his family.

Boxcar Jumping

Bernice Jenkins also lived on Adams Street not far from Faye Harris. Bernice, Faye and Gladys all worked together at the Tupelo Garment Factory. Lamar Croft, Bernice's oldest son, was about the same age as Elvis.

One Saturday, Gladys and Bernice took their sons shopping in downtown Tupelo. The boys took off to do whatever boys do, and by the time their mothers were ready to go home, they had disappeared. The boys were finally found at Lyles Feed Store, which was between Tupelo Hardware and the GM&O railroad tracks north of Main Street. Elvis and Lamar had climbed onto some stationary boxcars and were jumping from one to the other. It was about as much fun as boys could have in Tupelo!

Gladys, relieved and happy that Elvis was safe, reportedly smothered him with hugs and kisses. Bernice, however, was furious and gave Lamar a good whipping.

Elvis's First Contest

Mrs. Geraldine Franks Sheffield, another teacher at East Tupelo Consolidated School, told Julian about Elvis's first music contest. Geraldine's father, Tracy Franks, was assistant principal and teacher at the school and lived at 811 Allen Street next door to the brother of a popular entertainer, Mississippi Slim, who was an idol of Elvis.

Hillbilly singer Mississippi Slim, born Carvel Lee Ausborn, recorded for Tennessee Records, taught Elvis a few guitar chords and had his own radio show on WELO in Tupelo. In 1946, he

Mississippi Slim was an idol of Elvis while living in Tupelo.

arranged for eleven-year-old Elvis to sing on the weekly jamboree broadcast from the Tupelo courthouse, a big moment for a young performer.

Tracy Franks was a genuinely good guy who cared about his neighbors and students, often brought food to Vernon and Gladys and occasionally gave Elvis money. Julian believes that Tracy Franks may have known the family before they moved into the school district.

One day, Mr. Franks announced to the school that the regional talent contest would be held October 3, 1945, at the Mississippi Alabama Fair and Dairy Show. He urged Elvis to enter the contest. Elaine Dundy claimed it was Elvis's fifth-grade teacher, Mrs. Grimes, who prompted him to enter the contest. It's possible, of course, that both of them did.

The second day of the fair was Children's Day, and all the schools had closed so students could attend. The contest was broadcast on WELO Radio in Tupelo, but no recording of it has been found. Contestants were told that the winner would be determined by the amount of applause they generated. Wearing glasses, ten-year-old Elvis stood on a chair to reach the microphone and confidently sang the ballad "Old Shep" that Rev. Frank Smith had taught him.

Some biographers have said he won second place, but Elvis corrected this later by affirming he had placed fifth. This is verified by the photo above that shows first and second place winners holding trophies on the left and Elvis with no trophy second from right. Another common error has been that Elvis placed third, a conclusion perhaps deduced from the photo that shows Elvis standing next to the second-place winner.

Elvis (in glasses) earned fifth place in his first singing competition at the Mississippi Alabama State Fair and Dairy Show in 1945.

The first-place winner that day was nine-year-old Shirley (Jones) Gillentine who had traveled to the fair with Elvis on the school bus. Elvis believed Shirley had impressed the audience by accompanying herself on a guitar and decided that he should learn to play an instrument too.

Geraldine Franks told Julian that her father, Tracy, had given Vernon and Gladys the money to buy his first guitar at Tupelo Hardware as a gift for Elvis's eleventh birthday. Geraldine also confided that Elvis, after becoming a star, would sometimes come back to Tupelo and take her father out to lunch.

Gladys's sister, Retha Smith, died shortly after the fair ended when a kerosene can exploded and destroyed her home. To Gladys, it must have seemed like her family was doomed to suffer catastrophe. Friends recall that she literally threw herself on the floor, sobbing inconsolably and speaking in tongues, or more likely, incoherent words of unbearable pain.

Elvis's Second Contest

Elvis's first singing contest is a popular anecdote in the Elvis origin story. Few people, however, know about Elvis's second music competition. It occurred in Tupelo during the summer of 1950. The Presleys, who were living in Memphis, had returned to Tupelo to spend the summer with friends and family. Each Thursday night, a preliminary music competition was held at at the Lyric Theater, and the winner would be invited to a final competition to be held later in the summer.

A man named Wayne Hamilton had won the preliminary round in which Elvis competed, but little is known about that event, so Julian found Wayne in Idaho and placed a phone call to get the true story. Wayne, of course, was fully aware that he had beaten one of the world's most popular singers in a music competition, and he had a vivid recollection of the event. Wayne had played the immensely popular song "Are You from Dixie?" on the accordion.

"How could you beat that song for a southern audience?" Julian interjected as he told me Wayne's account of the contest.

Wayne didn't remember Elvis very well but recalled that the fourteen-year-old had sung a slow ballad called "Tenderly" and accompanied himself on the guitar.

"Well," Julian said, "you pretty much know that 'Are You from Dixie?' won that competition. Anyway, Wayne went on to win the main event and got an electric stove as his prize—just what every teenager wanted. When I heard about that, it made me remember the tiny shotgun shack Vernon built for the family and how they had electricity but couldn't afford to use it."

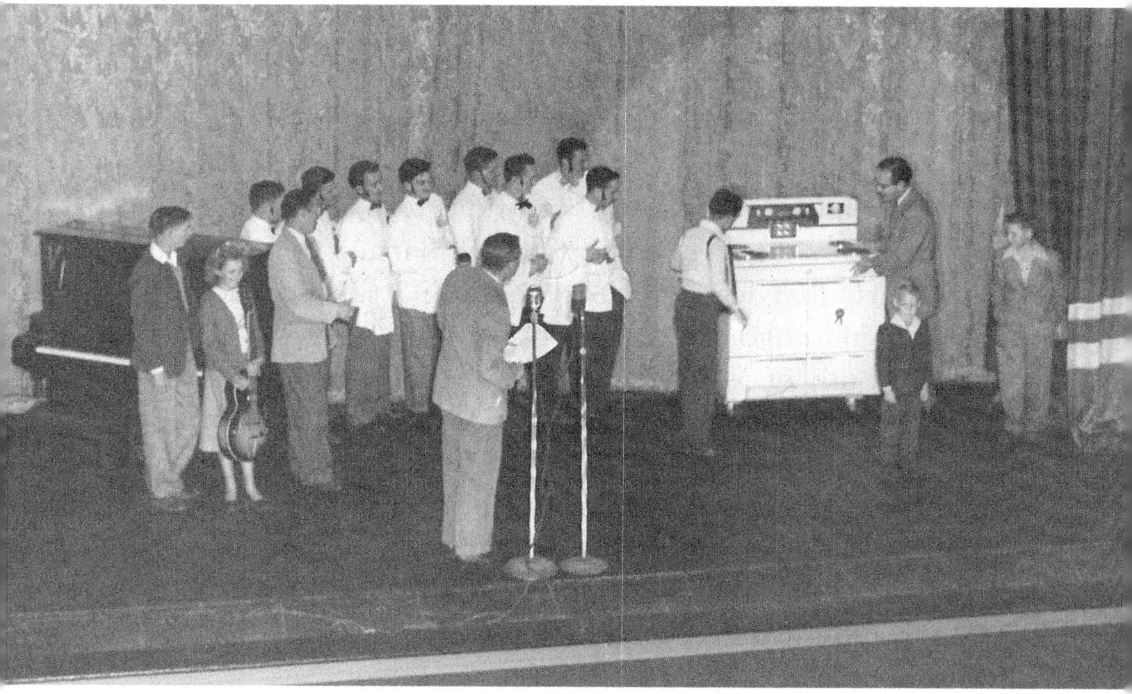

Wayne Hamilton, with an accordion strapped to him, stands to the left of the electric stove he won. Uninterested in the stove, Hamilton eventually exchanged it. The boy at the far right is Billy Boren, who would go on to win the nationally televised talent contest *Ted Mack's Amateur Hour*.

Somehow, though this sensitive young man had lost both of his music contests, he kept moving forward, never imagining that he would overcome these minor setbacks and become a legend in his time. Wayne Hamilton had won a stove, but Elvis Presley would win the hearts of millions of fans.

Unsettled Again

For the first time in his life, Vernon had a steady job, and his family was living in a good house. For unknown reasons, though, on July 18, 1946, he and Gladys lost the house on Berry Street and left East Tupelo forever, deeding the property to Vernon's close friend, Aaron Kennedy. A popular story in Elvis lore is that Elvis was given his middle name to honor Aaron, but Vernon and Gladys changed the spelling to "Aron" so it would more closely mirror infant Jesse's middle name "Garon."

The unsettled family was again on the move. They first took a house on the corner of Commerce and Main Street, which was on the edge of the notorious Shake Rag district. It was not a move up in status, but it was closer to Vernon's job at L. P. McCarty.

Then they moved again, this time to a small house on Mulberry Alley, a street behind Cockrell Banana Company and L. P. McCarty that dead ended at the GM&O railroad track. This house was in front of the current Tupelo City Hall.

Just south of Mulberry Alley sat the fairgrounds where Elvis had lost his first music contest but would make his famous homecoming appearance in 1956 and 1957. Ernest Bowen, who would later work as station manager for WELO Radio in Tupelo, remembered the Presleys living on that street because his father had a cabinet shop at 199 Mulberry Alley. Ernest said that his family would often take food to the Presleys because they were always in need of help.

Elvis's First Movie Role

Vernon, Gladys and Elvis moved around a lot. Most people, including Julian Riley, had thought Elvis had lived in East Tupelo most of his life before moving to Memphis. "We were wrong about that," Julian told me. "Elvis spent his first three years in East Tupelo, then was in South Tupelo for the next five years.

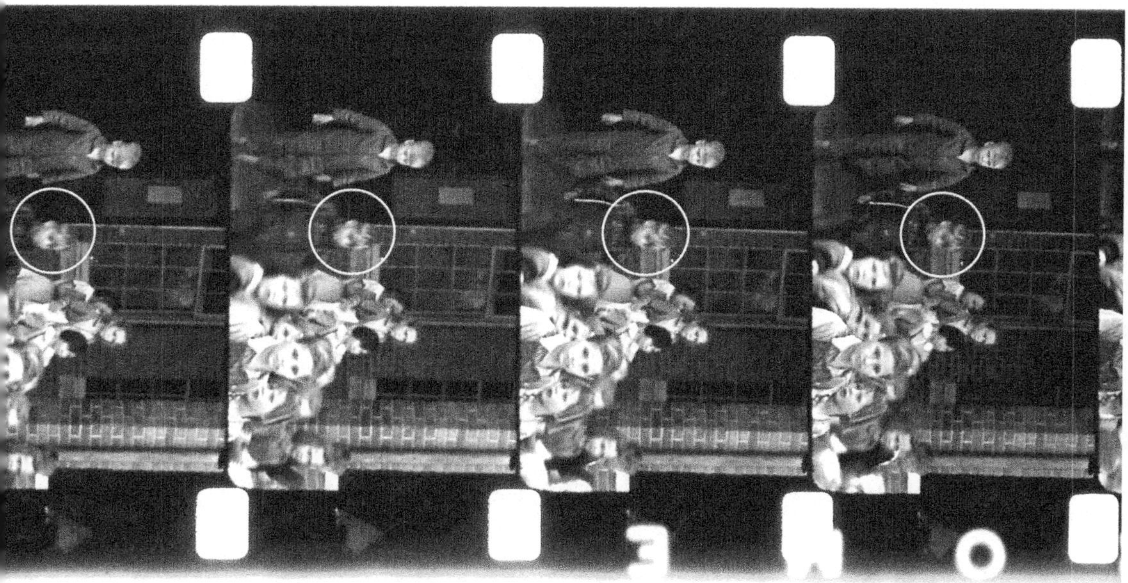

In the spring of 1946, while Elvis was closing out the fifth grade at East Tupelo Consolidated School, a film producer came to Tupelo. The producer, who had learned his craft in the army, had figured out a creative way to make money off his filmmaking talents. By filming the "story" of towns like Tupelo, with contemporary footage of its businesses and schools and parks and people, he could sell copies of the movie to the proud local residents. The producer notified East Tupelo Consolidated School and the other schools in advance of filming the students, staff and grounds. The families of all the students and teachers were prospective buyers of the movie. The school alerted the students to be on good behavior and wear their best clothing.

At the end of the school day on April 13, 1946, the filmmaker documented students exiting the building. The kids spilled out of the front doors in clusters, chatting and laughing as kids do. The camera kept rolling, capturing every last customer for the movie, until finally one blonde-haired boy emerged as if making his screen debut. He paused, looked around, and then confidently strolled out of the shot.

This was Elvis, and almost certainly he knew of the filmmaker's presence. Instinctively, it seems, he made the most of this cameo performance. The youngster, who had grown up watching movies in downtown Tupelo, had just appeared for the first time of many on celluloid.

Thanksgiving at Gloster Street Elementary

Elvis's sixth-grade class at Gloster Street Elementary. Photo provided by classmate Evelyn Helms, unidentified in the picture.

Two months after entering sixth grade, Elvis's class presented a Thanksgiving program in the Tupelo High School auditorium. Jack McKinney was listed on the printed program next to Elvis Presley and gave a copy of it to Julian. The program showed that Elvis had played two parts in the presentation—a judge in one skit and the month of October in another. An all-female group sang the Pilgrim song.

6-A ASSEMBLY PROGRAM
TUPELO HIGH-SCHOOL AUDITORIUM, TUESDAY, NOV. 26, 1946

I. WHAT IS THIS DAY WE CELEBRATE ? George Page, Home Room President

II. DEVOTIONAL AND PILGRIM SONG

Theresa McCormick	Lynda Clayton	Merial Johnston
Joan [illegible]	Mary Jo Godfrey	Geraldine Payne
Mary Bedford	Bettye Allred	Dorothy Palmer

III. WHO GIVES THE MOST FOR THANKSGIVING DINNER ?

THE TREE....................................Jimmie Anthony
THE VINE....................................Noah Beeding
THE BUSH....................................Jack McKinney
THE JUDGE...................................Elvis Presley
REPORTER FOR TREE...........................George Page
REPORTER FOR VINE...........................Dorothy Palmer
REPORTER FOR BUSH...........................Merial Johnston

IV. THE THANKFUL MONTHS:

SPEAKER.....................................Mary Bedford
DECEMBER....................................Leon Anderson
JANUARY.....................................Hayes Kelly
FEBRUARY....................................Theresa McCormick,
Bobby Dozier, and Mary Ann Christian
MARCH.......................................Ruth Cribbs
APRIL.......................................Mary Jo Godfrey
MAY...Bettye Allred
JUNE..James Ausborne
JULY..May Don Gibson
AUGUST......................................Geraldine Payne
SEPTEMBER...................................Gene Harrelson
OCTOBER.....................................Elvis Presley
NOVEMBER....................................Dorothy Palmer

V. ONE ACT THANKSGIVING PLAY....."AUNT ADELE REDUCES"

SCENE: LIVING-DINING ROOM AT AUNT ADELE'S HOUSE

CHARACTERS:

AUNT ADELE.........Charlotte Reynolds
AUNT MINNIE........Marjorie Eubanks
CHILDREN:

VIDA................Lynda Clayton
ROSE................Evelyn Carter
BEN.................Lassell Franklin
ART.................Billy Wayne Burks

FIRST DELIVERY BOY....................Joe Wallace, Jr.
SECOND DELIVERY BOY...................Dick Stone
THIRD DELIVERY BOY....................Hubert Gaither

Music by Mrs. Dewey Camp

Julian interviewed Joe Wallace, a schoolmate who was in one of the skits with Elvis, but Joe did not remember Elvis. Jack McKinney could not remember Elvis in the Thanksgiving presentation but recalled one time when Elvis brought his guitar to school and sang "Old Shep." Julian talked to many people who lived near Elvis during this period, but most of them had little or no memory of him. The flower had not yet bloomed.

Rev. Frank Smith

The year 1947 passed uneventfully. Gladys must have been grateful for that. The Presley family would continue to go to church with friends and family at the First Assembly of God Church over in East Tupelo. The pastor there, Rev. Frank Smith, who had taught Elvis the song "Old Shep," was working with Vernon packing and delivering wholesale groceries for L. P. McCarty and Sons. Gladys was now working at Long's Laundry.

Rev. Frank Smith was the minister at the Assembly of God church that Elvis and his family attended in Tupelo. He died in 2007.

Frank Smith, who was not related to Gladys, was a new nineteen-year-old minister who had replaced the previous preachers, Gladys's uncles Gains and Sims Mansell. Reverend Smith has been credited by many writers with teaching Elvis to play the guitar, but this is only partly true. Frank was a friend of Julian Riley, and in a conversation about this topic he personally set the record straight by claiming only to have shown Elvis the fingering for several basic chords. "That's about all I did," Frank confessed. Few of Elvis's relatives and acquaintances have been so honest in describing their relationships with the superstar.

Nevertheless, Elvis learned to play, and he continued to carry his guitar everywhere he went, never missing a chance to sing—even if almost no one could remember his music. The most consistent element in the Presley family's life, of course, was the constant moving to new homes, so it could not have surprised Gladys that they would relocate another two times before Elvis would enter seventh grade.

1010 North Green Street

We don't know why they left Mulberry Alley, but they moved to a house on Old Highway 45 North near the Ruff dairy farm, probably for a summer of sharecropping. Then, sometime before the 1947 school year began, the family moved to 1010 North Green Street in an area called "The Hill" where many of Tupelo's more affluent black families lived. The neighborhood had been destroyed by a tornado in 1936, so some of the homes there were relatively new. All around the center of this community were Black-owned stores, a pool hall, a barbershop and beauty salon, cafes, a funeral parlor, the Elks Club and African American Masonic Lodge, various churches, the Black graveyard and Black high school, and a library for the Black community.

Living in this four-room house, which they rented from neighbor James R. Parsons, was the first time Elvis and his family had enjoyed indoor plumbing with a flush toilet and a bathtub. Mr. Parson's wife, Lura, was a music teacher and she likely gave Elvis piano lessons.

Walking down Green Street past an old cemetery to Jefferson, Elvis could then take a right and go three blocks to Gloster Street

Junior High, or he could take a left and walk a couple blocks to the downtown area and see a movie at the Lyric Theater across from the stone Confederate soldier on the courthouse square.

Fans today trying to see the Presley house at 1010 North Green Street will not find it because Green Street was relocated in the early 1970s for construction of Highway 78. Two friends of the Presleys from the Black community on "The Hill," Sam Bell and Janice Davis (now Mrs. Janice Scales), showed Julian the original location of the Presley home, now a densely overgrown parcel.

Fans wishing to pay homage to the location of Elvis's last home in Tupelo can find it here (GPS location 34.27418, -88.71005). In the photo below, the building directly ahead is a church, Temple Compassion & Deliverance. The wooded land where the Presley house on Green Street once stood is directly to the left of the camera's position (GPS location 34.27418, -88.71005).

The Presley house that originally was at 1010 North Green Street was torn down. The overgrown lot on which it stood is to the left of the camera position in this photo. (GPS location 34.27418, -88.71005.)

Pitch, Plums and Parrots

Elvis met his buddy, William Claude "Billy" Welch, at Gloster Street Junior High. Billy lived about a mile from the Presleys on North Green Street, and Elvis was about nine months older. Billy came from a family of singers. In those days before television, the whole Welch family would sit out on their porch and sing together.

Elvis often strapped his guitar to his back and rode his bicycle over to Billy's house where he and his friend hid away in the back room behind a closed door and practiced their singing. Billy's voice had a higher pitch, so Elvis sang the main melody and Billy the harmony.

On one occasion, Billy's sister, Faye, remembered "Elvis calling Billy to chat about making some money by picking and selling wild plums," which they did for a while. If Elvis "called" Billy, it could mean the Presleys had a telephone in their Green Street home. The boys also earned some money picking cotton on a farm probably owned by Gladys's older sister Lavelle Smith and her husband Eddie, but one day of strenuous cotton picking was all the boys wanted.

Faye also recalled that Billy and Elvis liked reading comic books together and going to the movies. She told Julian that the neighborhood girls would often tease Elvis for wearing his cap backward.

The boys loved to play practical jokes on each other. One day, Elvis called Billy and told him that he had a parrot. They were both fascinated by a green parrot named Kiki that graced the pages of the children's book *Island of Adventure* by Enid Blyton. Excited to see the parrot, Billy climbed on his bike and raced over to Elvis's house. When he arrived, he was met by Elvis's wide grin and a painted chalk parrot like the ones given as prizes at the fair.

Billy's sister Faye shared these charming stories with Julian in 2006. She had been teaching drama at Shannon High when Julian met her, and she often helped find student actors to perform in Verona's annual reenactment of the marriage of Gladys and Vernon at the Verona town hall, the brainchild of Julian Riley.

The Piano

Janice Davis's father, John, was part owner of a grocery store on Green Street where Gladys often shopped. The Davis family was one of very few in the area to own a piano. Janice told Julian that Elvis would often come to her house to practice playing it. Even when other children were romping around outside, Elvis and Janice's brother, Eugene, would stay inside picking away at the keyboard.

Because there is no proof that Gladys allowed Elvis to wander around Shake Rag to be influenced directly by Black music, these piano adventures at Janice Davis's home provide one of just two provable experiences in which Elvis's music was influenced by Black people while he lived in Tupelo.

The other Black influence was by a man named John Andrew "Bubba" Collins who hawked newspapers and magazines for the owner of the stand in the lobbies of the Tupelo and Jeff Davis hotels. Most news sales were in the morning, so when things slowed down in the afternoons, Collins often sat outside and played his guitar, sometimes attracting a small crowd including Elvis, who would be walking home from school.

Except for these two examples, Julian has discovered no other documentary evidence of Black music influencing Elvis in his hometown.

The Library

Elvis entered the seventh grade at Gloster Street Junior High in September of 1947. A few weeks after Elvis's thirteenth birthday in January, Gladys took him to the Lee County Library so Elvis could get a library card. Fostering her son's interest in reading would have been important to Gladys, who at best had a sixth-grade education.

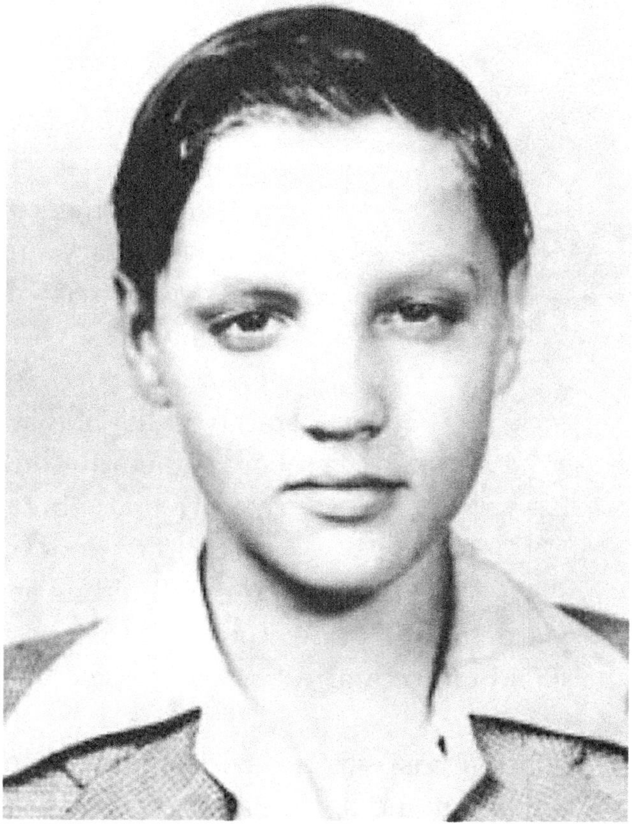

Elvis Presley's seventh grade school picture from Gloster Street Junior High.

We know that Elvis used his Tupelo library privileges because a book check-out card signed by young Elvis was found at the library and put up for auction. It shows that in 1948 he checked out a copy of *Courageous Heart, the Life of Andrew Jackson for Young Readers* by Bessie Rowland James. This was probably for a school assignment because two other children checked out the book shortly after Elvis. The check-out date was overwritten as "DEC 48," which cannot be correct because Elvis and his family moved to Memphis a month earlier in November of 1948.

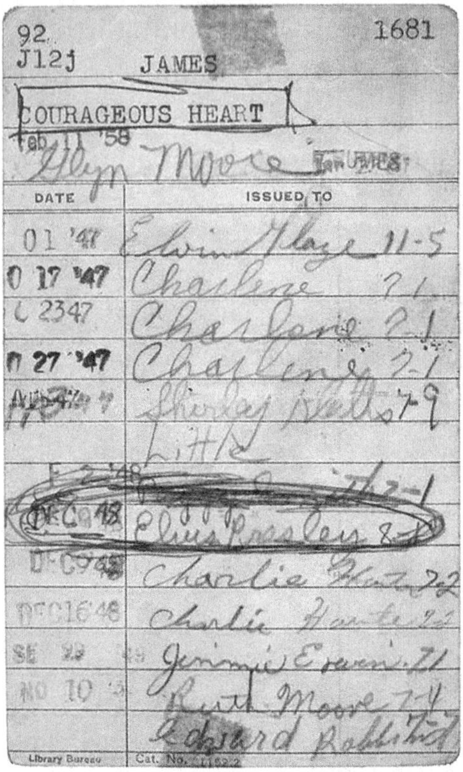

A library check-out card signed by Elvis Presley in 1948.

Many fans who make a pilgrimage to the library are sent to the current Lee County Library on Jefferson Street, which is misleading. Elvis never set foot in this newer building. In 1947, he received his library card and began checking out books at the original library located on the third floor of the City-County Building at 405 South Spring Street, a structure that now houses the Mississippi Dept. of Corrections Field Office and other businesses (GPS location 34.25430, -88.70431).

During his life, Elvis was an avid reader, often focusing on books about religion and spirituality. After he was reported dead at Graceland, a book about the Holy Shroud of Turin was found near him. Published in 1972, *A Scientific Search for the Face of Jesus* by Frank Adams argued that the image of Jesus Christ really was imprinted on the Turin shroud. Apparently, Elvis was also reading *Sex and Psychic Energy* by Betty Bethards. In *If I Can*

Dream: Elvis' Own Story, author Larry Geller, who was Elvis's hairdresser and spiritual advisor, lists other books on Elvis's reading list:

- The Bible
- *The Impersonal Life,* Anonymous
- *Aquarian Gospel of Jesus the Christ,* Levi H. Dowling
- *Autobiography of a Yogi,* Paramahansa Yogananda
- *Cosmic Consciousness: A Study in the Evolution of the Human Mind,* Richard Maurice Bucke
- *Esoteric Healing,* Alice A. Bailey
- *First and Last Freedom,* Jiddu Krishnamurti

Others have reported that he often consulted *The Power of Positive Thinking* by Dr. Norman Vincent Peale and *How to Live 365 Days a Year* by Dr. John A. Schindler. It is known that he read medical texts and was well-versed in *The Physician's Desk Reference,* which is a standard reference for medical professionals about prescription drugs. Among books he purchased in 1963 were:

- *Antique Guns,* various authors
- *An Eyewitness History of World War II,* Dorothy and Carl Schneider
- *First 100 Days of the Kennedy Administration,* various authors
- *Jokes for the John,* anonymous
- *The Infinite Way,* Joel S. Goldsmith
- *Isis Unveiled (2 Volume Set),* H. P. Blavatsky
- *Leaves of Morya's Garden, Book 1: The Call 1924,* Agni Yoga Society
- *Leaves of Morya's Garden, Book 2: Illumination 1925,* Agni Yoga Society

We cannot know how many of these books Elvis read. It is possible some were unread gifts by Larry Geller and others. But it seems that throughout his life Elvis had an enduring interest in philosophical and religious topics not limited to Christianity. By fostering his literacy, Gladys undoubtedly helped instill in him a love of books and a hunger for the ideas and knowledge they could convey.

The Bicycle Mystery

In 1993, a photo was discovered in Gladys's closet at Graceland. On the back of the picture, in which Elvis is riding a Firestone Pilot Classic bicycle with fenders and a light, Gladys had written "age 13." Some writers have stated that this bike was Elvis's birthday present when he turned thirteen on January 8, 1948, but that is another small error. Julian has interviewed Bobby Goff, who lived close to Elvis in East Tupelo, and Bobby said that sometimes Elvis borrowed that bicycle to ride around on.

Elvis at thirteen on a friend's Firestone Pilot Classic bicycle in Tupelo.

The discovery of this photo provided a glimpse of Elvis's

VANITY FAIR

Sign In | Subscribe

CULTURE

Elvis as a Teen? See a Never-Before-Published Photo From His Hometown in Tupelo, Mississippi

Is it really him? Elvis friends, relatives, and experts weigh in.

BY ALANNA NASH

JANUARY 8, 2014

Elvis Presley is one of the most photographed figures in music history. But in the nearly 37 years since his death, every significant picture of rock's swivel-hipped pioneer has been widely seen. Or has it?

life that was previously unknown, but it was hardly an earth-shattering event in the Elvisphere. Most fans were never aware of its existence. But then, the magazine *Vanity Fair* published another photo of Elvis on a bicycle in its January 2014 issue. The article was written by Elvis biographer Alanna Nash with fact-checking by Roy Turner, the Tupelo resident who had provided research for Elaine Dundy's biography *Elvis and Gladys*, a much-quoted source that unfortunately was riddled with errors.

According to author Nash, sometime during the summer of 1948, unaware of the sudden shift in his life that would occur later that year, thirteen-year-old Elvis was photographed leaning on his bike in North Tupelo. The picture wound up in the hands of Janelle McComb, a Tupelo resident and lifelong friend of Elvis. In 2005, responding to a fan request, Janelle sent the photo to Wade Jones, an Elvis admirer in Mount Holly, North Carolina.

In a phone call to Jones, Janelle, who died two months later, said that a female acquaintance was taking a roll of film to the drugstore to be developed but had one more exposure left to take. Elvis, who she knew from the neighborhood, was standing nearby with his bike, so the woman asked him to pose for the last picture on the roll. Commenting on the photo for the article, neighbor Sam Bell suspected that Elvis's mother, Gladys, was keeping an eye on her son. "Elvis wasn't ever running around by himself," he recalled. "If she wasn't with him, shopping and all that, we were."

In the photo, according to Roy Turner, Elvis was standing at the intersection of North Spring and Jefferson. On the west side of North Spring, he suggested, was a pool hall, barber shop and military surplus store that catered to a mostly Black clientele. To the east, a furniture store and a grocery-and-seafood market served mostly White customers. On the right-hand side of the picture, he claimed, was a squat, light-colored cafeteria where residents could get a milkshake or a soda, but the counter was not integrated, so Blacks couldn't go in and sit down. They would use the service window in the front of the building.

For a time, Ms. Nash stated, this was Elvis's neighborhood. Not far from his gaze, on the opposite side of Jefferson, she claimed, the Lee County Courthouse stood where he attended live WELO radio shows on Saturday afternoons, soaking up the

This photo of Elvis was featured in the January 2014 issue of *Vanity Fair*.

hillbilly sounds of local idol Mississippi Slim. If Elvis had ridden a block or so east on Jefferson, he would have arrived at Shake Rag, the destitute local Black community.

Vanity Fair prominently featured this entertaining story in its magazine. The headline proclaimed that this photo was "a Never-Before-Published Photo from His Hometown in Tupelo, Mississippi." The article flatly stated that the picture was taken a few months before the Presley family moved from Tupelo to Memphis.

Deeper research has shown that neither claim was true. This is another example of how countless small distortions can seep into

Elvis's origin story to create folklore that is far from the truth. Each falsehood replicates like a virus and merges with other untruths to become a platform for more egregious false assumptions.

When I first showed this photo to Julian, his first response was, "That's not a street anywhere in Tupelo!" Julian had been involved in the tearing down of property on Jefferson Street, the photo's location identified by Turner, to make room for a new Lee County Courthouse. "But you don't need to know that. In the background of the picture is a liquor store. But Mississippi was a dry state until 1972, so there were no liquor stores in Tupelo when this photo was taken."

With some deeper research, I found some of the answers at Elvis Australia, the official Elvis Presley fan club with a large website. They had posted an article by prolific contributor David Troedson, who had also questioned the location of the *Vanity Fair* photo. As noted by Roy Turner, if the location was Tupelo as he attested, the picture would be the only pictorial reference to Elvis living in the historically Black community of North Tupelo. If the location of the photo was not Tupelo… well, could the local residents who "remembered" that location fifty-five years later be wrong?

The research turned up an unattributed photo from around 1955 showing a location in Memphis that is a perfect match for the *Vanity Fair* photo. The photo surfaced during an exploration of historic Memphis photos that showed the neighborhood in which Elvis and his family first lived after moving to Memphis.

In the Memphis photo, looking east down Poplar Avenue at High Street, the S&S Drug Store is on the left (north side of Poplar.) Directly across the street is a distinctive twin gable building with three windows below each of the gables. This is the same structure that appears in the background of the *Vanity Fair* photo. The building to the west of the twin gabled building in the *Vanity Fair* photo had been removed a few years after the

The Memphis location of the Vanity Fair photo. In this picture circa 1955, the camera is pointed eastward down Poplar Avenue at High Street.

Vanity Fair picture was taken, and the façade of the remaining building had been changed somewhat by 1955, but clearly this picture shows the correct location of the *Vanity Fair* photo.

The Poplar Avenue site in Memphis is no random location. After Elvis's family moved to Memphis, their first two rental units were in this neighborhood. The following Sanborn Fire Insurance map of the Poplar Avenue neighborhood from the pre-1955 period shows the proximity of these Presley residences to the drug store.

They first moved into a small apartment at 370 Washington Ave. just two blocks south of the S&S Drug Store. Then they moved to a large rooming house at 572 Poplar Avenue barely a half-block from the drug store.

The Poplar Avenue neighborhood was home to Elvis for nearly a year before moving in the fall of 1949 to the Lauderdale Courts. While the *Vanity Fair* photo was erroneously said to be shot in Tupelo, it may be the earliest photo on record of young Elvis in Memphis, which he would call home for the rest of his life.

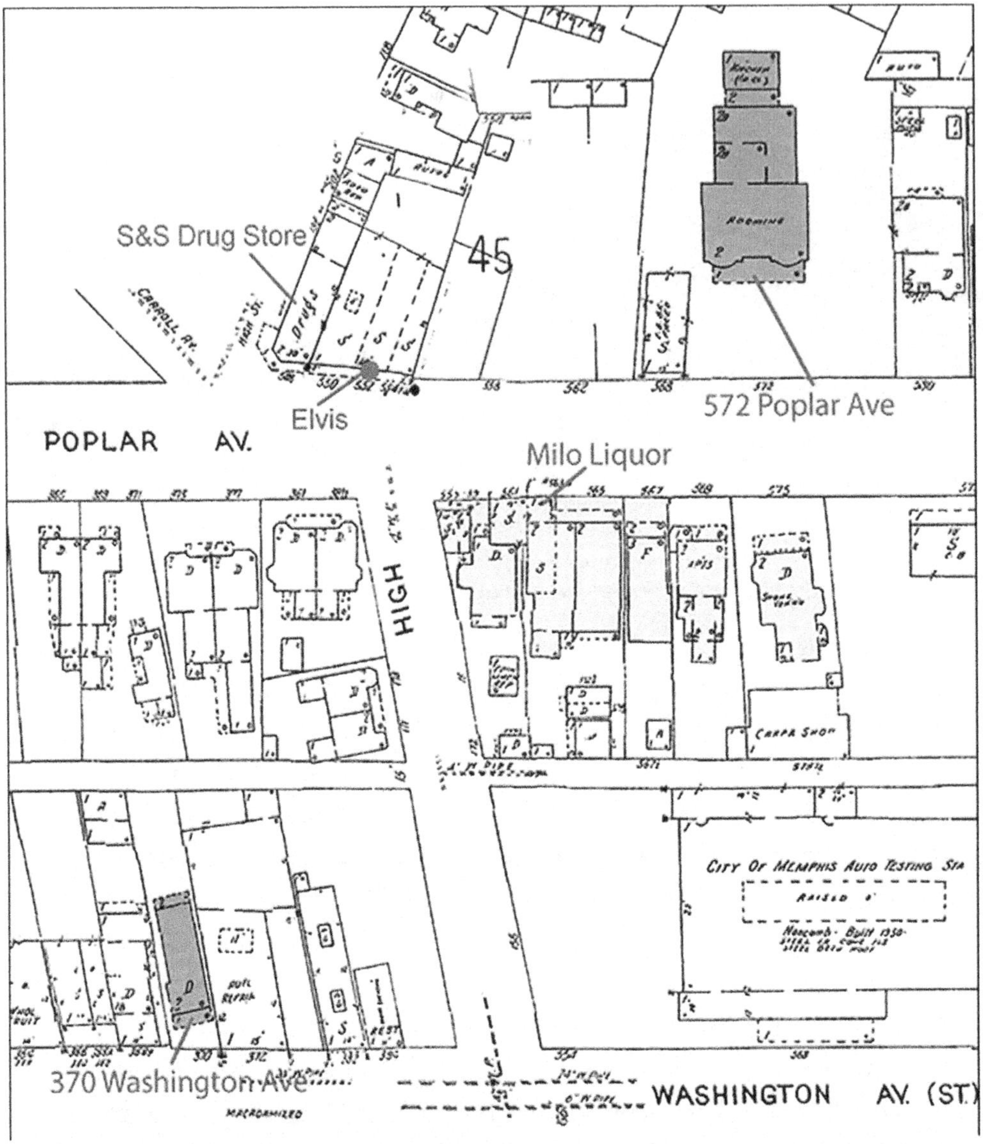

A Sanborn Insurance map shows the proximity of the Presley family's first two Memphis residences to the drug store.

City directories provide a list of businesses and residences by street names. The city directory shows S&S Drug Store located at 548 Poplar and Milo Liquor Store across the street at 563 Poplar. In the *Vanity Fair* photo, it is possible to make out the Milo Liquor sign across the street from young Elvis. The city directory also shows "Minnie M Mrs" living in apartment 1 at 572 Poplar Avenue. The Presley family moved out of this rooming house in September of 1949, but the city directory entry shows that Minnie Mae Presley, Elvis's paternal grandmother, continued to live in the Poplar apartment beyond 1950.

377 Howell Josie
381 Davis Elwood W pntr
Carroll av ends
High intersects
548 S & S Drug Store
Strauss Alvin
550 Sampietro & Co gros
552 Magic Cleaners
554 Knight Jas L baker
55 Marossi Lando restr
556 Sampietro Hdw & Appl Co
558 Curle Avery A restr
559 Solomito Rosario Mrs ©
563 Milo Liquor Store
563a McKimpson Ida M
563b Burnett Hettie L Mrs
565 Jones Wm R
Strickland Ollie furn rms
567 White Geo ©
568 Thompson B Lee barber and beauty shop
569 Jackson Nona Mrs
572 **Apartments**
1 Presley Minnie M Mrs
2 Spellings Milton
3 DeBerry W Ellis
4 Vacant

John Sampietro, whose father ran the S&S Drug Store in the late forties, remembered his father talking about how Elvis would frequently come into the drug store to play pinball. During this same time, Milo Solomito operated the Milo Liquor Store across the street. His son identified the store in the *Vanity Fair* photo as the one where Milo had spent many years. The Marossi Restaurant was next door to the liquor store until Lando Marossi moved to a nearby location in 1954, according to his son Jerry.

Elvis's First Marriage Certificate

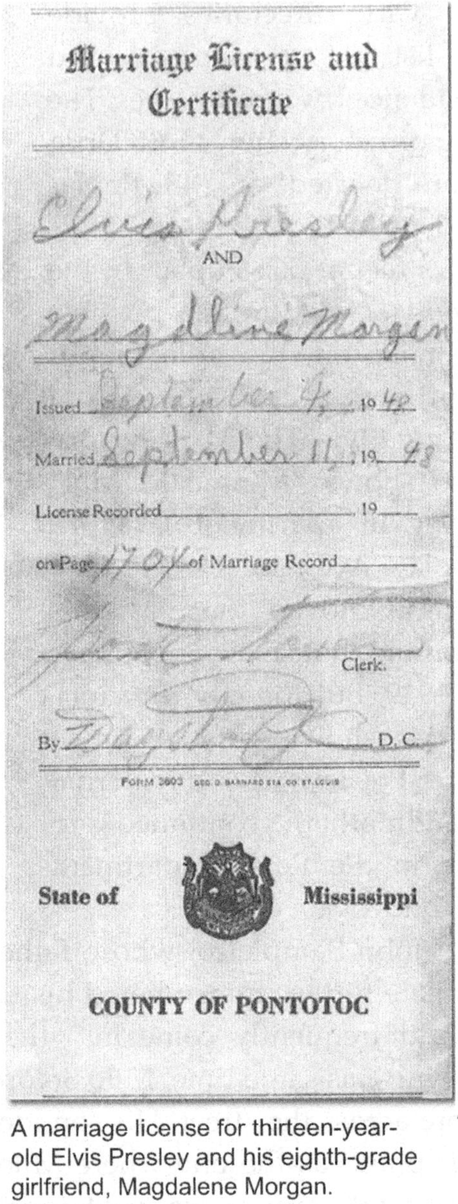
Marriage License and Certificate

Elvis Presley

AND

Magdline Morgan

Issued September 4, 1948

Married September 11, 1948

License Recorded ________ 19____

on Page 1704 of Marriage Record ________

________ Clerk.

By ________ D.C.

FORM 3603

State of Mississippi

COUNTY OF PONTOTOC

A marriage license for thirteen-year-old Elvis Presley and his eighth-grade girlfriend, Magdalene Morgan.

On September 4, 1948, before enrolling in the eighth grade at Gloster Street Junior High, thirteen-year-old Elvis married his close friend, Magdalene Morgan—or so the marriage license says. Doubters have claimed that the license must have been filled in and signed by Elvis as a prank. Others have disagreed.

Elvis had befriended a girl named Elois Bedford in 1947 and had taken her on a "date" to the Halloween party at Gloster Street Junior High. The next day, however, Elvis handed her a note as she was boarding the afternoon school bus. The note delivered a message perhaps as disturbing to the young girl as any Halloween horror: "I have found another girl."

That other girl was Magdalene Morgan.

In an interview with author Bill E. Burk, Magdalene said she had been eyeing the shy Elvis Presley for a long time and "just knew" that one day they would become close. "I guess my infatuation with Elvis started in that little [Assembly of God] church up in East Tupelo," Magdalene explained. "He sang and picked the guitar. I sang and played piano." In school, Magdalene was known as Maggie "because people, including Elvis, never got around to learning how to spell my name correctly."

Maggie claimed that when she was eight or nine, she was already the church pianist. "We were always in Christmas plays together up at the church. I always played opposite Elvis, which really thrilled me a lot. One time, I remember he was one of the wise men, and I was one of the angels. Another time he was Joseph, and I was Mary."

Maggie said that Elvis was pleasant and polite but wasn't very talkative. "He was kind of embarrassed a lot. He did not like crowds. He would talk to me a lot if we were by ourselves, like when my mother and I would visit the Presley home, which we did often because Gladys was my mom's best friend."

Maggie attended a couple of birthday parties for Elvis at the Presley house. "He and I would sing," she said. "We would hold hands and talk. We would go for walks in the woods out behind his house, and he would talk about what he wanted to be when he grew up. He always talked about wanting to be a singer and he would marry someone who would have to be a lot like his mama. This was when we were ten, eleven, on up in there. He was just my little guy, you know?"

For the parties, Gladys would serve the "usual meal—beans, potatoes and meat. And then some birthday cake. For birthday gifts, Elvis would receive a shirt, sometimes a handmade one made out of flour sack material. Gladys was very good at sewing. She worked in a sewing factory."

At the ripe old age of eleven or twelve, Maggie could not envision a life without Elvis. "I was right there with him when he sang his very first song on WELO Radio. I was so proud of him!" The station was not located above the Black and White store, as many authors have argued, but downtown on Spring Street over Nanny's Café, which was owned by Maggie's uncle and employed both Maggie and her mother.

When the mothers would get together, Maggie and Elvis would talk and share dreams. Once, Elvis got up the nerve to kiss Maggie for the first time. "We were just like any other kids. We would talk about school, church, singing… He always wanted to be a singer. Always!" They were "sweethearts" from the fourth grade until Elvis moved away early in the [eighth] grade. "We were so close at that time," she said. "I just thought we would always be together—in life, singing, everything."

When the marriage certificate of Elvis and "Magdlene" first surfaced, Maggie was astonished. "Where did this come from?" she wondered. And then she noticed that her name was misspelled, omitting the second "a," and that the signature was not her handwriting. Evidently, Elvis never learned to spell her name.

Thirteen-year-old Elvis in a fake version of a photograph in which his girlfriend was replaced by a shorter girl.

There are other problems with the certificate too. It was filled out in pencil, "Which would have not been done by an official," Julian said. The document is also missing the date for "License Recorded," which means the certificate was never recorded officially, thus is not a legal document.

There are other problems with the evidence

also. The photograph of Elvis and Magdalene Morgan so frequently exhibited on the internet is a fraud. This photograph has clearly been Photoshopped. The girl is shorter than Elvis. The timing of the photo, supposedly the summer of 1948 before Elvis left for Memphis, cannot be accurate either. Elvis has a buttoned-up jacket and is wearing gloves. The trees are missing leaves. This appears to have been taken during a Tupelo winter. And yet, the girl in the photo seems dressed for summer in a light blouse and no gloves. More tampering with Elvis's history.

Fortunately, the original negative of this photo fell into the hands of Rachel Shumpert of Tupelo, a researcher who for years had assisted Julian in his Elvis investigations. It was given to Rachel by Rev. Frank Smith, the preacher at the Assembly of God Church where Elvis and Gladys went to services. We do not know if he was the photographer. The image shows that the Photoshopped version has been flipped horizontally. The girl next to Elvis is the real Magdalene "Maggie" Morgan, and she is bundled up appropriately for a Tupelo winter. She is also several inches taller than Elvis.

The original photo of thirteen-year-old Elvis Presley and Magdalene Morgan.

Deeper research turned up several instances on the internet in which the girl was identified as Marilyn Monroe. After some detective work, I located a photo of Marilyn Monroe as a teenager that was identical to the shorter woman in the fake Magdalene picture. Obviously, a picture of Marilyn had replaced Magdalene who had originally been standing next to thirteen-year-old Elvis.

This made me wonder if Elvis had ever met Marilyn Monroe. There is almost nothing in the historical record to indicate there had been anything but a casual meeting. Several Memphis Mafia members had publicly stated that Elvis had once deflected Marilyn's suggestion of a date.

It turns out that Elvis did at least propose a rendezvous with Marilyn Monroe, which was revealed in an interview on the Classic Bands website with Byron Raphael, a William Morris agent who worked with both Elvis and Col. Parker. According to Raphael, at the time when Marilyn's marriage with playwright Arthur Miller was imploding, Marilyn was at the Fox studio for wardrobe tests for the movie *Let's Make Love,* and Elvis had a dressing room there. Raphael said, "We kind of urged him to ask her out," and Elvis finally approached Marilyn by asking if she wanted to go to a party that he was throwing the next night, but she declined.

"They didn't need each other," Raphael said in concluding his interview. "He was on his way up. And she was already a star. He was going to become immortally famous, and so was she. I think they both knew they were not right for each other."

We can't be sure of the motivation for the Photoshopped image of Marilyn and Elvis, but we are certain that the photo with the taller girl, the real Magdalene Morgan, is the original.

Though the pretend marriage license made out by Elvis is misleading today, I like to think that it was simply Elvis's way of expressing his love for the girl he was going to abruptly leave behind. His future would be taking many more sudden turns.

Mary Magdalene Morgan passed away on Feb. 15, 2021, at Sanctuary Hospice House in Tupelo after an extended illness.

Chapter 12
Memphis Bound

While still enjoying the indoor plumbing on North Green Street in Tupelo, Elvis enrolled in the eighth grade at Gloster Street Junior High in September of 1948. The book *The Ultimate Elvis: Elvis Presley Day by Day* presents a garbled chronology of this period, stating that Elvis enrolled in a Memphis school on September 13, 1948, which cannot be true because Elvis was still at Gloster Street Junior High in Tupelo.

Life in Tupelo must have seemed relatively stable for the young man. He was fitting in well with his new friends, the family's finances were still fragile but manageable and his musical talent was getting burnished by lessons and practice.

Then, in early November, Vernon was fired from his job and abruptly told the family to pack up their most precious possessions—they were leaving for Memphis across the state line. The family quickly sold their furniture and many of their belongings, a sign that this time they would not be returning.

At a junior high farewell party on his last day, Elvis sang and played his guitar for thirty minutes. For his last number, Elvis sang a well-known traditional song, *Leaf on a Tree*.

The leaf on the branch
the branch on the tree
the tree in a hole

the hole in the ground
and the green grass grew all around
all around

Elvis's teacher, Mrs. Camp, told researcher Roy Turner, "Elvis was always one of my main characters in homeroom and chapel programs. He would talk, sing and play anything you wanted."

To friends and family who didn't know Vernon had been fired, the sudden move to Memphis must have seemed like lunacy. After all, Vernon and Gladys both had stable jobs in Tupelo, they were living in the best house of their lives and Elvis was already eight weeks into a new school year. Close friends and relatives all lived nearby. Vernon and Gladys had no jobs lined up in Memphis, no friends in the new town to assist them, no living quarters arranged. Because of a housing shortage, Gladys's sister Lillian and her family moved from the country into the house vacated by the Presleys on Green Street.

Vernon, of course, had left town many times to seek work or take a job away from home, but only once had he taken his family with him. The story that circulated in Tupelo was that Vernon wanted "to find a better life for his family." But was Memphis in 1948 a better place to live than Tupelo? Most people would have said, "Not by a long shot."

A short time after the family moved to Memphis, Gladys's brother, Travis, and his family would join them there. Over time, especially after Elvis became famous, the magnetic pull of his success and generosity would attract other Smiths and Presleys to Memphis.

Julian, as well as many others, remained puzzled by the abruptness and apparent irrationality of the move. It seemed more like an escape.

Various theories about the move emerged, as they always do in the absence of facts. Some people have proposed that Vernon had been caught selling bootleg alcohol in Mississippi, which was a "dry" state until 1966. The Smith and Presley families both had numerous hard-drinking members who would have been familiar with sources of booze, and Gladys's father, Bob Smith, had experimented with bootlegging, so this was a reasonable speculation. Perhaps Vernon was fleeing to another state to avoid prosecution.

Another theory centered on Elvis's secret marriage to Magdalene Morgan. Though the marriage certificate had been forged, some people surmised that the family thought it was real and had fled Tupelo to avoid the humiliation of their thirteen-year-old son getting married. Yet another theory was that Gladys had become pregnant by another man and was beginning to show, thus forcing the family to seek the anonymity of another city.

The most plausible motive for moving so abruptly was suggested by a comment that Marcus Posey, Vernon's coworker, made to Julian. Marcus didn't know why Vernon had left but remembered that about that same time a large quantity of cigarettes had gone missing from the warehouse at L. P. McCarty and Sons.

Julian learned that Mr. McCarty had actually caught Vernon stealing cigarettes three times. This was told to Julian by Buddy McCarty, Mr. McCarty's grandson. Perhaps the family's modest increase in quality of life, which included owning a 1939 Plymouth automobile, had been due to Vernon profiting from the stolen cigarettes. By the third time Vernon was caught, however, Mr. McCarty may have run out of patience and threatened to report Vernon to the police. With Vernon's felony record, this would have been disastrous.

"When news of this offense leaked out, as it always does," Julian told me, "many of the townsfolk who had put their reputations on the line by signing the petition to get Vernon out of prison probably felt betrayed, so they ran his ass out of town."

All the Presleys had left was what could fit into an old trunk they strapped to the top of the Plymouth. For the rest of the year and most of 1949, they lived in a Memphis boardinghouse as Vernon and Gladys struggled to find jobs. Vernon's bad decisions had again brought hardship to the family and must have ruptured the relationship between Vernon and Gladys. On the other hand, this avoidable upheaval may have strengthened the already close bond between Elvis and his mother, forging an even more durable partnership to survive Vernon's erratic nature.

It seems, then, that statements by Elvis's cousin Billy Smith in Alanna Nash's book *Elvis Aaron Presley: Revelations from the Memphis Mafia* may have been an attempt to paper over the true story. This, of course, is how history gets rewritten. Smith wrote about Vernon's situation before departing Tupelo in these words: "My daddy [Gladys's brother Travis Smith] said that he wasn't any better off than when he first got out of prison, because he was sharecropping." That may be true for Travis, but Vernon had not sharecropped for five years—he had worked at L. P. McCarty and Sons that whole time. And we know that Vernon's family was considerably better off than after he had been released from prison.

In his book, Billy Smith remembered that "Vernon said [to Travis], 'Let's get out of town.' … Daddy and Vernon had gone there [Memphis] before. They stayed three weeks and couldn't find anything. Daddy sold two cows and a hog to get some money, about $105. I'm sure Vernon sold something too. I'm pretty sure we come in Daddy's car, a 1937 or 1939 green Plymouth. There were seven of us in that one car, Daddy and Mama, me and my older brother, Bobby, and Gladys, Vernon, and Elvis, and all of our belongings."

Billy Smith's memory defies logic. A '37 or '39 Plymouth certainly cannot hold seven people plus all their belongings. But

Billy was just five years old when the family moved to Memphis. Details of the trip are sparse, but most sources agree that Travis Smith and his family moved to Memphis shortly after Vernon, Gladys and Elvis arrived there. Family stories and distant memories are usually unreliable as evidence.

Memphis Blues

Upon arriving in Memphis, Gladys enrolled Elvis into the eighth grade at the Christine School on Third Street to complete the eighth grade. Some writers have confused details about this transition, claiming that Elvis entered the ninth grade at Humes High School after arriving in Memphis. He did, in fact, start Humes High School in the ninth grade, but not until the following year when he had completed eighth grade at the Christine School.

The Presleys moved into a rat-infested boardinghouse at 572 Poplar Avenue. After the comparative luxury of indoor plumbing for his small family in Tupelo, Elvis suddenly was sharing a bathroom with fifteen other families—close to fifty people. Baths were a rare luxury; running water was often unavailable, and cooking relied on a small community hot plate in a dingy kitchen. But the monthly rent was only thirty-five dollars.

To pay for rent, Vernon took a low-paying job at United Paint Company loading a truck and delivering boxes of paint to customers. Gladys found work as a factory seamstress and later took part-time jobs as a cafeteria waitress and a nurse's aide. Their combined monthly income was about thirty-five dollars, just enough to pay the rent.

After the relative comfort of Green Street in Tupelo, the entire family was experiencing the Memphis blues. Gladys and Elvis understood that this downward spiral was due to Vernon's bad decisions and found ways to let him know that he was to blame. Sharing their scorn undoubtedly drew mother and son together even more closely. If not for the company of some relatives and friends who had also moved to Memphis, this first year could have been much worse.

The students at the Christine School didn't know what to make of Elvis. The shy but mannerly new kid spoke with a thick, country accent and dressed in patched pants that were too short and shoes that had pieces of cardboard covering the holes. Elvis told his mother that no one liked him. Even worse, it seemed like he was invisible, he said. Except for attracting some teasing, no one noticed him. He badly wanted to find a way to be noticed.

By the summer of 1949, Gladys and Elvis began going to the Old First Assembly of God Church at 1084 East McLemore. The services were similar to the ones at their old church in East Tupelo, which must have been comforting. This is probably where Elvis attended singing practice with the popular Blackwood Brothers Gospel Quartet. Later, in his senior year, Elvis auditioned for the Quartet's teen group, the Songfellows, but was turned down because it was thought he could not blend his voice with the other singers. After he became famous, Elvis would often tease the Blackwood Brothers about this.

WDIA Radio

Although segregation was still a fact of life, Elvis found solace in listening to WDIA, a new music radio station that had been founded in 1947. The format featured pop, country and western, and light classical music. But by 1948, the station was near bankruptcy.

In a last-ditch effort to stay alive, the white owners of the station, John Pepper and Dick Ferguson, did something unprecedented in a strictly segregated Southern society—they hired Black professor Nat D. Williams ("Nat Dee") to host a new show called "Tan Town Jamboree," hoping to attract a larger audience during the late night and early morning hours. Featuring Black R&B groups, the show caught on, and hardworking Nat was scheduled to host a follow-on show called "Tan Town Coffee Club" at eight o'clock in the morning. The success of these shows spawned "Tan Town Jubilee" hosted by Maurice Hulbert, Jr., known as "Hard Rod."

Nat D. Williams broadcasts on WDIA radio in Memphis.

Pepper and Ferguson had stumbled upon the untapped power of the underserved and unrecognized African American community. Over the next year, offering only partial Black programming, the station rose to number two in the Memphis market. Despite bomb threats to the station, the owners stayed the course and made WDIA the first Black radio station with an all-Black on-air staff that programmed Black music all day long. It soon became the top radio station in Memphis and the first to gross a million dollars in a year.

Elvis loved the Black R&B, country and inspirational music played by the Sunset Travelers, the Southern Wonders and the Spirit of Memphis. Whenever Kay Starr or Mahalia Jackson, Elvis's two favorite female singers, were on the radio, Elvis insisted that everyone else be quiet so he could hear them.

He became a rabid fan of Hard Rod and the Black music he played. When inspirational readings were introduced in a new segment called "Sweet Talkin' Time," Hard Rod took on the persona of "Maurice the Mood Man." The growing audience, including young Elvis, Gladys and Vernon, were captivated by Hulbert's resonant and personal Bible-based messages often punctuated by riveting gospel "jubilees" and shout-singing numbers. The music on WDIA clearly influenced Elvis's singing and musical tastes.

Humes High School

In September of 1949, Elvis enrolled in the ninth grade at Humes High, an all-White, understaffed and ill-equipped school with 1,600 students at 659 Manassas Street. The frightening, first-day school experience at such a large institution traumatized the young man, who ran home "bug eyed" with nerves, according to Vernon.

Elvis eventually tried out for the school glee club, but music teacher, Miss Elsie Marmann, turned him down because, she said, he couldn't sing very well. Elvis was determined to "show her" she was wrong. He returned with his guitar, was allowed to sing to the students, and Miss Marmann admitted that her decision had been based on personal taste in music, not on his ability. In his first year at Humes, Elvis was given a C in music.

Shortly after starting at Humes, the family escaped the wretched boardinghouse and moved into a two-bedroom, ground-floor apartment at Lauderdale Courts where they would live for four years. Across the street was a slum of run-down shanties where the poorest blacks in Memphis lived, a constant reminder of how close to the edge of abject poverty the Presleys were living.

Lauderdale Courts was a federally funded complex at 185 Winchester Street that offered improved living conditions for the same monthly rent that the boardinghouse charged. Author Bill E. Burk, a friend of Elvis from his Humes years, claims that Elvis learned his crazy, wild moves in the "Courts." But this makes no sense, as abundant inspiration for those antics had been clearly available to him from the exuberance of preachers in East Tupelo and the showmanship of blues and R&B singers on legendary Beale Street just a half-mile from Lauderdale Courts.

The new apartment was a great improvement over the boardinghouse except for one minor irritation for Gladys. A neighbor, Mary Guy, continuously complained to the landlord that Elvis's late-night singing and guitar-picking was annoying.

As a sophomore at Humes, Elvis joined the JROTC—Junior Reserve Officers' Training Corps. He loved looking official in the uniforms but quit after a year because it didn't allow him enough time for his other interests. In addition to working on his music, he loved reading history and literature and became a library volunteer. His high school friends didn't understand his enthusiasm for books, so he started reading in private. For the rest of his adult life, according to Lamar Fike, he concealed his passion for reading and often brought boxes of books with him on tour, keeping them out of sight.

Elvis (center, top row) loved wearing his JROTC uniform.

A Change in Attitude

The summer before his junior year, Elvis took a job with Precision Tool. He liked having his own money to spend on records and clothes. This was about the time he started frequenting local pawn shops and stores along Beale Street. He replaced his worn-out, baggy clothes with garments from Lansky Brothers, which specialized in zoot suits, pegged trousers and vibrant hues that Bernard Lansky, the owner, called "LIFE SAVERS colors like red, orange, yellow, green and purple. The store often featured shirts and jackets with provocative names like "Date Bait," "Super Cool" and "The Hipster."

Two brothers owned the store located at 126 Beale Street in the music district. Bernard first noticed Elvis checking out the eye-catching store windows in the spring of 1952 and invited the lad in, but Elvis declined, saying he had no money. According to one story, possibly apocryphal, Elvis told Bernard, "When I get rich, I'll buy you out." Bernard came back with, "Do me a favor. Don't buy me out—just buy from me."

And Elvis did. He returned one day to buy a shirt for $3.95. For years after becoming famous, Lansky Brothers fitted him with iconic outfits including the navy jacket seen in the famous photo of Elvis and Muhammad Ali, the plaid jacket he wore on The Ed Sullivan Show and the red jacket in *Jailhouse Rock* promotional photos. Their relationship lasted until the end when Lansky provided the white suit for Elvis's funeral.

Bernard Lansky fits Elvis for a jacket at Lansky Brothers on Beale Street.

Besides wearing some outrageous outfits, Elvis also grew his hair longer, often slicking it back with pomade, a trick he learned from Black musicians on Beale Street. He started dying it black, like his musical icons. He loved bold, flashy patterns and bright pink shirts—which admittedly set off his piercing blue eyes.

Elvis was gaining confidence and expressing it in his manner of dress. Only Black people wore pink and black combos, and mostly truck drivers wore long, greasy hair and sideburns. Why not do something disruptive and put it all together?

During his senior year, Elvis assembled furniture full time for Marl Metal Products. He worked every day from 3:00 p.m. to 11:30 p.m. With his hard-earned income, he helped out his family financially and bought even more music and clothes.

Regis Wilson, the only girl Elvis ever took to a Humes prom, lived in Lauderdale Courts and had known Elvis for only four months. Though she was just fourteen and barely five feet tall, she loved to hang around with the guys, especially Elvis. She told interviewer Bill Burk, "While we were dating, sometimes he would show up on my front porch wearing a bright yellow sport coat with brown trim. I would always close my eyes because people just didn't dress like that in those days. But Elvis did."

About her prom date with Elvis at the Peabody Hotel, Regis explained, "So all through the evening, we just sat there and talked to each other. I don't remember a lot of people coming up to talk to us. So, we sat out the evening—never dancing once." Elvis never danced with a girl because he was intimidated by the prospect of dancing with a partner. His moves on stage were always solo acts.

"Later [after he became famous]," Regis said, "I saw him in *Jailhouse Rock* on TV, and I thought back to that evening and I said to myself, 'I thought he didn't know how to dance!'"

As prom night was coming to an end, Regis remembered, "It came time for us to line up with all the other couples to have our photographs taken to put in our scrapbooks. We walked into the 'heart' and posed, and the photographer snapped our picture."

Regis wore a pink carnation and a strapless pink taffeta dress for her Prom Date of the Century. Elvis showed up in a dark suit wearing, yes, blue suede shoes. Honest to God.

Regis Wilson Vaughn and Elvis have their picture taken in front of a giant red heart at the Humes High School Prom in the Continental Ballroom of the Peabody Hotel.

According to the Graceland website, "When prom season arrived, Elvis asked the tailors at Lansky's to create a unique suit for him—one with a pink coat, black pants and a pink and black cummerbund." This suggests that this outfit was for Elvis's senior prom, but it was not. The pink tux was made two years later after his girlfriend Dixie Locke invited him to be her date for her junior prom. Elvis was busy during this time performing in various towns on the *Lousiana Hayride* radio show circuit but took a break for Dixie's prom.

In 1955, Elvis took some time off his *Louisiana Hayride* performances to attend Dixie Locke's junior prom. He wore a pink jacket and pink-and-black cummerbund.

To other White people, Elvis's everyday clothing must have seemed outlandish, but his outfits forced people to take notice, which was important to him. How could his clothing not be stylish if it copied the look of great Black musicians? When his clothes caused stares or comments, even derision, that was a good thing—better, certainly, than being invisible. He could not have known that these adjustments to his appearance were his first tentative steps in profoundly altering American popular culture and music forever.

Accompanying his new threads, Elvis also evolved into a class clown, which attracted attention in the form of laughter—but this time, not *at* him but *with* him. His sense of humor would become a part of his performances later in life as he frequently ribbed the band, teased the audience and ad-libbed to make people wonder what was coming next.

Many stories have evolved about Elvis at Humes, many of them untrue—"Like the one that Bobby 'Red' West protected Elvis from guys who wanted to beat up on him because of his clothes or the sideburns," Evan "Buzzy" Forbess told interviewer Bill Burk. Red West, who had met Elvis in high school, would soon become a longtime member of "Memphis Mafia" and Elvis's bodyguard.

"Elvis never needed protection!" Buzzy insisted. "He could give it and take it with the best of us. He seemed to love mixing it up wrestling. He didn't go looking for trouble, but I never saw Elvis lose a fight."

One evening, when Buzzy was playing freshman football, Elvis came to watch him against the Treadwell team. Afterward, as Elvis and Buzzy were walking past the Treadwell bus, one of the opposing players stuck his head out the door and cursed at Buzzy's coach, Lee Thompson. "Elvis grabbed this guy and cold-cocked him," Buzzy said, "knocking him all the way back into the bus. None of this player's teammates came out to challenge him either."

Farley Guy, another close friend of Elvis at Humes, said, "I have read so much about guys at school picking on Elvis all the time because of his sideburns and loud clothes, but I don't remember any of these fights. Elvis was a scrapper. No one had to take up for him." Farley added, "I never cared for Red West. He was a smart mouth, a bully. One day we got into it, and I wrapped a footstool around his head."

"Buzzy" Forbess (left), Elvis and Farley Guy were close friends at Humes High School. This photo was taken in the fall of 1954 after Elvis returned from a Louisiana Hayride appearance.

Red West and Elvis on the set of *GI Blues* in 1960.

Other students have remembered Red West as one of the kids who picked on Elvis. But if there was animosity between Red and Elvis, it seemed to end when Elvis discovered that Red played the trumpet. Before long, the two of them and several other students were jamming together.

Each year, Humes would stage a big variety show in the auditorium with concession stands in the cafeteria. At about nine o'clock on the evening of the show, Malcolm Phillips, assistant football coach at Humes, was watching all the people go up the stairs from the cafeteria to the auditorium. Elvis loved playing football and had a good relationship with Malcolm.

Before long, Malcolm heard "strange thumping sounds coming from upstairs," he told interviewer Burk. To investigate, he climbed the fire escape up to the auditorium and entered at the end of the stage. "There was Red West playing trumpet," Malcolm said, "Elvis playing guitar and maybe two or three others in their band. Elvis was a sight, believe me. He was singing and wiggling and wobbling all over the place."

Malcolm went back to the cafeteria and found coach Rube Boyce. "I told Rube, 'That's Elvis and a couple others up there singin'. And Rube said, 'They will never amount to anything.'"

Well, not in football, anyway.

The 1953 Herald Yearbook

School yearbooks reveal interesting things about an individual. I was able to examine a copy of the 1953 Herald Yearbook owned by Gloria Trout, the girl named in it as the most popular girl in the Humes senior class. Gloria had put the book up for auction because it featured a very famous alumnus, Elvis Presley. The high bid at the time was $2,500.

You would expect Elvis, in a class of under one hundred boys, to be listed as special in some way, right? The Who's Who page in his senior yearbook presented twenty-two subjective "Best" and "Most" categories for recognition of standout students, so let's see.

- Best personality? No, that honor went to Bill Bishop.
- Cutest? That was Chris Kolives.

- How about most handsome? The yearbook said that was Gene Bernard.
- Most popular? No way, that was Gene Gann.
- Most likely to succeed? Not Elvis. In 1953, that was James Thomas.
- Elvis, considered one of the most talented men to ever live, had to be the most talented boy in his small high school class, right? No! That was Vernon Yarbrough.

The most popular girl in Elvis's senior class, Gloria Trout, was so popular, it seems, that almost everyone in her class signed her yearbook—even Elvis, who wrote next to his alphabetized photograph, "Best of Luck to a very Pretty girl, remember me, Elvis Presley."

I'm quite sure she remembered.

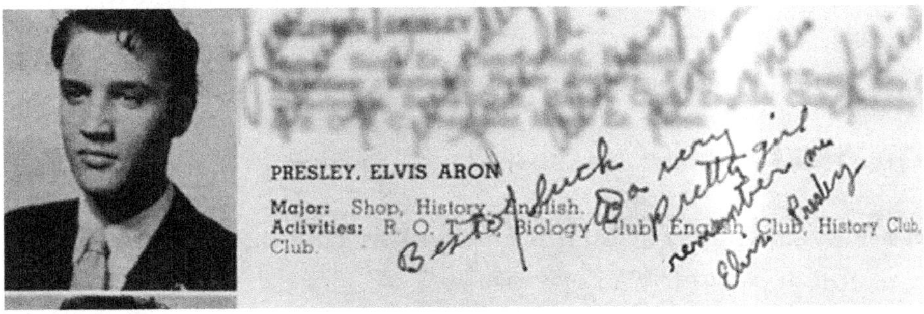

The inscription is remarkable not just for Elvis's quote, but because Elvis signed his full name, "Elvis Presley." He had signed a few other yearbooks, but never with his full name. Gloria got a large payoff not because she was the most popular senior girl at Humes in 1953, but because a strange boy she barely knew autographed his picture.

The Minstrel Show

In April of 1953, during his senior year, Elvis performed before an audience of 1,600 as the Humes High Band presented its annual Minstrel Show, a talent showcase for the school's students. Elvis, act 16, appeared relaxed and confident. He propped one leg on a chair, rested his guitar on it and sang "Keep Them Cold Icy Fingers Off of Me." After receiving the largest applause of the

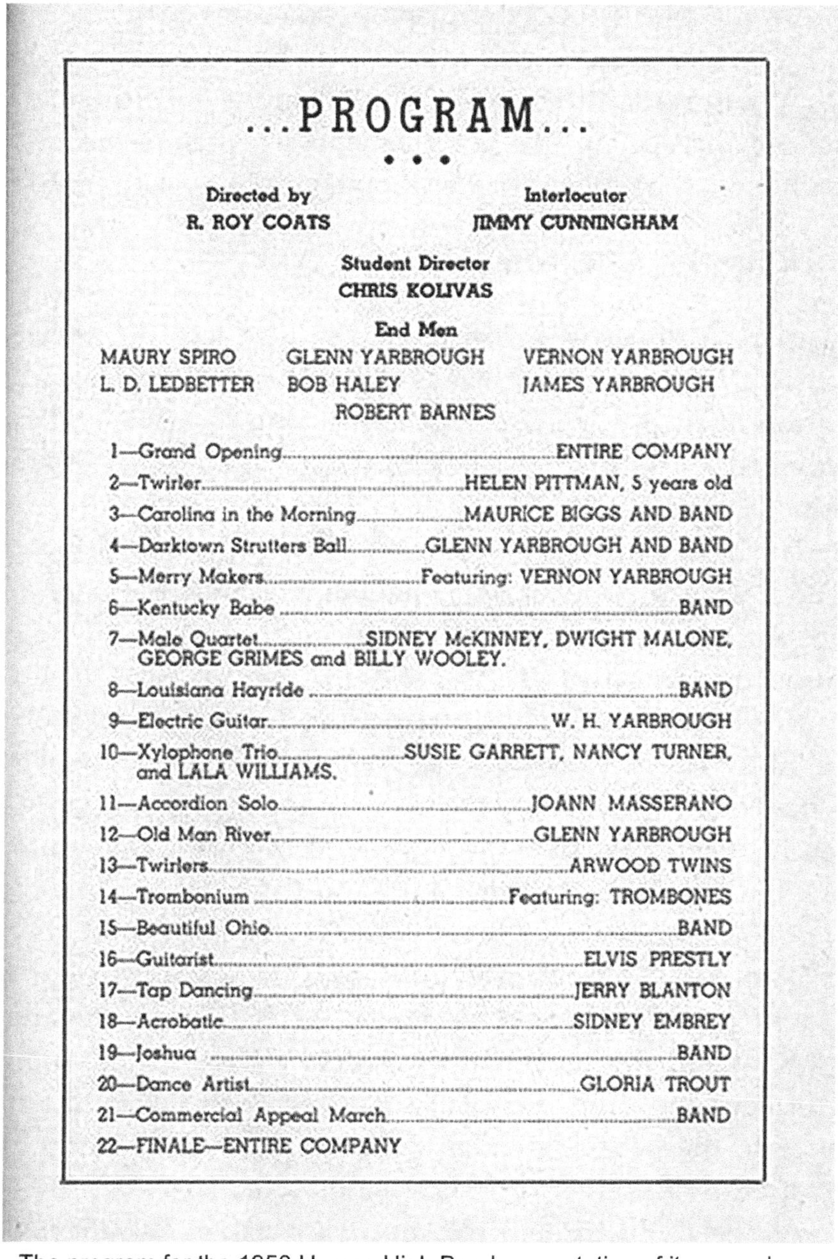

...PROGRAM...

• • •

Directed by
R. ROY COATS

Interlocutor
JIMMY CUNNINGHAM

Student Director
CHRIS KOLIVAS

End Men

MAURY SPIRO — GLENN YARBROUGH — VERNON YARBROUGH
L. D. LEDBETTER — BOB HALEY — JAMES YARBROUGH
ROBERT BARNES

1—Grand Opening....ENTIRE COMPANY
2—Twirler....HELEN PITTMAN, 5 years old
3—Carolina in the Morning....MAURICE BIGGS AND BAND
4—Darktown Strutters Ball....GLENN YARBROUGH AND BAND
5—Merry Makers....Featuring: VERNON YARBROUGH
6—Kentucky Babe....BAND
7—Male Quartet....SIDNEY McKINNEY, DWIGHT MALONE, GEORGE GRIMES and BILLY WOOLEY.
8—Louisiana Hayride....BAND
9—Electric Guitar....W. H. YARBROUGH
10—Xylophone Trio....SUSIE GARRETT, NANCY TURNER, and LALA WILLIAMS.
11—Accordion Solo....JOANN MASSERANO
12—Old Man River....GLENN YARBROUGH
13—Twirlers....ARWOOD TWINS
14—Trombonium....Featuring: TROMBONES
15—Beautiful Ohio....BAND
16—Guitarist....ELVIS PRESTLY
17—Tap Dancing....JERRY BLANTON
18—Acrobatic....SIDNEY EMBREY
19—Joshua....BAND
20—Dance Artist....GLORIA TROUT
21—Commercial Appeal March....BAND
22—FINALE—ENTIRE COMPANY

The program for the 1953 Humes High Band presentation of its annual Minstrel Show.

evening, he was asked to perform an encore for which he chose Teresa Brewer's "Till I Waltz Again with You."

Elvis was listed as "Guitarist," and his last name was misspelled "Prestly" on the printed program. Nevertheless, it was by far his biggest public event so far. Just three months later, Elvis would walk into Sam Phillips' Memphis recording studio to create the acetate of "My Happiness." That record would launch one of the greatest entertainment careers of all time.

Cracking the Overton Shell

It wasn't so much Elvis's first commercial recording for Sun Records that made him. It was his first big performance at the Overton Shell in Memphis that put a stamp on his style and captivated more than two thousand fans. After the Shell, there was no turning back.

The bill for the show on July 30, 1954, had been put together by Bob Neal, a popular radio personality and promoter. Sam Phillips, the owner of Sun Records, had prevailed on Neal to include upstart singer Elvis on the bill, even though it was promoted as a country and western show. The featured performer was Slim Whitman, whose latest hit was "Indian Love Call." Suddenly Elvis was going to have an opportunity do on stage what he'd done on his first big record. The A side featured a Black blues number called "That's All Right, Mama," and the flip side a country song, "Blue Moon Over Kentucky."

Before the show, a profoundly anxious Elvis worried that the audience would reject his music. After all, country singers like Whitman who starred on *The Grand Old Opry* were country performers and didn't do Black music. The audience had paid money to the hear relatively simple and familiar country and western hits. But Elvis's music was not that.

As Joel Williamson wrote in *Elvis Presley: A Southern Life*, "What Elvis and his guitarist, Scotty Moore, and his bass fiddle player, Bill Black, were doing was not country. It was not hillbilly, not pop, not gospel, and not blues. It was neither Black nor White, neither sacred nor—quite—profane. Yet it was somehow influenced by all these things."

As the younger singer marched onto the stage for his Overton Shell debut, he timidly adjusted the microphone, then stepped back and aggressively leaped into "That's All Right, Mama." He rose up on his toes, leaned forward and curled his upper lip into the sneer that would become a defiant trademark for the rest of his career.

"That's all right, mama," he sang, assaulting the audience with the words, "any—wa-ay you do." His body started to thrum with the beat, and as he stepped away from the mic for Scotty and Bill to take turns on the instrumental, they noticed the audience raucously moving with them and clapping their hands. As if fearing that silence would break the spell, they launched immediately into "Blue Moon over Kentucky." But instead of doing it like the King of bluegrass, Bill Monroe, with a high tenor slathered with nostalgia, Elvis turned the number upside down. In his hands, it was no longer hillbilly. As Williamson wrote, "It was joyous, country-come-to-town—and damn glad to be there."

The astonished crowd erupted in a spasm of ecstasy. As Elvis sang, he'd back off the mic, playing his guitar and shaking his body, and with each tremor the crowd would go wild. Scotty Moore said, "He thought they were actually making fun of him." Backstage, after the song, he asked his manager what he had done and was told the "wiggling your legs" had provoked all the excitement.

"I went out for an encore," Elvis said later, "and I did a little more, and the more I did, the wilder they went."

By "they" he meant the girls, mainly, and Elvis gave them more of what their screams demanded. This spontaneous yet somehow intimate call-and-response between performer and the females in his audience was the beginning of the Elvis phenomenon. As the crowds of young white women grew in size, the fans seemed determined to fearlessly and publicly express their joy and emotion and desire for a young man from Tupelo who had ignited their passions.

Remembering Old Friends

Elvis's sudden and prolonged popularity didn't seem to change him much. He still kept up with some of his former friends from Tupelo. One of them, Eugene "Ed" Christian, whom Elvis had known since childhood, revealed to Julian some personal stories of Elvis's early Memphis years.

> I remember that my aunt Floy May Frost and Gladys were good friends, and both moved to Memphis about the same time. My uncle Buster Frost and Aunt Floy moved to Memphis where Buster had a job keeping up a tract of rental houses just off South Cooper Parkway. Aunt Floy contacted Gladys and they began visiting. After Elvis moved into Graceland, he would send a car over to Aunt Floy's house to bring her to Graceland for lunch and sometimes for dinner. These visits continued until Mrs. Gladys's death.
>
> I lost touch with Elvis after they moved to Memphis until I ran into him on a street in Frankfurt, Germany, in the late 50s. I had enlisted in the Mississippi National Guard, and after about three months I transferred to the regular army. We were both in the Third Army, Third Armored Division, but in different companies. Even then he had his hangers-on. We stood on the street and talked about old times for a short while, but Colonel Parker seemed nervous about our talking of old

times, and he wanted to go.

Early in his music career, Elvis was generous to a fault, giving away new cars and money almost as if he was trying to buy friends. With all his fame and money, Elvis was just a poor, unhappy boy from East Tupelo trapped in a world he could not control. Many people have claimed to have known Elvis, and many fabrications have been concocted of him and places he is supposed to be connected with.

The next time Elvis and I met was in the mid-60s here in Tupelo. On that day, Richard Hill and I were returning to work at Western Auto after eating lunch. Richard's family operated the Western Auto store. We were walking south on North Spring Street, and as we came to the Phillips Seed and Hardware store, I noticed a long, black limousine parked in front. I remember saying to Richard, "I wonder who belongs to that." We had taken only a few steps when we heard someone calling my name. We turned to see who it was, and it was Elvis half in and half out of that black limousine. He asked me to get in, which I did. We talked about old times and how happy we were to see each other.

I asked Elvis what he was doing in Tupelo. He told me his attorneys were here to reclaim an iron fence that once had been at Graceland. He had given the fence to go around a little park that was to be built for the children of Tupelo. It seemed the fence went elsewhere, and Elvis was upset about it. We traded small talk for the next few minutes, and he told me how unhappy he was and how empty his life had become. I asked, "How could that be? You have anything and everything you want. You're on top of the world."

Elvis said, "No, the world is on top of me. I'm just a puppet on a string." Then he said, "Gene, I wish I could get out of this damned car and just walk around Tupelo without being mobbed." I can't imagine what it would be like not being able to go shopping, or to a restaurant for coffee, or just walk around without being mobbed by fans—such was his life.

He then asked if I would come to work for him. He said, "It won't be physical work, just be a companion." I said, "No, my life is here. I'm married to a good woman and don't want to leave her." I guess I was the only one to say no to Elvis at this period of his life. He seemed disappointed, but then his expression could have been one of relief. This was the last time I ever saw or talked to Elvis. I have often wondered if I had had said yes to his job offer, if things would have turned out different. I also wonder if Gladys had bought Elvis that rifle instead of a guitar how his life would have turned out.

I have never tried to capitalize on my friendship with Elvis. Just being his friend was good enough. Some things I know about Elvis are best left out of history. One thing about Elvis—he was never the macho man he often portrayed in his movie roles, but he was not particularly wimpy either. For the remainder of my days, I will remember Elvis and those carefree days when we ran wild in the streets of old South Tupelo. What I have stated here is true, and the truth is all that matters to me.

To our knowledge, this is the only interview Ed Christian has ever given about his friendship with Elvis Presley after he moved to Memphis. In a March 24, 1956, radio interview with Robert Carlton Brown, Elvis said, "The only kind of trouble I've ever been in is stealing eggs when I was real little." Most likely, the egg-stealing incident and the chicken-catching adventures occurred at about the same time.

Gene Christian's account of meeting Elvis after he became famous was confirmed to Julian by Gene's friend, Richard Hill. This is how he remembered the incident:

> Gene [Christian] and I had been to eat at Leon Blackwell's café on North Spring Street [in Tupelo] across the street from the Lee County Courthouse. On our way back to work, we passed a black Cadillac parked on the street. We heard someone call out, "Gene!" It was Elvis.
>
> Gene asked if I wanted to meet Elvis. We walked over to the car. Elvis had sent his driver into Leon's Café to get some hamburgers. Elvis invited him into the car. Gene got in but I had to get back to work at the store, so I talked to Elvis through the open window for about two minutes. I could tell that they wanted to talk about old friends and times, so I shook his hand and returned to the Western Auto store at 114 North Spring Street. Gene returned to work in about fifteen minutes.

A Link in the Ancestral Chain

Because of my obsession with uncovering the truth, Elvis's hardships and his family's stumble through life cause me to reflect on the Presley family's what-ifs and should haves. I have covered many of these in the preceding pages, but one enigma still looms large: Why did Vernon and Gladys have no more children? In a book largely about ancestry and DNA, this topic is highly relevant

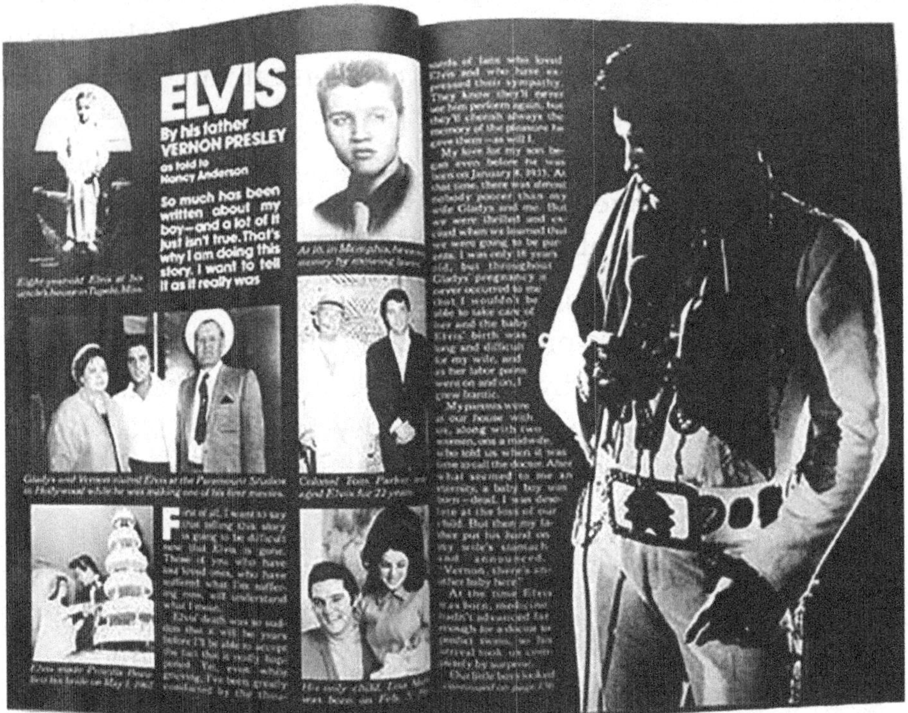
ELVIS

By his father VERNON PRESLEY as told to Nancy Anderson

So much has been written about my boy—and a lot of it just isn't true. That's why I am doing this story. I want to tell it as it really was

Vernon Presley was interviewed in the January 1978 edition of *Good Housekeeping*.

Thousands of pages have been written about Elvis as an only child, and if the handwritten letters I presented in *Letters from Elvis* were telling the truth and Vernon was not Elvis's biological father, then Vernon had no children with Gladys. In the Presley and Smith families, which generally had bunches of kids, this barrenness has always seemed odd. So has the fact that Vernon's brother, Vester, had only one child, and his daughter did not appear until five years after he married Gladys's sister, Clettes.

Many writers have attempted to blame Vernon's small immediate family on Gladys's health. With no proof, some have surmised that the difficult birth of her twins made it impossible to have children in the future. Others have claimed that complications from a miscarriage in 1942 prevented Gladys from having more children. In the absence of hard evidence, these are reasonable theories.

Gladys's husband, however, directly contradicts these notions. During an interview in the January 1978 issue of *Good Housekeeping*, Vernon said:

> Gladys and I were so proud of Elvis and enjoyed him so much that we immediately wanted more children. But, for reasons no doctor could understand, we had none. While Elvis grew from infant to toddler to lively little boy, we consulted doctors about our failure to have another child. We prayed about it, too. There was no medical reason why my wife didn't conceive again, but she didn't.

So, if the lack of other pregnancies was not due to Gladys's medical condition, I asked Julian, might the cause have been related to Vernon? No one had ever suggested that before, perhaps because it was commonly believed that he had fathered twins.

"But if Vernon was not Elvis's and Jesse's father," Julian answered, "then the existence of twins would have no bearing on Vernon's ability to get Gladys pregnant. Someone else, maybe Lawrence Riley, would have done that. In fact, if Vernon were sterile, it would prove that he *could not* be Elvis's father, so this is an important question."

In the *Good Housekeeping* interview, Vernon also specified when he became aware that he and Gladys would have no more children. "When Elvis was about ten years old," he said, "the reason was revealed very clearly to me . . . that Elvis was the only child we'd ever have and the only child we'd ever need. Elvis was a special gift who would fill our lives completely."

I was still troubled by the fact that there were no children attributed to Vernon after Elvis and Jesse, but also that his brother

Vester did not have a child for five years after his marriage. It seemed too coincidental that two brothers were sterile.

"We don't know for sure that either or both of them were sterile," Julian said. "But if so, the likely cause would be an outbreak of the mumps, which occasionally would sweep through Mississippi."

During Vernon's and Vester's childhood, mumps often ran unabated through families. An experimental vaccine for the mumps was not created until 1948 and vaccination was not mandatory for children until 1977. Two of the most frightening outcomes of the disease were sterility or subfertility—a lowering of the sperm count. But infertility issues can also be genetic, affecting kin just like syndactyly (webbed toes.)

There is considerable anecdotal evidence that Vernon could not father children, and at some point, he knew it, probably because he and Gladys had no additional offspring though they had tried to conceive and even consulted doctors about the problem. Compelling clues arose after Vernon's second marriage.

Two years after Gladys died, Vernon married thirty-five-year-old Dee Stanley, who had divorced her husband for a more glamorous life in the Presley family. More than anything, Dee wanted to have a child with Vernon—to be the mother of an Elvis sibling. According to the book *Elvis: We Love You Tender,* on which Dee closely collaborated, "Like women in days of yore who bore children to 'royalty,' bearing Vernon's child—a half-sister to Elvis—would have no doubt entrenched her more solidly in the bosom of the family…"

Anxious and frustrated at the lack of a quick pregnancy, Dee relentlessly complained that the reason she had not conceived was probably because Vernon was uncircumcised. Vernon finally relented and went through painful surgery to satisfy his wife. Vernon's circumcision was corroborated in Albert Goldman's biography, *Elvis,* which stated, "Vernon . . . was circumcised after he became involved with a young woman." Apparently, that young woman was Dee Stanley.

This raises a question. If Vernon knew he was sterile, why would he inflict upon himself such a terrible experience? Why not just explain that he could not father children? To my mind, he did it because confessing his condition to Dee would mean divulging the long-held secret that he could not possibly be Elvis's biological father. This would shatter the family legend and reveal that he had wooed Dee under false pretenses.

After a year of marriage, as Dee and Vernon were visiting Elvis in Florida while he was shooting the movie *Follow That Dream* at the Crystal River, she received confirmation from a doctor that she was carrying a girl. According to the account Dee gave to author Martin Torgoff, "He [Vernon] was in one of his jealous moods when she told him. Staring at her icily for a moment, he said, 'Well, that's fine, Dee. Who does it belong too?'"

Vernon's response, seemingly cruel, takes on a new meaning in light of a statement Dee Stanley made over the phone to Julian Riley after Vernon had passed away. In one of three long calls, a bitter and lonely Dee Stanly said that Vernon had told her during a later argument about the matter, "Everybody knows I can't do that." By "everybody," I think he meant those close to the family.

The theory of Vernon's sterility requires more proof but is a provocative link in the ancestral chain. If true, Elvis's origin story would be pregnant with new possibilities. It seems that no matter how hard we search for answers or poke the mythical beasts, we end up just short of the complete truth. Each new find exposes more missing pieces in the puzzle. Yet, as that long-running TV series, *The X-Files*, promised, "The Truth is Out There."

Remembering Elvis

Elvis deserves a better story. A true story. Apparently, enormous talent, global fame, financial success and legions of adoring fans does not guarantee that one's personal story will be told honestly. The hundreds, perhaps thousands of falsehoods and inaccuracies in Elvis's origin story, some of which are exposed here, degrade his true identity and insult his legacy, as if he were not *good enough* without sanding off the rough edges, retouching his history and burnishing the reputations of his friends and relatives.

Everyone who knew Elvis has tried to remake him, myself included, I suppose. I have often wondered if I have reinterpreted certain facts to help create an Elvis icon in keeping with my own conclusions. And yet it is impossible, I think, to study the facts about a man without seeking to understand how they inform his motives, passions, fears and behaviors.

For thirty-four years, I have been studying Elvis through his correspondence, his actions and finally his people and their culture. I still don't understand this complex man. In the end, I have decided that perhaps it is enough to pay tribute to him by helping straighten out the "mess of myth" that surrounds him. The very least that he deserves is that when we tell stories about him, they be true. That when we describe his family and ancestors, they be presented fairly, honestly and without shame or façade. That when we document his life, it be a faithful rendition of exactly how and where he lived. That when we judge his life, if we must, it be based on facts, not fantasy.

After humorist Dave Barry went to Graceland seeking to understand the "cult of Elvis," he wrote: "Talk to a True Fan, and odds are she won't talk about Elvis's art, his genius, the way fans of, say, Bob Dylan will talk. Odds are she'll tell you how, when he performed, he always seemed to be looking at her, singing to her. The True Fans really believe that Elvis loves them, just as much as they love him. They talk about how much he cared for them, how much he gave them, how, in a way, he died for them."

But how can we love a legend without loving the man behind it? I believe that what Dave Barry wrote is true of the typical fan, the impressionable, worshipful individual who is in love with the superficial image and the emotional connection. The True Fan, I believe, wants to know the man behind the mask—the details, the nitty gritty, the humanity!

And yet, because of countless cover-ups, legions of lies and a host of PR distortions, Elvis remains an enigma, a man of mysteries, and they tantalize us. While this book may resolve some of those mysteries and clear up a lot of confusion, many more issues exist. So, *Roots of Elvis* along with its forebears, *Letters from Elvis* and *Brando on Elvis* may be only the beginning of trying to get at the truth for the True Fans among us.

Be a Part of the Story

I chose not to end this book with a Conclusion, because there are still too many unanswered questions and unsolved mysteries in Elvis's origin story. I am proud, of course, of the many issues we have resolved. We have identified the missing fathers of Elvis's paternal great-uncles and other kinfolk; straightened out the major bloodlines of Elvis's ancestry starting with the earliest immigrants to America; debunked the popular myth of Morning White Dove and the family's Cherokee heritage; exposed the fiction about Elvis's Jewish genes; unearthed the true story of Elvis's birthplace; located numerous important sites and graves with directions of how to find them; corrected countless errors and inconsistencies in previous biographies and the general historical record; and I hope provided some insights into the roots of Elvis that helped make him who he was.

While we were working hard to find answers to difficult questions, however, we also discovered new mysteries that so far have defied solutions. We have found considerable evidence that Vernon Presley was not Elvis's biological father, but we are missing critical DNA to prove the identity of the real father; one sample from the right person could solve this mystery.

We have found tantalizing clues that Gladys Presley may have been an illegitimate daughter; but again, we are lacking one critical DNA sample to prove that theory and the identity of her biological father. We have proven the connection of numerous individuals to Elvis's family tree, many of which were previously unidentified; but many other relatives are still unproven members of the family.

The Elvis DNA Project

Because our Elvis DNA project holds in one database over a hundred DNA samples from every major bloodline of Elvis family heritage, and our interactive family tree now contains about forty thousand names, we have the unique ability to identify family members and their relationships to Elvis. Voluntarily donated DNA samples are a chief means by which we can continue to solve the many Elvis family mysteries and locate more family members.

The Elvis DNA project is a resource for all individuals who have reason to believe they or a friend or relative may be related to Elvis Presley. We use a variety of genetic labs and do not charge for DNA processing or analysis. We can sign a Non-Disclosure Agreement guaranteeing that we cannot make public the results of a DNA test or any matches to the Elvis family tree without the donor's permission.

Why are we doing this? Because your DNA may not only make you part of the Elvis story, but also help us solve some of the thorny mysteries surrounding Elvis Presley and his enigmatic family.

If you have questions about submitting DNA, or are ready to submit a sample, please contact us at ElvisDNA@calumeteditions.com.

If you have information you believe may be relevant to the Elvis story, please contact us at Elvis@calumeteditions.com.

Appendix A

The Smith Branch of Elvis Presley's Family Tree

This appendix illustrates the origin of Elvis Presley's direct ancestors beginning with the first Smith immigrant to the United States and ending with Elvis's mother, Gladys Love Smith. This appendix assumes the traditional view that Robert Lee Smith is the biological father of Gladys Presley, Elvis's mother.

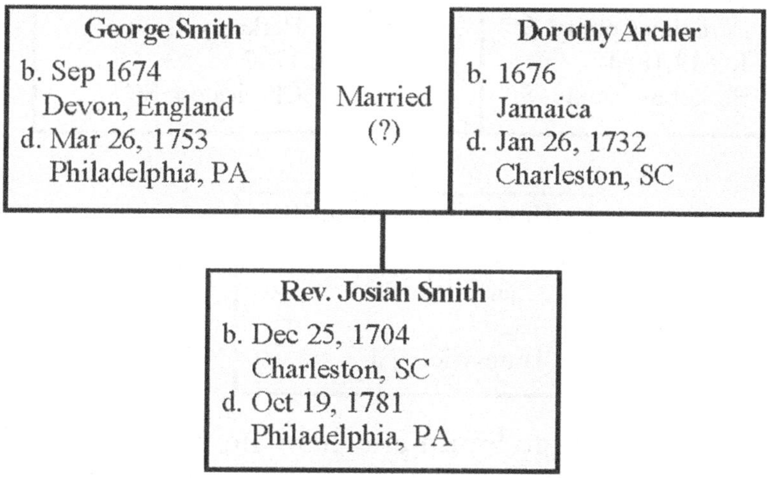

George Smith, born 1674 in England, was the first maternal ancestor of Elvis to emigrate to the United States of America. Jamaican-born Dorothy gave him eight children, including Elvis Presley's great-great-great-great-great-grandfather, Josiah Smith.

Rev. Josiah Smith		Edith Darrell
b. Dec 25, 1704 Charleston, SC d. Oct 19, 1781 Philadelphia, PA	Married 1730	b. October 1709 South Carolina d. Jun 10, 1759 South Carolina

George Elias Smith
b. Jan 3, 1733
Berkeley County, SC
d. Jun 12,1824
Berkeley County, SC

Josiah Smith and his wife Edith had eight children, including George Smith, named for Josiah's father. This second George Smith is Elvis Presley's great-great-great-great-grandfather.

George Elias Smith		Mary Alken
b. Jan 3, 1733 Berkeley County, SC d. Jun 12,1824 Berkeley County, SC	Married 1765	b. Oct 8, 1745 Berkeley, SC d. 1797 Charleston, SC

Thomas Alken Smith, Sr.
b. 1770
Charleston, SC
d. 1820
Brunswick, NC

The second George Smith and his wife, Mary Alken, had one child, Thomas Alken Smith. They honored Mary's maiden name by using it for their son's middle name. Thomas was Elvis Presley's great-great-great-grandfather.

Thomas Alken Smith, Sr.		Jane Jordan
b. 1770 Charleston, SC d. 1820 Brunswick, NC	Married 1765	b. 1722 Horry, SC d. 1820 Brunswick, NC

Thomas Alken Smith, Jr.
b. Feb 26, 1801 Horry, SC d. After 1870 Heard County, GA

Thomas and his wife Jane had five children including Thomas Alken Smith, Jr., who was Elvis Presley's great-grandfather. At least four of these children moved to Lee County, Mississippi. They all lived in the northeast part of the county. Thomas Newton Smith was the first one to make the move from Georgia to Lee County.

Thomas Alken Smith, Jr.		Elizabeth Heard Lock
b. Feb 26, 1801 Horry, SC d. After 1870 Heard County, GA	Married Dec 13, 1874	b. Jan 17,1800 South Carolina d. After 1847

Mileage Obadiah Smith
b. Feb 1843 South Carolina d. May 2, 1909 Lee County, MS

Thomas Jr., and Elizabeth had eight children, including Mileage Obadiah Smith, Elvis Presley's great-grandfather.

Many people who have studied the Presley genealogy have proposed that Obadiah's father was a man named John Smith from the Birmingham, Alabama region. This is clearly wrong because the census shows Obadiah and three brothers—Thomas Newton, Steven Samuel and John W.—living with Thomas Alken Smith, Jr.

Thomas was living in Edgeville, South Carolina, when his first wife, Jane Jordan, died in 1820. Elizabeth was his second wife. The census shows that in 1860 Thomas was living in Heard County, Georgia. Elizabeth's maiden name was Heard, so the county to which he and his family moved may have been named after her family.

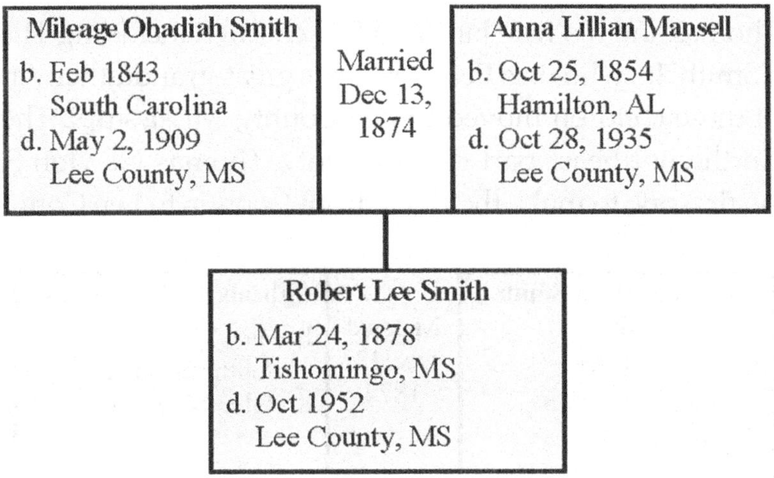

Obadiah and Anna had six children, including Robert Lee Smith, who was Elvis Presley's grandfather. Obadiah was not much of a provider. He served in the 4th Georgia Infantry during the American Civil War and may have suffered an injury. He happened to be single in 1874 when Anna was looking for a husband.

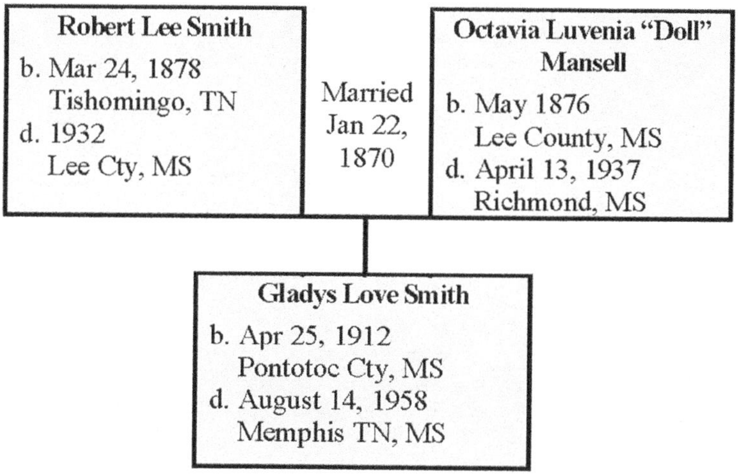

Robert Lee Smith, Elvis's grandfather, married "Doll" Mansell after she had divorced his brother, Hallie. He and "Doll" had nine Smith children including Gladys Love Smith, Elvis Presley's mother.

Appendix B

The Mansell Branch of Elvis Presley's Family Tree

This appendix illustrates the origination of Elvis Presley's direct ancestors from the family of the first Mansell immigrant to America to Elvis's mother, Gladys Love Smith. NOTE: in public records, the name Mansell is spelled in a variety of ways. To avoid confusion and simplify searches in our interactive family tree, with one exception, we have applied the "Mansell" spelling to the variants after ensuring they are part of this ancestral branch.

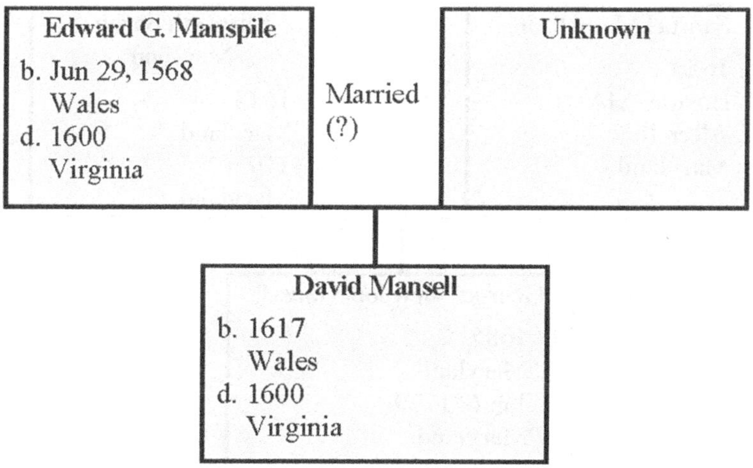

Edward Manspile, who was born in Glamorganshire, Wales, is the father of the first Mansell to immigrate to the United States. We can find no record of a marriage though Mary Mordent gave him one son, David Mansell.

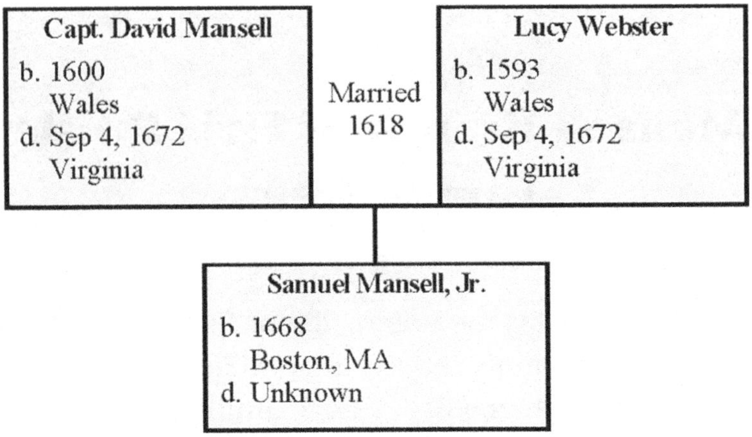

Capt. David Mansell is the first member of the Mansell branch of Elvis's family to immigrate to the United States. He came from Glamorganshire, Wales with his wife, Lucy. Their son, Samuel, Jr., continued the Mansell family line in the US.

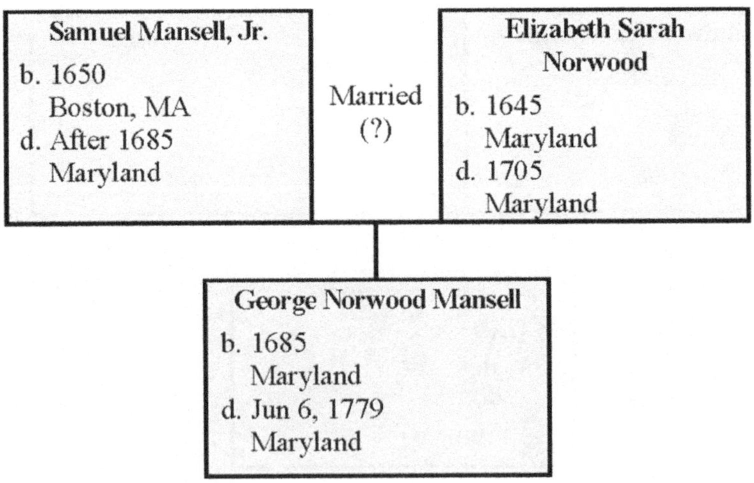

In these early years of the United States, public records for females were not regularly kept, so we know almost nothing about Samuel, Jr.'s wife, Elizabeth Norwood, except for her name. Samuel, Jr. and Elizabeth had one son, George Norwood Mansell.

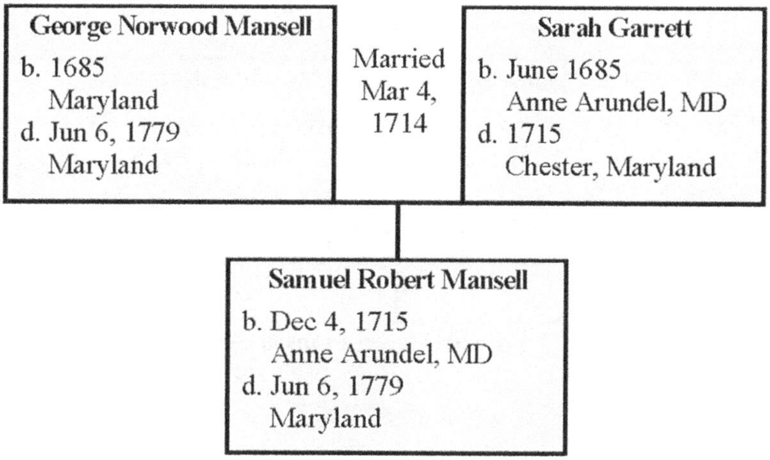

When he was twenty-nine, George Norwood Mansell married Sarah Garrett in 1714. Dates on the public records tell a tragic story. It appears that Sarah became pregnant, giving birth in December of 1715 to an only child, Samuel Mansell, the namesake of his grandfather and great-grandfather. Sarah died in 1715, either during childbirth or possibly as a result of complications following the birth of Samuel.

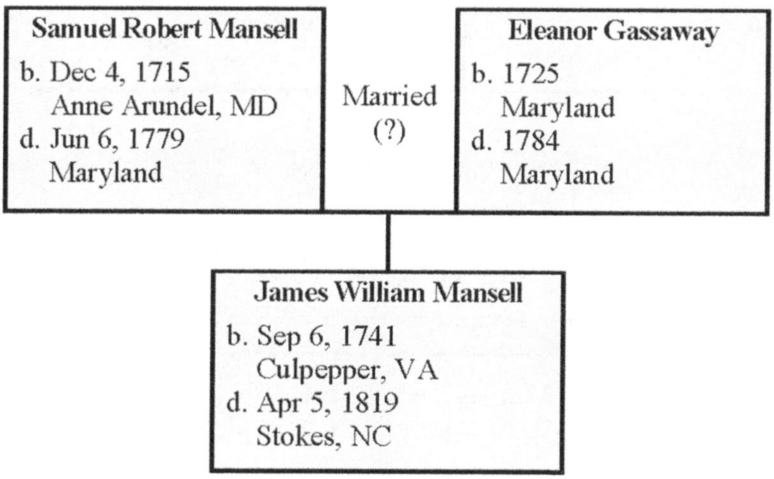

The eighteenth-century Samuel Robert Mansell was a soldier in the Revolutionary War. He married Eleanor Susannah Gassaway and had five offspring, including firstborn son Robert John Mansell, Elvis's great great-great-great-great-grandfather.

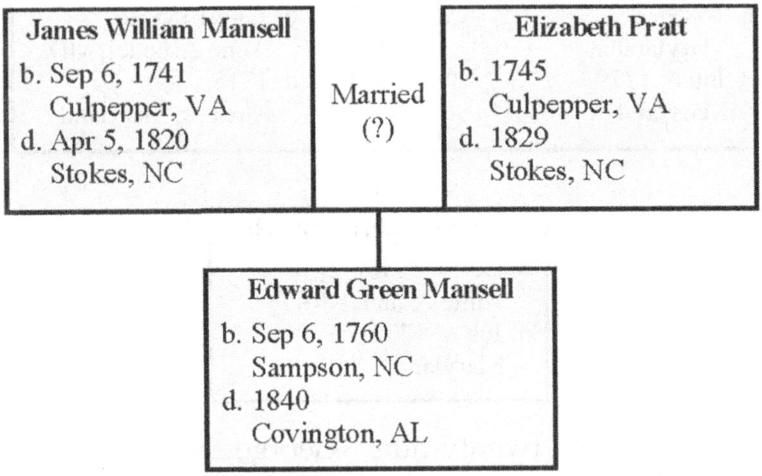

James William Mansell and Elizabeth Pratt had nine Mansell children, including Edward Green Mansell.

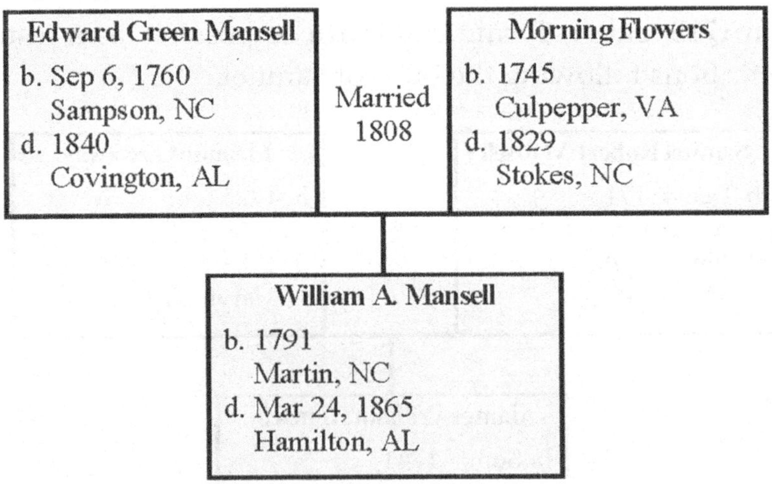

Edward Green Mansell was Elvis's great-great-great-great-grandfather. He was the first Mansell to move into Alabama. He had eleven children with Morning Flowers, including firstborn son William A. Mansell, who is Elvis's great-great-great-grandfather.

Because of the popular myth of "Morning White Dove," who was thought to be a Cherokee princess, some researchers have mistakenly identified Edward's wife, Morning Flowers, as a Native American. Several census reports, however, show her identified as a "free white woman." The name "Morning" was a popular name for white women in that era.

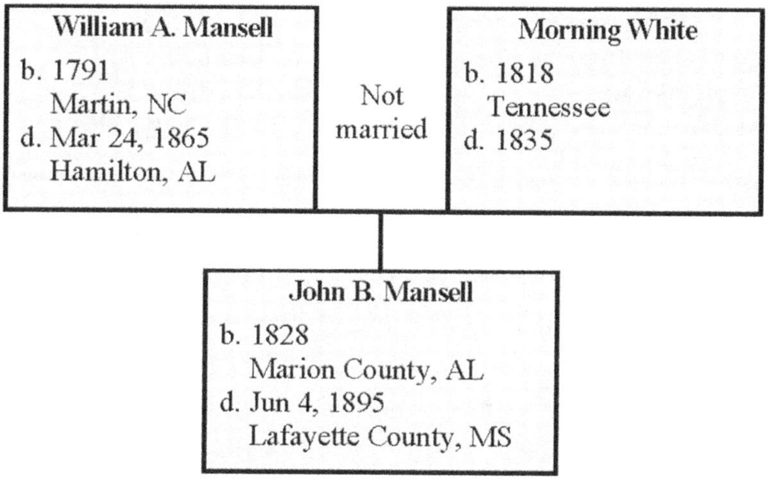

William A. Mansell, Elvis's great-great-great-grandfather, married Jane Ellender Egar in 1808 and had six children with her. While married, he settled down with another woman named Morning White, who was declared to be a Cherokee princess by ill-informed individuals who also transformed her name into "Morning White Dove." (Read more about this myth in "Chapter 8: A Cherokee Princess.") Morning White's father was Mr. White, first name unknown, and her mother was Maphy Arnett. Neither parent was American Indian.

William and Morning White had four children including Morning Dizenzie, who was also given the popular first name Morning to honor her mother, and John B. Mansell, who is directly connected to Elvis's bloodline.

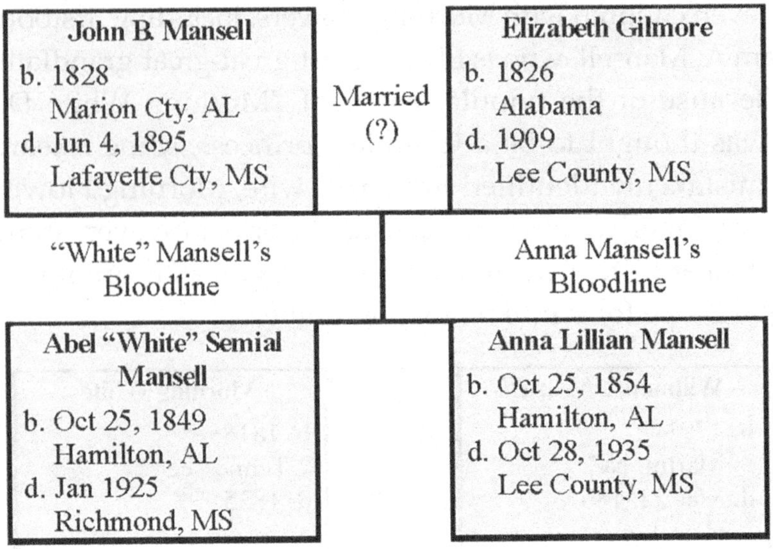

John B. Mansell, Elvis's great-great-grandfather, and Elizabeth "Betsy" Gilmore, his great-great-grandmother, had as many as ten children. Two of these children, "White" and Anna, directly contributed a unique bloodline to Elvis.

John and Betsy's son, "White" Mansell, became Elvis's great-grandfather (see "'White'" Mansell's Bloodline" in this appendix) by marrying Martha Tackett and fathering Octavia "Doll" Mansell, Elvis's grandmother.

John and Betsy's daughter, Anna Mansell, became Elvis's great-grandmother (see "Anna Mansell's Bloodline" in this appendix) by marrying Mileage Obadiah Smith and giving birth to their son Robert "Bob" Smith, Elvis's grandfather.

With these two children, the Mansell and Gilmore branches of Elvis's family tree independently enter the bloodline twice. In other words, Elvis had a great-grandfather and a great-grandmother who were brother and sister but not married to each other.

"White" Mansell's Bloodline

Abel White Semial Mansell b. Oct 25, 1849 Hamilton, AL d. Jan 1925 Richmond, MS	Married Jan 20, 1870	**Martha Tackett** b. 1800 Tennessee d. 1835

Octavia Luvenia "Doll" Mansell
b. May 1876
Lee County, MS
d. April 13, 1937
Richmond, MS

"White" Mansell is the son of Betsy Gilmore and is Elvis Presley's great-grandfather. He married Martha Tackett in 1870, and they produced eight children including Octavia Luvenia "Doll" Mansell, Elvis's grandmother.

Octavia Luvenia "Doll" Mansell b. May 1876 Lee County, MS d. April 13, 1937 Richmond, MS	Married Jan 22, 1870	**Robert Lee Smith** b. Mar 24, 1878 Tishomingo, TN d. 1932 Lee Cty, MS

Gladys Love Smith
b. Apr 25, 1912
Pontotoc Cty, MS
d. August 14, 1958
Memphis TN, MS

"Doll" Mansell's first husband was Hallie Jefferson Smith. They divorced and Doll married Hallie's brother, Robert Lee Smith. They had nine children, including Gladys Love Smith, Elvis's mother.

Anna Mansell's Bloodline

Anna Lillian Mansell		Mileage Obadiah Smith
b. Oct 25, 1854 Hamilton, AL d. Oct 28, 1935 Lee County, MS	Married Dec 13, 1874	b. Feb 1943 South Carolina d. After 1820 Heard County, GA

Robert Lee Smith
b. Mar 24, 1878
Tishomingo, MS
d. Oct 1952
Lee County, MS

Anna Mansell is the daughter of Betsy Gilmore and is Elvis Presley's great grandmother. She married Mileage Obadiah Smith in 1874 after bearing the child of Mr. Cowley, first name unknown. She and Obadiah produced six children including Robert Lee Smith, Elvis's grandfather.

Robert Lee Smith		Octavia Luvenia "Doll" Mansell
b. Mar 24, 1878 Tishomingo, TN d. 1932 Lee Cty, MS	Married Jan 22, 1870	b. May 1876 Lee County, MS d. April 13, 1937 Richmond, MS

Gladys Love Smith
b. Apr 25, 1912
Pontotoc Cty, MS
d. August 14, 1958
Memphis TN, MS

Robert Lee Smith, Elvis's grandfather, married "Doll" Mansell after she had divorced his brother, Hallie. He and "Doll" had nine Smith children including Gladys Love Smith.

Appendix C

The Gilmore Branch of Elvis Presley's Family Tree

This appendix illustrates the origination of Elvis Presley's direct ancestors from the family of the first Gilmore immigrant to America to Elvis's mother, Gladys Love Smith Presley. The Gilmore branch is one of the least known and studied bloodlines in Elvis's family tree, but arguably one of the most important because two individual Gilmore women independently entered the family tree as blood relatives.

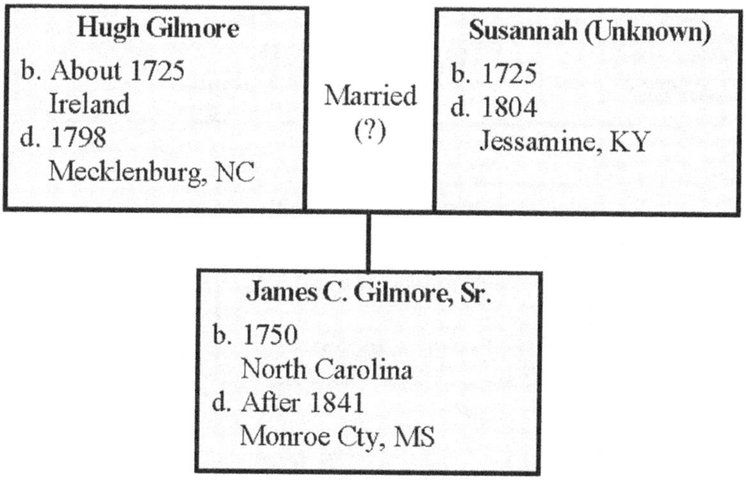

Hugh Gilmore is the first of Elvis's Gilmore bloodline to immigrate to the United States. He was born in Londonderry, Ulster, Ireland. He met Susannah in Ireland and brought her to America with him. He died at the age of seventy-three in North Carolina.

James C. Gilmore, Sr.
b. 1750
North Carolina
d. After 1841
Monroe Cty, MS

Married
(?)

Ann Wylie
b. 1751
d. 1875
Georgia

John Gilmore
b. Aug 2, 1776
North Carolina
d. After 1870
Fayette Cty, AL

John Gilmore
b. Aug 2, 1776
North Carolina
d. After 1870
Fayette Cty, AL

Married
(?)

Nancy Thomas
b. 1772
Wilkes, GA
d. 1826
Alabama

John Joyner Gilmore
b. Dec 17, 1795
Marion Cty, AL
d. Jun 4, 1895
Lafayette Cty, MS

John Gilmore and Nancy are Elvis's great great-great-great grandparents.

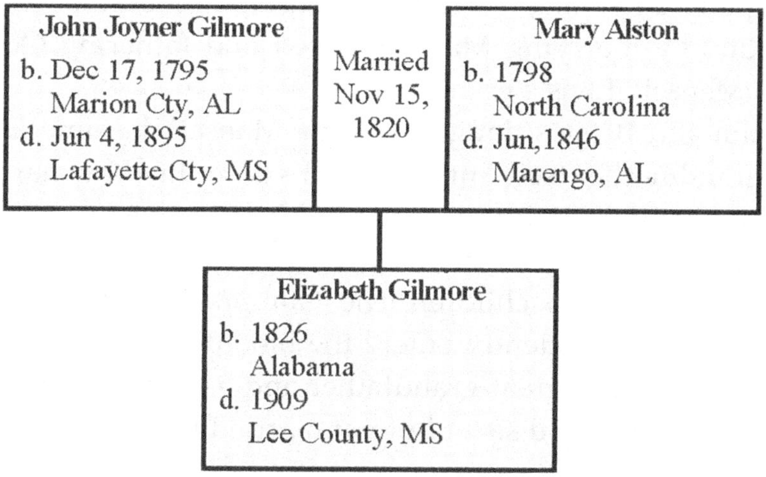

John Joyner Gilmore and Mary Alston had twelve children together between 1819 and 1846. They are Elvis's great-great-great-grandparents.

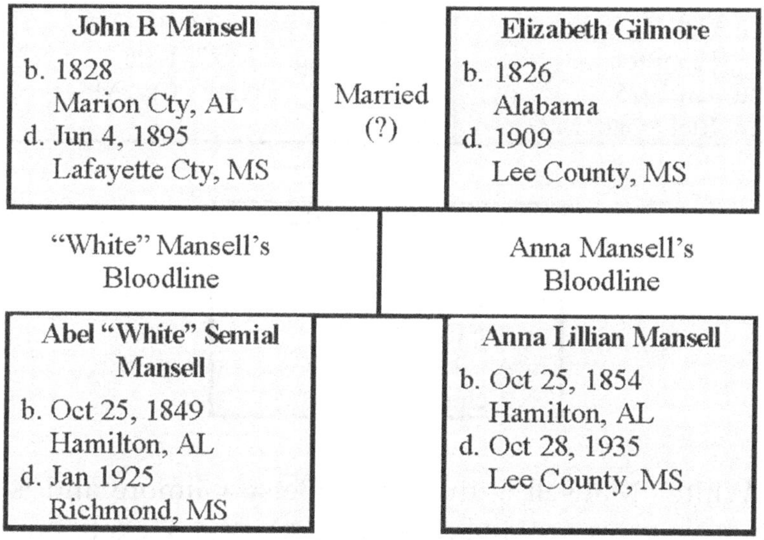

John B. Mansell, Elvis's great-great-grandfather, and Elizabeth "Betsy" Gilmore, his great-great-grandmother, had as many as ten children. Two of these children, "White" and Anna, directly contributed a unique bloodline to Elvis.

John and Betsy's son, "White" Mansell, became Elvis's

great-grandfather (see "'White'" Mansell's Bloodline" in this appendix) by marrying Martha Tackett and fathering Octavia "Doll" Mansell, Elvis's grandmother.

John and Betsy's daughter, Anna Mansell, became Elvis's great-grandmother (see Anna Mansell's Bloodline) by marrying Mileage Obadiah Smith and giving birth to their son Robert "Bob" Smith, Elvis's grandfather.

With these two children, the Gilmore branch of Elvis's family tree independently enters the bloodline twice. In other words, Elvis had a great-grandfather and a great-grandmother who were brother and sister but not married to each other.

"White" Mansell's Bloodline

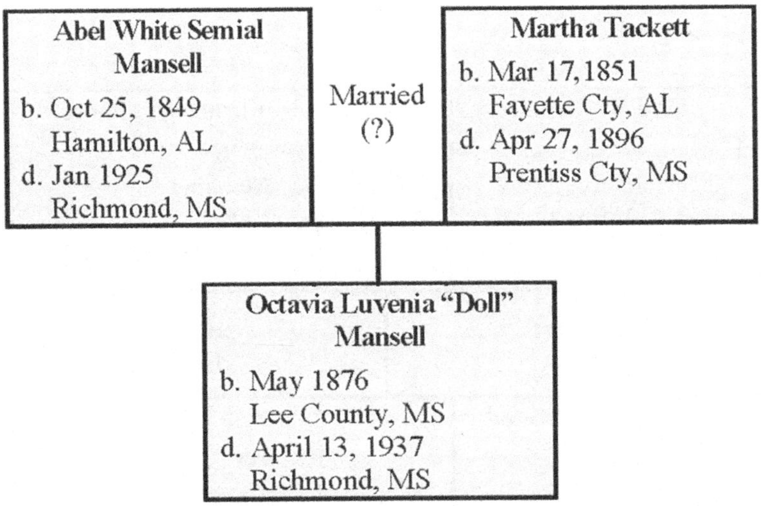

"White" Mansell is the son of Betsy Gilmore and is Elvis Presley's great-grandfather. He and Martha Tackett produced eight children including Octavia Luvenia "Doll" Mansell, Elvis's grandmother. Martha was buried at Carolina Cemetery next to the Carolina United Methodist Church in Booneville, Mississippi (GPS location 34.68173, -88.60520).

Octavia Luvenia "Doll" Mansell		Robert Lee Smith
b. May 1876 Lee County, MS d. April 13, 1937 Richmond, MS	Married Jan 22, 1870	b. Mar 24, 1878 Tishomingo, TN d. 1932 Lee Cty, MS

Gladys Love Smith
b. Apr 25, 1912 Pontotoc Cty, MS d. August 14, 1958 Memphis TN, MS

"Doll" Mansell's first husband was Hallie Jefferson Smith. They divorced and Doll married Hallie's brother, Robert Lee Smith. They had nine children, including Gladys Love Smith, Elvis's mother.

Anna Lillian Mansell		Mileage Obadiah Smith
b. Oct 25, 1854 Hamilton, AL d. Oct 28, 1935 Lee County, MS	Married Dec 13, 1874	b. Feb 1943 South Carolina d. After 1820 Heard County, GA

Robert Lee Smith
b. Mar 24, 1878 Tishomingo, MS d. Oct 1952 Lee County, MS

Anna Mansell is the daughter of Betsy Gilmore and is Elvis Presley's great-grandmother. She married Mileage Obadiah Smith in 1874 after bearing the child of Mr. Cowley, first name unavailable. She and Obadiah produced six children including Robert Lee Smith, Elvis's grandfather.

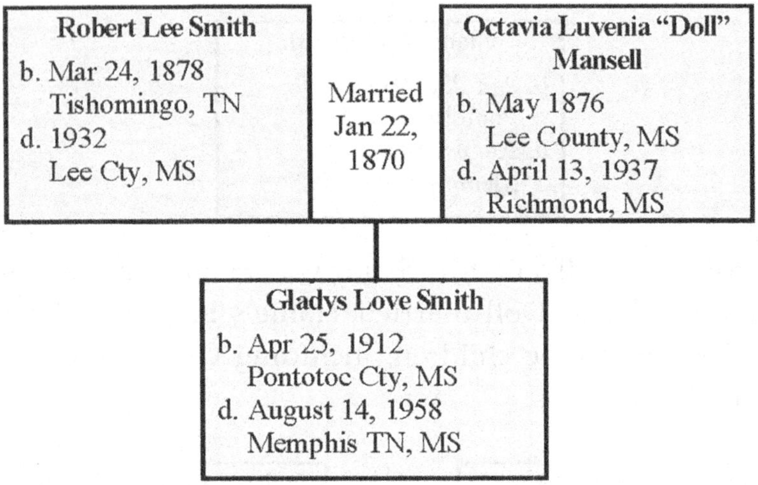

Robert Lee Smith married "Doll" Mansell after she had divorced his brother, Hallie. Robert and "Doll" had nine Smith children including Gladys Love Smith, Elvis Presley's mother.

Appendix D

The Hood Branch of Elvis Presley's Family Tree

This appendix illustrates the origination of Elvis Presley's direct ancestors from the family of the first Hood immigrant to America to Elvis's mother, Gladys Love Smith.

Jasper Hood
b. 1670
Holland
d. January 1740

Married
Jun 7,
1696

Catherina Andries
b. 1673
d. 1713
France

Jan Hood
b. Feb 12, 1699
New York
d. Feb 26, 1742

Jasper Hood was the first of the Hood branch to immigrate to America. He and his wife, Catherina Andries, had one child, Jan Hood, who was Elvis's great-great-great-great-great-great-grandfather.

Jan Hood
b. Feb 12, 1699
New York
d. Feb 26, 1742
Virginia

Married
(?)

Rachel Van Bunschoten
b. Feb 22, 1695
d. Aug 17, 1780

Theunis (Tunis) Hood
b. Feb 22, 1719
Kingston, NY
d. May 12, 1797
Mecklenburg Cty, NC

Jan Hood and Rachel Van Bunschoten had ten children including Theunis (Tunis) Hood, Elvis's great-great-great-great-great-grandfather. It is not known where Jan Hood was born, but his father was originally from Holland.

Theunis (Tunis) Hood
b. Feb 22, 1719
Kingston, NY
d. May 12, 1797
North Carolina

Married
(?)

Elizabeth Harrison
b. Aug 18, 1720
Sussex, DE
d. 1790
North Carolina

John Hood
b. Nov 11, 1745
Augusta Cty, VA
d. 1835
Ashville, AL

Theunis Hood and Elizabeth Harrison had nine children including John Hood, Elvis's great-great-great-great-grandfather. Theunis became one of the largest landowners and slaveholders in Mecklenburg County, North Carolina.

John Hood		**Sarah (Sallie) Austin**
b. Nov 11, 1745 Augusta Cty, VA d. 1835 Ashville, AL	Married (?)	b. Sep 3, 1766 North Carolina d. Jun 1, 1860 St. Clair, AL

James Hood
b. 1782 South Carolina d. 1849 St. Clair, AL

John Hood and Sarah Austin had seven children, all of them sons including James Hood, Elvis's great-great-great-grandfather.

James Hood		**Margaret Summerville**
b. 1782 North Carolina d. 1845 St. Clair, AL	Married (?)	b. 1789 Georgia d. After 1850

Joshua H. Hood
b. Sep 13, 1831 St. Clair, AL d. Apr 17, 1885 Itawamba Cty, MS

James Hood and Margaret Summerville had four children, including lastborn Joshua Harrison Hood, Elvis's great-great-grandfather.

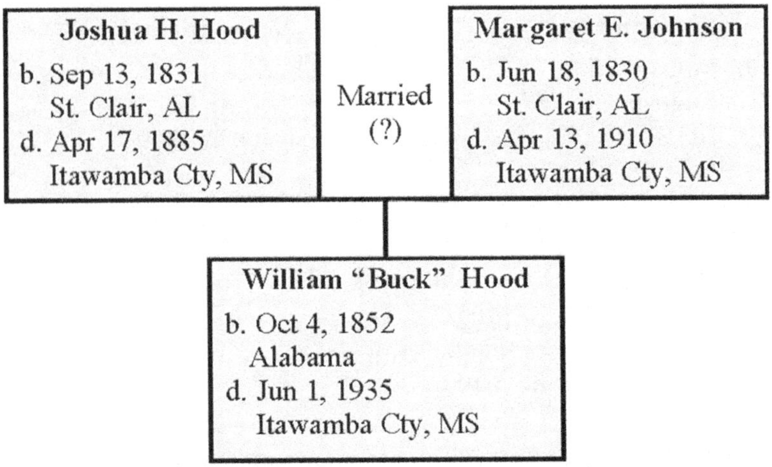

Joshua Hood and Margaret Johnson had twelve children, including William "Buck" Hood, Elvis's great-grandfather. Originally, "Buck" Hood had no tombstone for his grave at Mount Pleasant Cemetery in Itawamba County, Mississippi. Later, a family member made a crude marker out of concrete on which his name was inscribed.

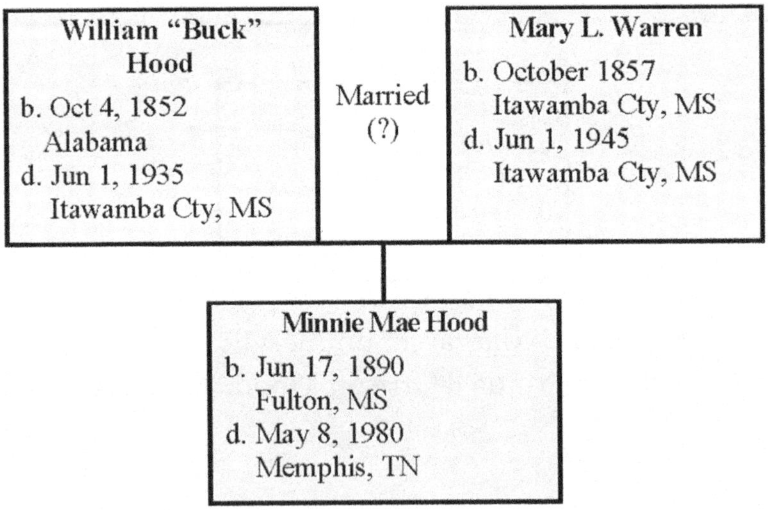

William "Buck" Hood and Mary Warren had seven children, including Minnie Mae, who was Elvis's grandmother.

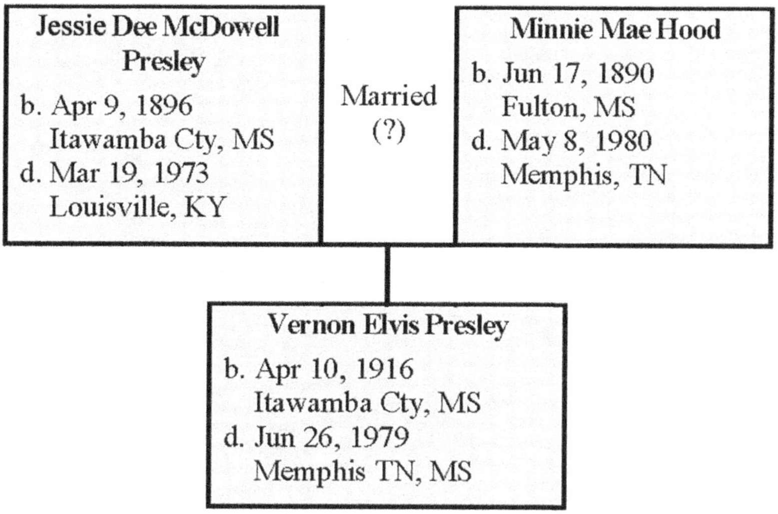

Jessie Dee McDowell Presley and Minnie Mae Hood had two sons and three daughters, including Vernon Elvis Presley, Elvis's father.

Appendix E

The Presley Branch of Elvis Presley's Family Tree

This appendix illustrates the origin of Elvis Presley's direct ancestors beginning with the first Presley immigrant to the United States and ending with Elvis's father, Vernon Elvis Presley. This appendix assumes the traditional view that Vernon Presley is the biological father of Elvis Presley.

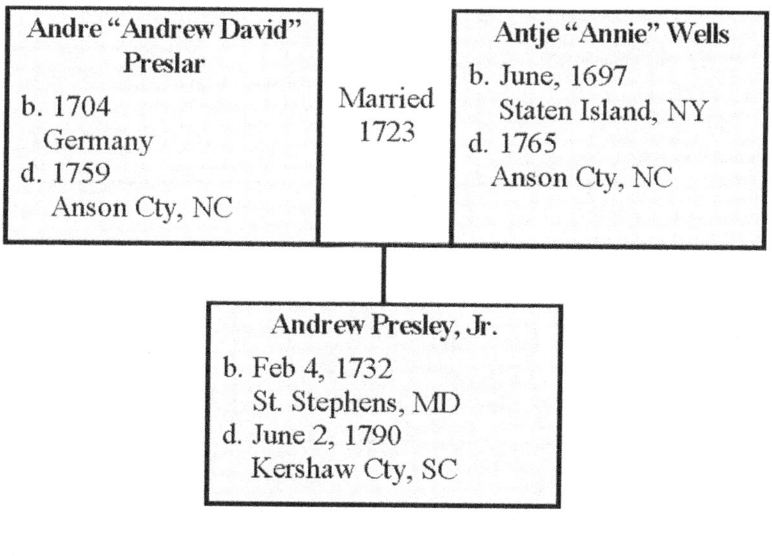

Andre "Andrew David" Preslar was the first Presley ancestor to immigrate to America. He arrived in 1754, changed his last name to Presley and married Antje "Annie" Wells. They had five children including Andrew Presley, Jr.

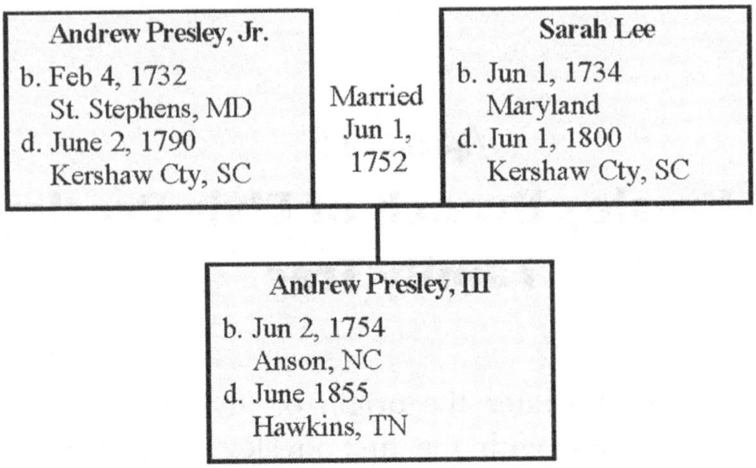

Andrew Presley, Jr. and his wife Sarah Lee had seven children including Andrew Presley, III.

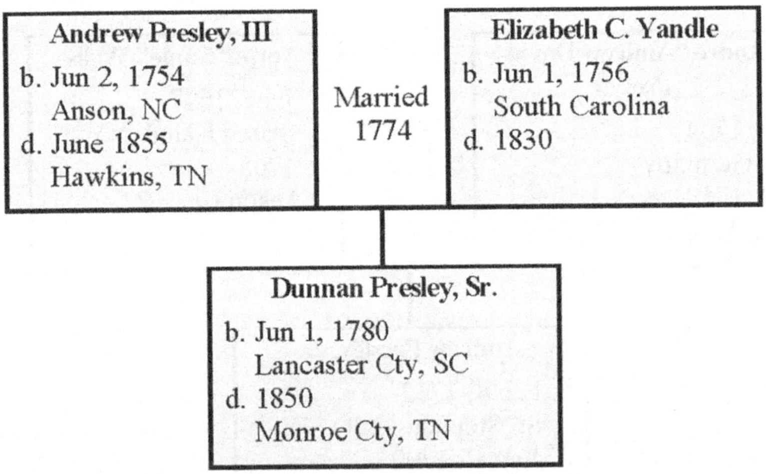

Andrew Presley, III and his wife Elizabeth had four children including Dunnan Presley, Sr., Elvis's great-great-great-grandfather.

Dunnan Presley, Sr.		**Mary C. Warren**
b. Jun 1, 1780 Lancaster Cty, SC d. 1850 Monroe Cty, TN	Married 1808	b. Jun 1, 1782 South Carolina d. Jun 1, 1860 Itawamba Cty, MS

Dunnan Presley, Jr.
b. Jul 1, 1827 Madisonville, TN d. Mar 10, 1900 Washburn, MO

Dunnan Presley, Sr. was married twice and had four children with his first wife. His second wife, Mary C. Warren, gave him six children, including Dunnan Presley, Jr., Elvis's great-great-grandfather.

Dunnan Presley, Jr.		**Martha Jane Wesson**
b. Jul 1, 1827 Madisonville, TN d. Mar 10, 1900 Washburn, MO	Married (?)	b. 1840 Rutherford, NC d. 1868 Itawamba Cty, MS

Rosella Elizabeth Presley
b. Feb 16, 1863 Itawamba Cty, MS d. Jul 30, 1924 Itawamba Cty, MS

Dunnan Presley Jr., was married four times, sometimes without divorcing a previous wife. He had a total of eleven children. His second wife, Martha Jane Wesson, had six children with Dunnan including Rosella Elizabeth Presley, Elvis's great-grandmother.

John Henry Wallace
b. Aug 1, 1853
Itawamba Cty, MS
d. Nov 17, 1935
Itawamba Cty, MS

Not married

Rosella Elizabeth Presley
b. Feb 16, 1863
Itawamba Cty, MS
d. Jul 30, 1924
Itawamba Cty, MS

Jessie Dee McDowell Presley
b. Apr 9, 1896
Itawamba Cty, MS
d. Mar 19, 1973
Louisville, KY

Rosella Presley, who was never married, had nine children with at least five men. All of her children took their mother's last name because they did not know the identify of their fathers. Rosella's fifth child, Jessie Dee was Elvis's grandfather.

Jessie Dee McDowell Presley
b. Apr 9, 1896
Itawamba Cty, MS
d. Mar 19, 1973
Louisville, KY

Married (?)

Minnie Mae Hood
b. Jun 17, 1890
Fulton, MS
d. May 8, 1980
Memphis, TN

Vernon Elvis Presley
b. Apr 10, 1916
Itawamba Cty, MS
d. Jun 26, 1979
Memphis TN, MS

Jessie Dee McDowell Presley and Minnie Mae Hood had two sons and three daughters, including Vernon Elvis Presley, Elvis's father.

Appendix F

The Wallace Branch of Elvis Presley's Family Tree

This appendix illustrates the origin of Elvis Presley's direct ancestors beginning with the first Wallace immigrant to the United States and ending with Elvis's father, Vernon Elvis Presley. In the Wallace branch, the repetitive use of the given names "Hugh" and "John" have confused many genealogists. These tables should help clear up the individuality of these ancestors.

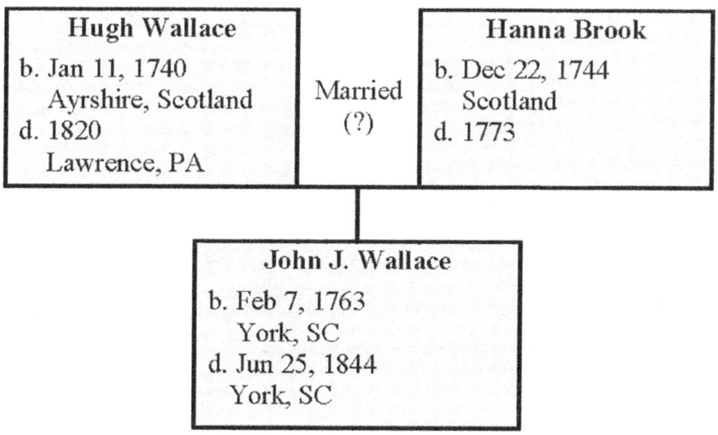

Hugh Wallace, from Scotland, was the first member of the Wallace branch to immigrate to America. With his Scottish wife, Hannah Brook, he had ten children in his new homeland, including John J. Wallace, Elvis's great-great-great-great-great-grandfather.

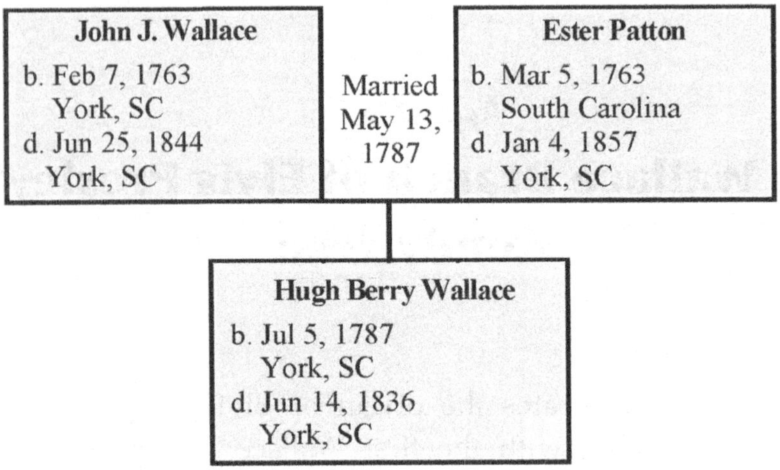

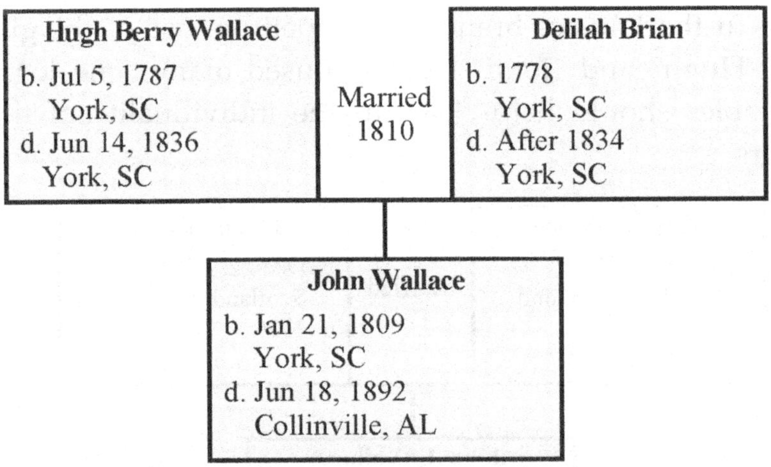

Hugh Berry Wallace and Delilah Brian had five children including John Wallace, Elvis's great-great-great-grandfather.

John Wallace		**Malinda Mattox**
b. Jan 21, 1809 York, SC d. Jun 18, 1892 Collinville, AL	Married Dec 19 1827	b. 1808 Pulaski, TN d. March 1880 Itawamba Cty, MS

Hugh (Henry) Wallace
b. December 1830
Lincoln Cty, TN
d. 1909
Itawamba Cty, MS

John Wallace (not to be confused with John Henry Wallace, his grandson) was one of the first settlers of Itawamba County, Mississippi. At some point he also set up a residence in DeKalb County, Alabama. It appears that he had a family in Mississippi, with ten children by Malinda Mattox, and another family at the same time in Alabama with thirteen children by Nancy Templeton. He and Malinda were the parents of Hugh Wallace, Elvis's great-great-grandfather.

Hugh (Henry) Wallace		**Lydia Gideon**
b. December 1830 Lincoln Cty, TN d. 1909 Itawamba Cty, MS	Married Oct 6, 1852	b. 1833 Itawamba Cty, MS d. July 1860 Itawamba Cty, MS

John Henry Wallace
b. Aug 1, 1853
Itawamba Cty, MS
d. Nov 17, 1935
Itawamba Cty, MS

Hugh (Henry) Wallace was married three times. Lydia Gideon was his second wife. He and Lidya had four children, including John Henry Wallace, Elvis's great-grandfather.

John Henry Wallace		Rosella Elizabeth Presley
b. Aug 1, 1853 Itawamba Cty, MS d. Nov 17, 1935 Itawamba Cty, MS	Not married	b. Feb 16, 1863 Itawamba Cty, MS d. Jul 30, 1924 Itawamba Cty, MS

Jessie Dee McDowell Presley
b. Apr 9, 1896
Itawamba Cty, MS
d. Mar 19, 1973
Louisville, KY

John Henry Wallace fathered twelve children with five different women, two of whom were his wives. He had a longstanding affair with Rosella Presley, with whom he fathered one son, Jessie Dee McDowell Presley, Elvis's grandfather.

Jessie Dee McDowell Presley		Minnie Mae Hood
b. Apr 9, 1896 Itawamba Cty, MS d. Mar 19, 1973 Louisville, KY	Married (?)	b. Jun 17, 1890 Fulton, MS d. May 8, 1980 Memphis, TN

Vernon Elvis Presley
b. Apr 10, 1916
Itawamba Cty, MS
d. Jun 26, 1979
Memphis TN, MS

Jessie Dee McDowell Presley and Minnie Mae Hood had two sons and three daughters, including Vernon Elvis Presley, Elvis's father.

Appendix G

The Tackett Branch of Elvis Presley's Family Tree

This appendix illustrates the origin of Elvis Presley's direct ancestors beginning with the first Tackett immigrant to the United States and ending with Elvis's mother, Gladys Love Smith Presley. He and his wife, Mary, had two sons of which Phillip Moses was the first. The Tackett bloodline is widely overlooked in Elvis's genealogy, and sloppy research has added confusion as explained earlier. The bloodline below is confirmed by extensive study and DNA findings.

Lewis Tackett
b. Mar 12, 1676
France
d. 1743
Prince William, VA

Married
1709

Mary Sarah Spiller
b.1674
England
d.1748
England

John Moses Tackett
b. 1712
Cedar Run, VA
d. Aug 27, 1775
Rowan City, NC

Lewis Tackett, originally from France, was the first Tackett to emigrate to America. He was Elvis's great great-great-great-great-great-grandfather. He had three sons with his wife Mary, including his second child, John Moses.

John Moses Tackett		**Priscilla Rosanna Rose**
b. 1712 Cedar Run, VA d. Aug 27, 1775 Rowan City, NC	Married 1737	b. 1715 Virginia d. 1812 Virginia

Phillip Moses Tackett
b. 1745
Cedar Run, VA
d. Jan 1, 1830
Shelby Valley, KY

John Moses Tackett was Elvis's great-great-great-great-great-grandfather. He had three sons with his wife Mary, including his second child, Phillip Moses.

Phillip Moses Tackett		**Sarah Rice**
b. 1745 Cedar Run, VA d. Jan 1, 1830 Shelby Valley, KY	Married (?)	b. 1745 Virginia d. 1850 Pike, KY

Lancaster H. Tackett
b. 1780
Prince Wm. Cty, VA
d. Jul 9, 1848
Fayette Cty, AL

Phillip Moses Tackett was Elvis's great-great-great-great-grandfather. He and his wife, Sarah, had only one son, Lancaster.

Lancaster H. Tackett		Ellender Burgess Hampton
b. 1780 Prince Wm. Cty, VA d. Jul 9, 1848 Fayette Cty, AL	Married Apr 16, 1855	b. 1782 North Carolina d. Apr 16, 1855 Pontotoc Cty, MS

Abner Hampton Tackett
b. Feb 6, 1803
Knox Cty, KY
d. Jun 20, 1889
Lee Cty, MS

Lancaster Tackett was Elvis's great-great-great-grandfather. By 1830, he had moved to Fayette County, Alabama. He would have twelve children with his wife, Ellender, including his second child, Abner Hampton.

Abner Hampton Tackett		Celia Ann Butler
b. Feb 6, 1803 Knox Cty, KY d. Jun 20, 1889 Lee Cty, MS	Married 1827	b. Dec 12, 1809 North Carolina d. Feb 28, 1873 Franklin Cty, AL

Martha Tackett
b. Mar 17, 1851
Fayette Cty, AL
d. Apr 27, 1896
Prentiss Cty, MS

Abner Tackett is Elvis's great-great-grandfather. His name was misspelled on the 1850 census as Abner Sackett, which made him difficult to find. After fathering eleven children with his wife, he had a child with another woman, Elizabeth Willett, in 1851. Two months after Elizabeth gave birth, Abner's wife also gave birth to a daughter, Martha Sue Tackett, who would become Elvis's great-grandmother.

Celia also gave Abner two more children in 1854. By 1860, eight of Abner's fourteen children with these two women were still living with him. By 1870, however, Celia was still alive but no longer living with Abner, who went on to have an additional seven children with a woman named Sarah Willett. In 1873, after having four children with her, Abner finally married Sarah. In total, Abner was the father of twenty-one children with three women.

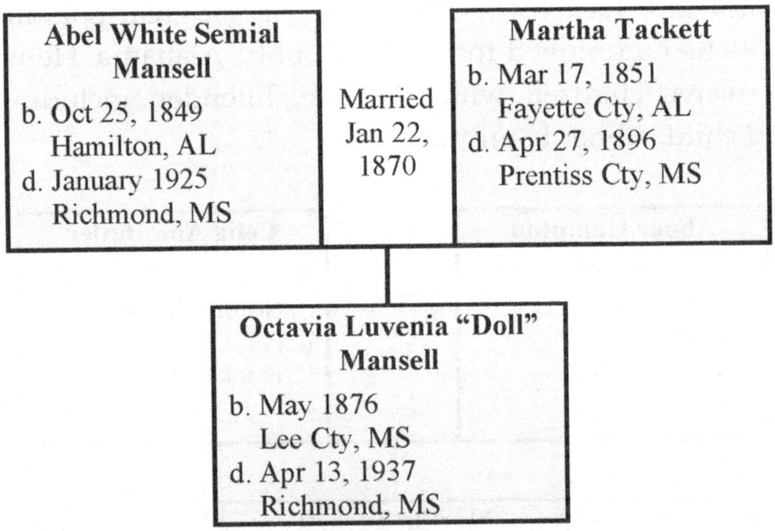

Martha Tackett, Elvis's great-grandmother, married "White" Mansell in 1870, and they produced eight children including Octavia Luvenia "Doll" Mansell.

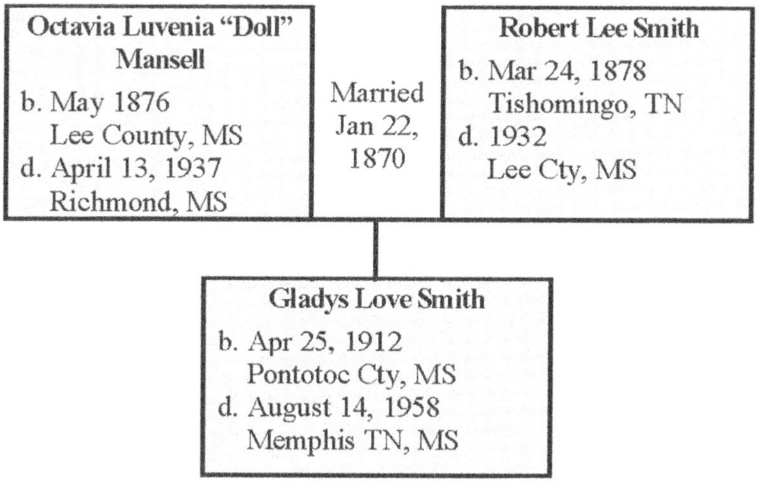

"Doll" Mansell's first husband was Hallie Jefferson Smith. They divorced, and Doll married Hallie's brother, Robert Lee Smith. They had nine children, including Gladys Love Smith, Elvis's mother.

Appendix H

Table of GPS Locations

CEMETERIES	GPS LOCATION
Abbeville Cemetery	34.51671, -89.50227
• *John B. Mansell*	
Andrews Chapel Cemetery	34.22678, -88.56241
• *Effie Smith*	
• *Martha Jane Presley*	
• *Thomas Eleanach Canan Presley*	
• *White Mansell*	
Carolina Methodist Church Cemetery	34.68173, -88.60520
• *Martha (Tackett) Mansell*	
Crosslawn Cemetery	35.26734, -90.79135
• *Nashval Lorene Presley*	
Fairview Cemetery	34.45013, -88.17990
• *Doshie Presley*	
Forest Hill Home & Memorial Park – Midtown, Memphis	35.09920, -90.01732

• *Clettes (Smith) Presley*	
• *Delta Mae Presley*	
• *Johney Lee Smith*	
• *Lillian Panther Smith*	
• *Linnie Lavelle Smith*	
• *Tracy Smith*	
• *Travis Smith*	
• *Vester Presley*	
Graceland Memorial Garden	35.04531, -90.02297
• *Gladys Love (Smith) Presley*	
• *Vernon Presley*	
Hopewell Cemetery	34.33055, -88.21699
• *William Marion Steele*	
Louisville Memorial Gardens	38.18876, -85.81876
• *Jessie Dee McDowell Presley*	
Mt. Pleasant Cemetery	34.22178, -88.21109
• *Mack Presley*	
• *Robbie Presley*	
New Spring Hill Cemetery	34.33639, -88.60719
• *Retha Smith*	
• *Robert Lee "Bob" Smith*	
• *Octavia "Doll" (Mansell) Smith*	
Priceville Cemetery	34.26684, -88.65732
• *Noah Persell Presley*	
Ridge Cemetery	34.45013, -88.17990
• *Rosella Elizabeth Presley*	
• *Joseph Warren Presley*	

Roselawn Cemetery, Tallahassee, FL	30.48662, -84.26570
• *Gladys Erlene Presley*	
OTHER LOCATIONS	
Elvis's last home in Tupelo (site only)	34.27418, -88.71005
Frank Richards' home at 509 Maple Street	34.25218, -88.70591
James Alford Love's homesite	34.33427, -88.55188
Jessie Dee's home in Fulton, MS (site)	34.34881, -88.34749
Elvis Presley birth house (replica)	34.25998, -88.68006
Rosella's cabin on White Springs Road (site)	34.17591, -88.36828
Tupelo Garment Factory	34.25376, -88.70677
Tupelo Public Library (original location)	34.25430, -88.70431
Vernon Presley's birthplace	34.34881, -88.34749
Verona Town Hall	34.19399, -88.71619

Appendix I

Petition Signatories

Gladys Love Presley and Zora Riley, in 1938 Gladys's best friend and trusted keeper of secrets, collected the signatures for a petition requesting Vernon Presley's early release from Parchman Prison. Over a hundred individuals lent their names to the petition, and they are listed below in the order of signing. Many signatures were difficult to read, so we are providing typed versions below. All have been meticulously cross-checked with Tupelo city records.

Oddly, none of Gladys Smith's family signed the petition. There were no Presley signatures except for Jessie Dee and Minnie Mae, Vernon's parents, which appear at the very end. The first dozen signatures were mainly friends and relatives of Zora Riley. This reveals yet another provocative mystery we have not yet solved—why did the Smith and Presley families refuse to support Vernon's petition?

	SIGNATORY	HOME LOCATION
1	Claude Buse	East Tupelo
2	Luna Buse	East Tupelo
3	Lawrence D. Riley	East Tupelo
4	Zora Riley	East Tupelo
5	Paul D. Clark	Main St.
6	Mrs. Daisy Mears	East Tupelo
7	Mr. Norman Mears	East Tupelo

8	Ola Clark	Main St.
9	Rebecca Wilson	N. Church St.
10	Russell Wilson	N. Church St.
11	[Illegible] Brown	[Unknown]
12	[Illegible] Brown	[Unknown]
13	Mrs. Beatrice Sanderson	East Tupelo
14	Dew Drop Hutchins	East Tupelo
15	Mrs. James Hutchins	East Tupelo
16	Mrs. James McGill	East Tupelo
17	Mrs. J. I. Hutchins	East Tupelo
18	Mrs. Lillie Hand	East Tupelo
19	Rufus Hand	East Tupelo
20	Grady Hand	East Tupelo
21	Classie Hand	East Tupelo
22	Mrs. Nonie Hand	East Tupelo
23	Mr. John Hand	East Tupelo
24	Mrs. Clara Stewart	East Tupelo
25	Mrs. Della Martin	East Tupelo
26	Tressie Miller	East Tupelo
27	Delmath Miller	East Tupelo
28	Mrs. Fay Harris	East Tupelo
29	Mr. [Illegible] Harris	East Tupelo
30	Myrtle Harris	East Tupelo
31	[Illegible]	[Unknown]
32	Miss Dora Harris	East Tupelo
33	James V. Harris	East Tupelo
34	Mrs. Myrtle Holloway	[Unknown]
35	Mr. Elmo Holloway	[Unknown]
36	Mrs. Novie Clark	South Tupelo
37	Mr. Oliver Clark	South Tupelo

38	Mrs. Orbie McCollum	West Tupelo
39	Mr. Orbie McCollum	West Tupelo
40	Mr. Dink Allred	East Tupelo
41	Mrs. Dora Allred	East Tupelo
42	Luther L. Roberson	East Tupelo
43	Mrs. Addie Roberson	East Tupelo
44	Albert W. Roberson	East Tupelo
45	Lee (Illegible] Roberson	East Tupelo
46	Mrs. J. T. McCoy	East Tupelo
47	W. R. Mitchell	East Tupelo
48	Clark Daugherty	Tupelo
49	W. C. Payne	East Tupelo
50	Condry V. Harris	East Tupelo
51	Lillian Griffin	East Tupelo
52	Mrs. R. L. Pannell	West Tupelo
53	R. L. Pannell	West Tupelo
54	M. S. Roland	Blair St.
55	W. E. Martin	Route 2
56	J. D. Christian	East Tupelo
57	Etta Bailey	East Tupelo
58	[Illegible]	[Unknown]
59	John W. Repult	East Tupelo
60	W. P. Anthony	Blair St.
61	[Illegible]	[Unknown]
62	[Illegible]	[Unknown]
63	[Illegible]	[Unknown]
64	D. D. Smith	Star Rt.
65	M. L. Bedford	South Tupelo
66	H. L. Whitten	South Tupelo
67	H. M. Murphy	Itawamba County

68	G. C. Grissom	South Tupelo
69	[Illegible]	[Unknown]
70	Gilbert McCollum	East Tupelo
71	James Oscar Bishop	South Tupelo
72	George McCollum	East Tupelo
73	Chois Fox	East Tupelo
79	Andrew Brookman	[Unknown]
80	William Griffin	East Tupelo
81	Mrs. J. C. Watkins	East Tupelo
82	Mrs. C. V. Woods	East Tupelo
83	Rev. Floyd H. Coleman	East Tupelo
84	Hazel Kennedy	East Tupelo
85	Mrs. F. H. Coleman	East Tupelo
86	Mattie Sue Kennedy	East Tupelo
87	Aaron S. Kennedy	East Tupelo
88	Sally Ballard	West Tupelo
89	Pirnie Lovelady	East Tupelo
90	Mrs. A. E. Montgomery	East Tupelo
91	Novel Taylor	[Unknown]
92	Lillian Griffin	East Tupelo
93	Ava Funderbork	East Tupelo
94	A. R. O'Neal	East Tupelo
95	Lottie O'Neal	East Tupelo
96	James Bishop	East Tupelo
97	Hazel Bishop	East Tupelo
98	Thomas J. Hatley	East Tupelo
99	Anna Mae Hatley	East Tupelo
100	J. D. Presley	East Tupelo
101	Minnie Mae Presley	East Tupelo
102	Gladys Presley	East Tupelo

Appendix J
Aerial Photo

On the next page is an aerial photo of Tupelo taken around the time Elvis had come back to his hometown for a triumphant Homecoming concert. In this photo, you can see the following sites:

1. Tupelo Garment Factory where Gladys worked.
2. Tupelo Cotton Mill.
3. The home on Maple St. where Gladys and Elvis lived when he entered the first grade.
4. The Ledyard School where Elvis attended the first grade.
5. Cotton compressors.
6. The Fairgrounds where Elvis performed his Homecoming concert.
7. The railroad depot, which sits at the intersection of two tracks..
8. The original Tupelo Library where Elvis got his library card.
9. A Black neighborhood generally referred to as Front Street. This is distinctly different from Shake Rag or The Hill, two other Black districts. Front Street was where the Panama Hotel was located, the place where Black musicians and singers stayed when visiting Tupelo.

1
2
Maple St.
3
4
Spring St.

8
6
9
7
5

Index

N

O

R

S

Y

Acknowledgments

Without Julian Riley, this book would not exist. If not for his persistence, remarkable memory, attention to detail and good fortune to be born and raised in Tupelo, much of this information would have remained hidden or uncorrected in the historical record. But because he called me one day to complain about several errors in my first Elvis book, *Letters from Elvis,* we discovered an opportunity to fulfill a mutual dream together.

My partner at Calumet Editions, Ian Graham Leask, provided his superb editing, which made this book better that it would have been, but more importantly, gave me the support and courage to plunge into this "mess of myth" and try to make some sense of it.

I must also thank Rick Polad, for his excellent copyediting and wise counsel, and Beth Williams, for her marvelous indexing skills and for catching those final pesky mistakes before publication. Without Joshua Weber helping Ian run the shop while I was exploring the Elvisphere, this book would never had been completed.

I would also like to thank Mackay Hargett for his stories, photographs, encouragement, and for helping Julian Riley solve one of the biggest mysteries in Elvis's origin story. Countless others contributed their thoughts, information, and most importantly, bits and pieces of truth. Thank you all.

About the Author

Gary Lindberg has spent his entire adult life as a screenwriter, movie director and producer, author of fiction and nonfiction, and book publisher. He is the author of four Amazon #1 bestselling novels. His first two books about Elvis were *Letters from Elvis,* based on a large cache of unpublished correspondence to a secret confidante, and *Brando on Elvis,* a detailed account of letters written by Marlon Brando about Elvis Presley. He co-wrote and co-produced the Paramount motion picture *That Was Then, This Is Now* starring Morgan Freeman and Emilio Estevez. Currently he is researching his fourth book about Elvis.

Made in the USA
Monee, IL
18 October 2026

66036549R00194